Literature in our Lives

This book recreates in written form seventeen of the most popular, frankly personal and engaging lectures on literature given by the award-winning teacher Richard Jacobs, who has been working with students for over forty years. This is a book written for students, whether starting their studies or more experienced, and also for all lovers of literature. At its heart is the conviction that reading, thinking about, and writing or talking about literature involves us all personally: texts talk to us intimately and urgently, inviting us to talk back, intervening in and changing our lives.

These lectures discuss, in an open but richly informed way, a wide range of texts that are regularly studied and enjoyed. They model what it means to be excited about reading and studying literature, and how the study of literature can be life-changing – perhaps even with the effect of changing the lives of readers of this eloquent and remarkable book.

Richard Jacobs is an Honorary Fellow at the University of Brighton, School of Humanities, where he was subject leader for literature and Principal Lecturer for many years and where he received teaching excellence awards. His publications include *A Beginner's Guide to Critical Reading: An Anthology of Literary Texts* (Routledge), *Teaching Narrative* (Palgrave), chapters on the 20th century novel (Penguin and Palgrave), editions for Penguin Classics, articles on literature and the teaching of literature, and several reviews.

Literature in our Lives

Talking about Texts from Shakespeare
to Philip Pullman

Richard Jacobs

Routledge
Taylor & Francis Group

NEW YORK AND LONDON

First published 2020
by Routledge
52 Vanderbilt Avenue, New York, NY 10017

and by Routledge
2 Park Square, Milton Park, Abingdon, Oxon, OX14 4RN

Routledge is an imprint of the Taylor & Francis Group, an informa business

Library of Congress Cataloging-in-Publication Data
A catalog record for this title has been requested

ISBN: 978-0-367-18931-0 (hbk)
ISBN: 978-0-367-18934-1 (pbk)
ISBN: 978-0-429-19930-1 (ebk)

Typeset in Sabon
by codeMantra

MIX
Paper from
responsible sources
FSC
www.fsc.org FSC™ C013985

Printed in the United Kingdom
by Henry Ling Limited

For Winnie and Rose, with love and gratitude for mutual support in difficult times.

Contents

Acknowledgements

Formal acknowledgments are recorded below with thanks for permissions to quote from copyright material but I'd like first to express some more personal thanks to those who have been so kind and supportive over very many years, from before this book was even planned and then continuing through its composition.

Warm thanks to friends and colleagues at the University of Brighton, especially Kate Aughterson and Jess Moriarty, and more latterly Craig Jordan-Baker, Emma Bell and Liam Connell (who first suggested I look towards publication). The staff at Falmer Library were very helpful with inter-library loans. James Grieve not only kindly gave permission for the use of extensive extracts from his Proust translation for Penguin (see below), but also translated specially for this book a passage from a later volume in the novel (see the Introduction). He also read the lecture and suggested improvements – and sent me a very rare copy of his *Swann's Way*. James died in early 2020. His Proust will long be cherished.

The readers for Routledge were more than generous in their comments on the proposal. Thanks so much to Ben Knights, Rachel Trousdale, Will Norman and, especially, Sean McEvoy who also read many of the chapters: his friendship has been very sustaining over the years.

This book would have been unthinkable without the innumerable students who, especially at Brighton, I've been lucky enough to know and teach over decades. Teaching that works is only possible with willing and supportive students, participating with enthusiastic engagement in lectures and seminars, and it's impossible for me to offer adequate thanks to them all. So I'll restrict myself to thanking just a few of the many ex-students who have become friends, almost all of whom have gone on to further successful academic work: Emma-Louise Day, Luke Edmeades, Mollie Gilliland, Lauren Keen, Joel Roberts and Rosanna Wood. Thanks also to Tasha Cook (now in her final undergraduate year) whose support has been so friendly and unstinting. Above all, warm thanks to Chloe Murphy who read all the lectures, improved most of them with detailed written feedback and helped shape the design and order of the book. Chloe was a dedicated student and is an equally dedicated reader and editor.

Finally, and most pertinently, I'm very grateful to Jennifer Abbott at Routledge for her warm support for this book from the proposal stage and throughout – including throughout Hurricane Dorian. Thanks also to the Routledge editorial and production teams.

For permission to reprint copyright material I'm very grateful to the following:

The Magician's Nephew by C.S. Lewis copyright © C.S. Lewis Pte. Ltd. 1955. *The Last Battle* by C.S. Lewis copyright © C.S. Lewis Pte. Ltd. 1956. Extracts reprinted by permission.

The Amber Spyglass Text © Phillip Pullman, 2000. Reproduced with permission of Scholastic Limited. All rights reserved. Thanks also to Penguin Random House USA.

Quotations from *The Catcher in the Rye* by kind permission of The J. D. Salinger Trust.

Quotations from *Waiting for Godot* by Samuel Beckett by kind permission of Faber and Faber (UK) and Grove/Atlantic, Inc. (USA).

Proust: *In Search of Lost Time, Volume 2: In the Shadow of Young Girls in Flower* (Penguin Books, 2002). Copyright © James Grieve, 2002. Extracts reprinted by kind permission of James Grieve.

All quotations from *Good Morning, Midnight* (Penguin Books, 1969), *Voyage in the Dark* (Penguin Books, 1969) and *Sleep It Off Lady* (Penguin Books, 1979) by Jean Rhys by kind permission from Jean Rhys Ltd. All Jean Rhys material is protected by copyright and therefore may not be quoted without prior permission in writing from Jean Rhys Ltd.

The following articles are reproduced by kind permission of the English and Media Centre, publishers of emagazine (www.englishandmedia. co.uk): *Claribel's Story* (Issue 28, April 2005); *Transformed by Godot* (Issue 20, April 2003); *Narrative and the Reader in Two 19th Century Novels: Jane Eyre and Wuthering Heights* (Issue 77, September 2017).

The lecture on 'The Musgrave Ritual' was originally published in *The Victorian Newsletter*, No. 118 (Fall 2010): 54–65. Reprinted by kind permission.

Some passages in the Introduction were first published in *The Use of English*, Volume 70, Number 1, Autumn 2018. A brief passage in the Introduction and a passage in the lecture on *Hamlet* and *King Lear* were first published in *Teaching English*, Issue 16, Spring 2018. Reprinted by kind permission.

Quotations from pre-20th century texts – including from The King James Version of the Bible and Shakespeare – are from editions in the public domain, with spelling lightly modernised. Those from Emily Dickinson are from the edition edited by Martha Dickinson Bianchi (Little, Brown: 1924). I'm grateful to Harvard University Press for their advice.

Introduction

The seventeen chapters of this book have their origin in seventeen lectures (in a few cases, shorter seminar papers) given at the University of Brighton and other institutions in forty years of teaching. Because they were spoken lectures I've been encouraged by friends, colleagues and students who heard about this book to stick very closely to the words actually spoken, to reproduce if possible a sense of occasion and the informality of the speaking voice, and, particularly, to retain the often personal nature of the material.

For this is a personal book, one devoted to the idea, which I'm sure we all share, that reading, thinking about and writing or talking about literature is a very personal matter, that texts talk to us with degrees of personal intimacy and urgency and, above all, that literature intervenes in our lives – in ways ranging from the insinuating to the explosive – and changing our lives in the process. So I've been quite open about how literature has had a profound (and often unsettling) effect on me, especially when I was a student. And that's of course why my title is *Literature in our Lives*. And my sub-title starts with *Talking about Texts* not just because this is a book of lectures but also because we're all talking back, in the various ways we express our responses, to the texts that are talking to us, and changing us. Literature changes lives, our lives, as well as dramatising, in its plots and those irreversible and unforgettable moments of suddenly enhanced perception, the life-changing effects on people within texts.

So what I'm aiming to do here is to discuss, in an accessible and, I hope, engaging way, a wide range of texts that are regularly studied and enjoyed and also to model what it means to be excited about reading and studying literature, to model how the study of literature can be life-changing, and perhaps even change your lives a little.

Let me say a little bit more about this matter of changing lives. I'll do so by asking a more basic question now and that's: why study literature at all? (Perhaps, in some less confident moments in your studies, you may well have asked yourself this.) And as this is a personal book I'll try and think about this personally.

As it happens, the question 'why study literature?' would rarely have been asked when I started teaching literature forty years ago. That was the time when, for instance, George Steiner could confidently pronounce that to teach *King Lear* was to have the responsibility of holding students' souls (or was it their heart strings?) in one's hands. But from about the early 1970s continental 'theory' was beginning to unsettle such notions, as was clear when I arrived at Oxford and was soon told, at a student essay-society meeting, that liberal humanism was dead, but then, as a privately educated adolescent, I hadn't heard of liberal humanism either. A few years later, when I was a hardly less callow postgraduate, the principal of the most exclusive Oxford college (so exclusive it excluded students, almost literally) told me that he didn't actually agree with anyone at his college studying English literature, but that wasn't because he belittled the subject (as might be the case now) but because he thought all properly educated students (at least at Oxford) were doing it all the time anyway just by reading books, so there was no need for research grants and prize fellowships for them to get on with it.

Today the question 'why study literature?' has urgency for different reasons, especially because of the instrumentalist-utilitarian ideology infecting education in the UK (and I hope less so elsewhere in the English-speaking world). The 'humanities' have to argue their case or fight their corner (for money and resources, for a place in the curriculum). But the answer to my basic question might be simply that studying literature enhances, as I hope you've found, our powers in critical literacy, by which I mean the shared experience in class on the individual text empowering us with the ability, and the need, to read the world and its texts on our own, with critical insight and the awareness of other possible readings, other possibilities for yourself and for lives in the world.

In the lectures that follow I speak openly about my own readings of the world (and myself) in relation to (for instance) Beckett's *Waiting for Godot*, Emily Dickinson, Jane Austen's *Emma*, *Hamlet* and *King Lear*, Keats (and Beethoven) and others, but let me add a few more examples here, in the knowledge we all share that great literary texts simultaneously explore, dramatise and thematise changes in and to lives and also enact that process of change upon the reader, a dynamic that is at the heart of the reading-experience.

**

My first example is from Chaucer, not of course because he chronologically kicks things off but because this, I think, is the purest example of what I'm exploring. It's also, for me, the most wonderful textual moment in the entire *Canterbury Tales* (first published 1476).

It's the climax of 'The Franklin's Tale' in which the devoted wife Dorigen has playfully and pityingly indulged her besotted courtly-lover Aurelius that she will yield to his demands for love if he performs an impossible task which, of course, he sort-of does. In desperation she confesses to her husband, the knight Arveragus who, in another wonderful moment, says (in effect) 'oh, is that all? Well, you must keep your word as that's always our first duty' – and then bursts into tears. Dorigen starts off to the garden where the promised assignation is to take place and in the street on the way bumps into Aurelius whom, in her despair, she doesn't seem to recognise. He asks her where she's going. In a state of near madness she cries that she's going, as instructed by her husband, 'to the garden, to keep my word, alas, alas!' This onrush of true feeling so profoundly affects the young lover that he feels a great surge of pity and, under that impulse, he releases her from her promised word.

I read this as a schoolboy but it wasn't till teaching it to 17- and 18-year-olds in my first job that it hit me with the force of revelation. For what became so clear was that Dorigen, but also Aurelius, were as-if sleepwalking into the coerciveness of allegory, in the form of the garden beyond the city-street, in imminent danger of succumbing to a paper-thin fictiveness – the pseudo-world of courtly love becoming 'real', where it suddenly matters and is irrevocable. Aurelius has occupied that allegory as his daily life, a dream; the threat so nearly not averted is that Dorigen will be folded into it, as a text into a text. Of course, the students I was teaching realised that we weren't talking about one 'real' life or world and one 'fictive' life or world, because 'The Franklin's Tale' is fictive and its characters are made up of Chaucer's words. But they saw clearly that the dangers of Dorigen and Aurelius collapsing into allegory can only be averted by that semi-conscious cry in the street, her tears (and those of Arveragus), and that onrushing surge of pity. The fact that my own adolescence, hardly behind me at the time, was, like Aurelius', a matter of fictive romantic entanglements, little to do with true feeling, and nothing to do with pity, sharpened further the revelatory power of this moment.

I was, like everyone else, stunned and astonished by Philip Pullman's trilogy *His Dark Materials* (2000), which, both for literary and political reasons, I'd love to be placed in the hands of all schoolchildren. I'll be saying more about this great work in the first lecture but let me say now that at one point in *The Amber Spyglass*, the third and last volume, Pullman makes a crucial distinction which we can compare with the Chaucer passage we've just been looking at.

Lyra and Will have travelled to the world of the dead. Harpies guard and harry the ghosts in the region and when Lyra offers to tell them a story to make the Harpies let them through to search for her friend she thinks she's on safe ground, being (as her name hints) used to spinning lies. So, after she does a quick mental check-through of her usual repertoire of plot clichés, she launches into the fantasy narrative only to be viciously attacked by the Harpies screaming 'Liar! Liar!'. Pages later she tries telling stories again, this time simply drawing on the world she knows, its this-ness, and now legions of ghosts as well as the Harpies are listening to her. And this time the Harpies listen 'solemn and spellbound'. Will asks them why. Their leader replies, in a paragraph that for me is Pullman at his eloquent best.

> 'Because it was true ... Because she spoke the truth. Because it was nourishing. Because it was feeding us. Because we couldn't help it. Because it was true. Because we had no idea that there was anything but wickedness. Because it brought us news of the world and the sun and the wind and the rain. Because it was true.'
>
> (Chapter 23)

The distinction here is no simple one between true and false, and of course Pullman is the first to be aware of that (as his fiction, like the Chaucer tale, like all fiction, is 'false'), nor is the narrative implying that only the biographically factual (Lyra's life) can make for 'true' stories. The distinction, I think, is between narrative as empty fantasy (like courtly love), manipulative and merely lying for routine and other purposes (as in our world of Trump and Brexit), and narrative as 'nourishing' and 'feeding': and it is literature of that kind that changes lives, as it changes the lives of the Harpies. And this is the literature that as students and readers we celebrate above all.

I want to pick up on that word nourishing and turn to what I'll offer here as the most miraculous moment (almost literally miraculous, as we'll see) in the lovely poetry of the 17th-century poet George Herbert. He gave up a potentially glittering career at court (he was born into a grand family) and became a humble parish priest in a quiet part of the west of England. In perhaps the greatest of his poems, 'The Flower', he writes about the surprise and delight in being able to 'bud again' after earlier unhappiness in his relations with God, and being so grateful to be able to 'relish versing' – and the relish he takes in writing poems is, the word quietly insists, as necessary as the nourishing taste of food. But it's lines from one of his other poems, 'Affliction', that I want to share with you. Here he's suffering from what we would call depression, as is clear from the vivid analysis of the illness in the first three lines of my example: but it's the miracle of the fourth line that is about lives changing – Herbert's own but also, and for him more importantly, other people's lives.

> My thoughts are all a case of knives
> Wounding my heart
> With scattered smart:
> As watering-pots give flowers their lives.

There can be gasps of pleasure in class when students see (literally) that the image of the poet's heart with perforated knife wounds is magicked in the gap between lines 3 and 4 into the (pictorially duplicating) image of the rose of the watering-can, a moment when Herbert realises – in a rush of unexpected access to his selfless duty – that his own personal experience of depression might serve to nourish and cheer his parishioners in their every-day sufferings. (That's miracle enough for me.) I'll just add that the dying Herbert told a friend to burn his book of poems, unless the friend thought it might do good in the world. This 1633 book, *The Temple*, proved to be one of the most popular and reprinted of its time. Lives were changed.

I've implied already that when lives change – for characters in texts, for us as students in reading about them – there is a political dimension, even if political issues are not explicitly evoked. I mean that the kind of enhanced reading that we're thinking about has the effect of enlarging our conscious-ness and sympathies – simply put, our capacities to identify with and feel for others, especially for those demonised as the 'other'. An example I've written about more than once is the radical transformation of Melville's lawyer in *Bartleby* (1853) as he feels, for the first time in his life (he admits that), profound sympathy for another human being. In effect, the elderly lawyer, like the callow young Aurelius, grows up. It's a blunt point to make about our cultural moment (Brexit, Trump) that the successful demonis-ing of the 'other' is the ugliest and most dangerous of its manifestations. We should feel no embarrassment, as students and readers, in wanting to counteract this thinking – or rather the active encouragement, fed in frenzy especially in England by the western world's most rabidly irresponsible and vindictively partisan press, not to think properly at all, and certainly not to think about and not to feel for others different from ourselves. We can all subscribe to many aspects of contemporary theory without losing sight of how reading can change lives for others as well as ourselves.

Of my other examples the next two are openly political. In the first, a character becomes politicised and as readers we are made to negotiate our own political responses to this process. This is Stevie in *The Secret Agent* (1907). I only got to know this novel when teaching it – and, as it happens, this was during the 1980s miners' strike in England which (very belatedly) politicised me. Conrad made the challenging decision to base his account of a character becoming politicised on someone himself 'othered' (by everyone apart from his sister) because of being 'simple'. There's an attendant com-edy lurking in Stevie's discovery of the brutal social realities of poverty and exploitation from talking to the cabby with his suffering horse. Conrad's flickering ironic narrative voice is always tempting us to keep our distance from the rawness of the pain. But he knows we can't but be moved, not least because, perhaps like Bartleby, Stevie is missing the usual human layer by which we limit our susceptibility to the pain of others.

Though it's 'funny', Stevie's wish to take the suffering cabby and his horse into his bed, and his child-like gnomic utterances, "'Bad! Bad!... Poor! Poor!'", spoken 'with convulsive sympathy' and culminating in the suddenly flashing accumulated insight "'Bad world for poor people ... Beastly!'" (Chapter 8), have exactly the 'simple' immediacy that can awaken us all to our own enlarged political understanding, as raw and odd and unsettling as Stevie's, and more powerful as an agent of change in our lives than any economics textbook.

Stevie's awakened political understanding allows me to turn to the only example that's from a critical book, rather than the creative texts that the rest of this introduction and all the lectures are about. Like countless others, I was very personally affected and influenced by the exemplary critical work of the great Raymond Williams, certainly the most important British cultural critic of the 20th century (and in effect the founder of what we call cultural materialism) and I can vividly recall feeling awe-struck and completely humbled by one particular page of his 1973 masterpiece *The Country and the City*. Here, as his tone is suddenly charged with passion and anger (the book is very openly personalised), Williams urges us to respond with our fully sentient selves when we visit the grand country-houses of England and turn from them, as he says we should, to look at the small and isolated working farms and cottages in the area. What shocked me – and changed me – was the sudden realisation that 'literary-criticism' can, and should, speak with such moral eloquence and political authority. I was expecting to learn about country-house poetry; I wasn't expecting to learn how to 'read' a country-house, and to read it feelingly.

> But stand at any point and look at that land ... Think it through as labour and see how long and systematic the exploitation and seizure must have been to ... to produce that degree of disparity, that barbarous disproportion of scale ... What these 'great' houses do is ... a visible stamping of power, of displayed wealth and command ... And will you then think of community? You will see modern community ... in the surviving exploiters and in their modern relations – the corporation country-house, the industrial seat, the ruling-class school.
>
> (Williams 1975: 132–133)

(Reading that not many years after leaving a 'ruling-class school' only increased its impact.)

Before my last example, a brief word on two texts that my own students have regularly reported back as having had an enormous impact on them, making their lives feel very different. (I very much hope you get the opportunity to read these texts one day, if you haven't yet.) The power of these texts derives largely from the fact that they are compressed into the smallest possible space and use language of the utmost concentration and with almost incantatory powers. These are Geoffrey Hill's 1967 Holocaust poem 'September Song' and Beckett's tiny 1973 play *Not I*. I've written about these before, so I'll just say here that in both instances students are forced to struggle in language's grip, in the case of the Hill poem having to negotiate, through the thorny series of furious puns, issues of history, entitlement, collusion and guilt, and in the case of *Not I* being locked into a space and forced to listen for a few terrible minutes to, to bear witness to, a woman whose torrent of words is a refusal to own the narrative of her anguished life. The texture of language, its text-ness, is where the life-changing power inheres, as in all great poems, as in the textures of music and painting.

My last example is very different and concerns a painting. I came to Proust late in life and I wouldn't pretend for a moment that you'll be easily urged to climb that particular mountain. (The next to last lecture in this book encourages you to try.) With self-help and other books arguing how Proust changes our lives you don't need me to add to the list. But one passage did change my life in a particularly acute way (rather than cumulatively through the 3300 pages) and that's the very moving passage on the death of the writer Bergotte, following a revelatory moment of self-scrutiny about his work.

Ailing and only partly aware of how ill he is, he feels he must visit a Paris exhibition of Dutch art to see a painting he particularly loves and thinks he knows intimately, Vermeer's *The View of Delft*. A review of the exhibition has mentioned the wonderful effect in the painting of a 'little patch of yellow wall' that Bergotte can't recall. So, with his head now spinning and on the edge of a stroke, he goes up to the painting. He sees it afresh, noticing details he didn't recognise, especially 'the precious substance of the tiny area of wall'.

(I'm privileged to add here that the translation that follows was done especially for this book by James Grieve whose wonderful translation of the second volume of Proust forms the backbone of the Proust lecture in this book.)

> Feeling dizzier now, he peered at the precious little patch of wall, as intently as a child will focus on the yellow butterfly he is trying to catch. 'That's how I should have written,' he was thinking. 'There's a thinness to my last books. I should have layered on the colour, to make my actual sentences precious, like that little patch of yellow wall.'
>
> He was quite aware of how serious this dizzy spell was. His whole life seemed to be hanging in one scale of a heavenly balance, the other of which contained the little patch of wall so nicely painted in yellow. And he sensed that he had been unwise to give the former for the latter. 'Mind you, I wouldn't want to be the item of the day in the evening papers' account of this exhibition.'
>
> He said over to himself the words: 'A little patch of yellow wall with a canopy on top, a little patch of yellow wall.' Then he collapsed onto a circular couch, just as suddenly stopped thinking that his life was in the balance and told himself with renewed optimism, 'It's just indigestion, those potatoes weren't properly done, it's nothing.' Another stroke felled him and he tumbled to the floor as visitors and gallery attendants rushed to him.

**

A few words about the book that follows. This collection is purposely non-chronological, with lectures of varying length, which should make for a fresh reading-experience: though of course the book can be read in any way that you like. There are threads that connect the lectures and one of them – desire, loss and the Fall – structures the book in the form of the first, the central and the last lectures. Other threads concern women and sexuality, myth, republican politics, conflicted texts and the realism/ modernism dynamic. I've tried to make explicit connections between the texts discussed wherever possible in the belief that comparative reading can be especially enhancing and illuminating in critical work.

As I mentioned at the outset this book tries to replicate the informal and personal speaking-voice of actual lectures and that means the book is not a typically academic textbook. References are kept to a minimum to make sure the text moves in as unimpeded a way as possible. (References to the primary texts discussed are restricted to chapter or act/scene numbers. The very selective secondary critical sources quoted are listed in the 'further reading' section that follows each lecture.)

The lectures were, with a few exceptions (the first and central lectures, which range widely across texts, and the Proust lecture which assumes no prior knowledge at all), delivered in front of students who either had read or were about to read the texts concerned. But, as in the original lectures, I've tried wherever I can to avoid plot-spoilers (for instance, avoiding discussions of the endings – though that hasn't always been possible) so I hope the book will appeal to those who know the texts only by reputation as well as those who are studying the texts. Not being a heavy-duty academic text-book (and because of my personal history) I'd be the last to claim that there's a great deal of original thought or cutting-edge research in what follows (and being the age I am there may well be things I read in critical books so long ago that I've genuinely made them part of what I take to be my own thinking – and if so I apologise). On the other hand, I would hope that there are several new or fresh insights and ideas in the discussions that follow, and I sometimes take the liberty of flagging these up.

It just remains for me to wish you a very productive and positive experience in your own literary-critical journeys. I very much hope this book can serve as a pleasurable and helpful companion for you in those journeys.

Further Reading

Geoffrey Chaucer, *The Canterbury Tales: Seventeen Tales and the General Prologue*, edd. V.A. Kolve and Glending Olson (Norton: 2018).

Joseph Conrad, *The Secret Agent*, ed. Richard Niland (Norton: 2016).

Richard Jacobs, *A Beginner's Guide to Critical Reading: An Anthology of Literary Texts* (Routledge: 2001. Contains texts and commentaries on material discussed above: Melville's *Bartleby*, Conrad's *The Secret Agent*, Beckett's *Not I* and Hill's 'September Song').

David Norbrook and H.R. Woudhuysen edd., *The Penguin Book of Renaissance Verse: 1509–1659* (Penguin: 1993. Norbrook's Introduction is a landmark critical statement).

Philip Pullman, *His Dark Materials* (Scholastic: 2000).

Marcel Proust, *In Search of Lost Time*, ed. Christopher Prendergast (Penguin: 2002).

* *

As this is a personal book, I want to highlight here twenty critics whose work has had a shaping influence on how I think and feel about texts and the world, and texts in the world.

Janet Adelman, *The Common Liar: An Essay on Anthony and Cleopatra* (Yale UP: 1973); *Suffocating Mothers: Fantasies of Maternal Origin in Shakespeare's Plays* (Routledge: 1992).

Francis Barker, *The Tremulous Private Body: Essays on Subjection* (Methuen: 1984).

Roland Barthes, *A Lover's Discourse* trs. Richard Howard (Jonathan Cape: 1979); *Camera Lucida* trs. Richard Howard (Jonathan Cape: 1982).

Catherine Belsey, *Critical Practice* (2nd ed., Routledge: 2002).

Peter Brooks, *Reading for the Plot: Design and Intention in Narrative* (Harvard U.P.: 1992).

Judith Butler, *Gender Trouble: Feminism and the Subversion of Identity* (Routledge: 1990).

Marilyn Butler, *Jane Austen and the War of Ideas* (2nd ed., Oxford UP: 1988); *Romantics, Rebels and Reactionaries* (Oxford UP: 1985).

Rosalie Colie, *Shakespeare's Living Art* (Princeton UP: 1974); *My Echoing Song: Andrew Marvell's Poetry of Criticism* (Princeton U.P.: 1970).

Denis de Rougemont, *Love in the Western World* trs. Montgomery Belgion (Princeton U.P.: 1983).

Jonathan Dollimore, *Death, Desire and Loss in Western Culture* (Routledge: 1998).

William Empson, *The Structure of Complex Words* (1951; new ed. Harvard U.P.: 1989).

Barbara Johnson, *The Critical Difference: Essays in the Contemporary Rhetoric of Reading* (Johns Hopkins U.P.: 1980).

Hugh Kenner, *The Stoic Comedians: Flaubert, Joyce and Beckett* (University of California Press: 1972); *The Pound Era* (University of California Press: 1973).

D.A. Miller, *The Novel and its Discontents* (Princeton U.P.: 1981); *The Novel and the Police* (University of California Press: 1988).

Toril Moi, *Sexual/Textual Politics* (Methuen: 1985).

Edward Said, *The World, the Text, and the Critic* (Harvard U.P.: 1983); *Culture and Imperialism* (Knopf: 1993).

Imre Salusinszky, *Criticism in Society* (interviews with nine leading theorists, including Jacques Derrida, Geoffrey Hartman and J. Hillis Miller) (Routledge: 1987).

Eve Kosofsky Sedgwick, *Between Men: English Literature and Male Homosocial Desire* (Columbia U.P.: 1985).

Raymond Williams, *The Country and the City* (Chatto and Windus: 1973); *Politics and Letters* (Verso: 1979).

Janet Wolff, *The Social Production of Art* (Macmillan: 1981).

* *

In the Further Reading sections that follow each lecture I regularly recommend volumes in three excellent series that should be among the first resources for your critical reading. University libraries will almost certainly stock many of the volumes in the three series.

Norton Critical Editions (Norton). A very wide-ranging series, regularly updated, that presents complete and reliable editions of texts with very substantial critical materials drawn from articles and books, including original reviews and key contextual information.

Cambridge Companions (Cambridge U.P.). These are cutting-edge collections of essays edited by leading authorities. There are Companions to single texts, single authors, as well as periods and genres. Many universities subscribe to the series online.

Cambridge Introductions (Cambridge U.P.). These are single-authored and pitched at a less academic level than the Companions. Similarly wide-ranging. One volume that belies the 'introduction' in the name is Jean-Michel Rabaté's thrilling *The Cambridge Introduction to Literature and Psychoanalysis* (Cambridge U.P.: 2014).

1 The Myth of the Fall and its Impact
Pullman, Lewis and Others

A very warm welcome to the first lecture in this series and this book. It's rather longer than almost all the other lectures because, unlike the others apart from the lecture at the centre of the book on 'fallen women', it ranges quite widely across texts many of which I think you'll know. The other lectures are almost all focused on single texts which are widely studied and enjoyed.

My starting point here is the biblical story of the Fall and its impact and cultural significance. I approach it in terms of myth as a way of discussing it in the context of a rich sampling of literary texts and in the light of psychoanalytic ideas. And I'll add that the final lecture on Milton's treatment of the Fall in his great *Paradise Lost* means that the beginning, middle and end of this book make up one of the threads that connect these lectures in ways that I hope you find productive in your reading-lives.

** **

Myths serve to relieve anxiety. They start from a difficult question or problem and guess backwards with a narrative that ends with 'explaining' or 'answering' what was otherwise inexplicable, relieving the anxiety caused by the original problem. The myth of the Fall, and the subsequent loss of Eden, has such a tentacular reach and power to suggest that the anxieties to which it ministers are the most urgent and elementary of all. There are some pressingly specific anxious questions that the myth 'answers', like why are women's child-labours so painful, why do men 'rule' over women, why do we wear clothes and feel shame about our private parts – oh, and why do we have to die? But there are more generalised but just as pressing anxieties at stake. Why am I not happy? Why do I not get what I want? Why does what I want, when I get it, not make me happy? Why is desire bound to fail to reach its object? Why have I lost what I had? And what am I being punished in this way for? Why can't I stay with mummy, at her breast, in her bed?

Why are you not happy? You were, but Eve (and then Adam) contrived to make sure you'd never be, any more, properly. The anxiety of unhappiness is narrated as a myth which relieves the burden: a myth in which there is an othering of good and bad, Eden and Fall. Gerard Manley Hopkins calls it, and his sweetly poisonous poem, 'Spring and Fall' and in it he addresses a child who is weeping over leaves falling in Autumn. He tells her that the 'springs' for all sorrows are identical and reside in the 'blight man was born for', the Fall that is death, her own death for which she unknowingly weeps. The blight man was born for. Why are you going to die? You weren't, once. I'm reminded of the moment Alice returns to her world from Wonderland and her sister is brushing dead leaves off her face: her journey started at the height of summer so, in a subtly muted way, the year has fallen and died, intimating a kind of death for Alice herself. But that makes sense because, for Carroll, Alice growing into a mature woman (in what he pointedly calls the after-time) is a kind of death, certainly for him and even for her.

The root anxiety which the Fall myth most elementally answers to is our collective need to believe in guilt itself – it being preferable (to paraphrase Elaine Pagels) to feel guilty than helpless, better than subsisting in a void of meaninglessness. To believe in guilt is to believe that things were better once, that we were happy once but that something happened which is my fault or someone else's fault, or everyone's, and that things now, like gardens, aren't what they used to be, before we grew up, before language, before daddy. The myth of the Fall is everyday pathology. This is what the post-Freudian psychoanalyst Jacques Lacan realised in his ideas about the infant having to negotiate a series of wounding separations after losing the primal and nurturing illusion that its world consists exclusively of one unified entity, infant-plus-mummy. Separation from the breast, from the bed, the recognition that mummy has needs focused elsewhere, notably on daddy – these are the psychic losses of the child's garden, of Eden. Garden is mother. What Freud and Lacan had to say about the infant's negotiation of mother-loss and its subsequent insertion in forms of exile and deferred desire is, in this sense, just the story of Adam and Eve losing their garden told in a grown-up way or, an example at random, the story of David Copperfield now barred by the padlocked gate and the high fence from the garden where 'fruit clusters on the trees, riper and richer than fruit has ever been since, in any other garden, and where my mother gathers some in a basket' (Chapter 2). We are exiles from that garden/mother.

Hamlet knows this as painfully as anyone when he describes his post-Edenic and fallen world, where his mother has in effect exiled him from her love by marrying a hated brute, as 'an unweeded garden / That grows to seed; things rank (= disgusting) and gross in nature / Possess it merely' (= completely: his hated uncle's grossly complete possession of his mother). He now feels that his own flesh, as well as what was the beautiful garden of a world, is 'sullied' (= fouled; Act 1, Sc. 2. Reading supplied from second quarto). Before this evidence of his mother's sexual appetite Hamlet fed off (as all children do) an idealised family romance where he, mother and (first) father were the Edenically unsullied unit. Old Hamlet (as ghost), describing the official account of his murder in the Edenic garden ('sleeping in my orchard') as the work of a 'serpent', pointedly colludes in this fantasy-romance when claiming that his love for Gertrude was of a chaste and simple purity: 'what a falling-off was there' is his phrase for Gertrude then choosing Claudius (Act 1, Sc. 5).

When Alice falls into Wonderland she wants to and can't get into the most beautiful garden – she's either too big or too small – and when she does eventually get there it's a nightmare world of cardboard cut-outs with a pseudo-mother wanting to decapitate her (and everyone else). The opening fall down the rabbit-hole itself is a death-fall (into the underworld) and birth-fall (down the birth-canal) combined, as well as a flying-penetration-orgasm-fall, and therefore none of these; the same may be said of the other child-fantasy or adult-nightmare scenes (according to how they're read), like Alice in the White Rabbit's house, which is at once the child small enough to play in the doll's house, the terror of claustrophobia, the foetus constricted in the womb, the vagina about to be penetrated by Bill the lizard (whose pencil Alice famously deprives him of in the trial scene). The garden which Alice longs to enter functions equivalently, attracting multiple connotations which, somehow, float into each other, neutralising their forces. It's Eden as mother, Alice wanting to go home, Carroll wanting his mother and to be her mother, the womb, the place where we're always too big or too small to enter (or re-enter), the 'real' Eden we're all locked out of, the 'real' world Alice wants to grow into, the Deanery garden in which, from his rooms, Carroll can get glimpses of Alice at play.

Too big or too small: the wonderful 17th-century priest-poet George Herbert, wanting to be an orange-tree in his poem 'Employment', reflects bleakly that he can never reach God to offer back his fruit: 'But we are still too young or old; / The man is gone / Before we can our wares unfold: / So we freeze on / Until the grave increase our cold'. Why do I not get what I want? Why does what I want (like Alice's garden), when I get it, turn out so wrong? Desire never reaches its goal, as Lacan also said about language. Meaning like desire is always deferred. In effect the garden disappears as soon as Alice enters it, in the way that all objects of desire turn out to be not the ones we thought we wanted. That itself is not the least of the falls intimated in these stories, the garden that collapses into playing-card world.

Our attempts to love are acts of recovery from these wounding psychic separations. That's why it's impossible to read Cathy and Heathcliff's love as anything other than as constituted in and structured by separations and loss – for, in effect, they are each other's lost mother. (More on this great novel in the third lecture.) The novel insists that loss is the principal fact of our psychic lives, and Emily Dickinson notices this more than once in her poems, one of them even suggesting that her first moment of consciousness was of being bereft, having lost something – but not knowing what.

The need to believe in guilt is also the need to believe in significant events, significantly connected, to believe in narratives. The pre-Fall Eden, like the infant's earliest bonded bliss with the mother, by definition cannot be narrated. Adam and Eve are happy, for ever. That is not narrative. Narratives are by definition fallen as they end in closure, which is death. The Fall narrative is narrative at its most elemental or pure – perhaps the only narrative we have to tell. Eden/happy/forever; temptation; fall; punishment/ exile/death. The need for narrative may in turn be related to the most primitive moment of the infant at the breast. Hunger > satisfaction > sleep. This meta-narrative is as close to the Edenic non-narrative as we can get. Related perhaps also is an equally urgent need, that of the infant's later need for the bed-time story. Tell me a narrative > the narrative is told > sleep. Hunger for food and hunger for story > satisfaction > sleep is also the narrative of desire: desire > sex > orgasm. And if pre-Fall Eden is hunger > satisfaction > sleep in an endless cycle in what has been called time as *mythos*, the Fall is hunger > satisfaction > death where food is sex and death is punishment, in what is called time as *chronos*, time as linear.

And if there is this psychic connection between need for food and need for story, in that for the infant they both lead to the desired sleep, that might suggest why, in Philip Pullman's dazzling *His Dark Materials* trilogy, Mary Malone is told to play Satan, to awaken the budding sexuality of Lyra and Will's desire for each other, and she does so by telling them a story of her own first sexualised love, with its own context of significantly charged eating. She feeds them her story and they fall. And it was good.

The need for narrative may account for the fact that we prefer, and tend to know much better, the story of Adam and Eve's creation in Genesis 2 and 3 rather than the one in Genesis 1. In terms of sexual politics the difference is vital. In Genesis 1 'God created man in his own image ... male and female created he them', in effect simultaneously and equal. In Genesis 2 and 3, Adam is created first and superior and Eve is only secondarily created from Adam's rib as 'an help meet' for Adam as 'it is not good' for Adam to be alone. But Genesis 1, God the workman working then resting, is only a linear narrative in the sense that he stops working and we prefer the narrative action of the Fall in Genesis 2 and 3 – which incidentally was written much earlier than Genesis 1 (and their writers were different). The former earlier narrative (the Fall) was apparently written to warn the Jews not to be too complacent; the latter later narrative was written to console them in their captivity.

Northrop Frye notes that the story of the Fall seems originally to have been one of many 'sardonic' folktales explaining how mankind was cheated out of immortality by malign deities. He also points to a strange moment at Genesis 3.22 in which God 'seems to be telling other Gods that man is now "as one of us" and in a position to threaten their power unless they do something about it at once' (Frye 1982: 109). But the early Christian church fathers would have had no time for such sceptical reflections on the origin of their founding myth. It's those church fathers whose readings of Genesis 2 and 3 set the pattern for all the later repressive and misogynistic doctrines that have so disfigured Western culture and which Milton and Pullman rebel against – and, I would add, Blake. (Mind you, the early fathers disagreed about the reason why Eve and Adam fell: was it because they were children, because they were gluttonous, because they were lustful?)

The Judeo-Christian tradition is unashamedly misogynistic. Orthodox Jewish men still thank their God for not being created women. Clement of Alexandria said that every woman should blush at the thought that she was a woman. For Thomas Aquinas women are defective. In Leviticus a woman who gives birth to a son is considered unclean for 40 days; in the case of a daughter's birth the unclean period is 80 days. Earliest human cultures had believed that creation was the work of earth-goddesses and that everything in life was sacred because of its place in that matriarchal wholeness. This world-view was replaced by the Hebrew invention of a single male God; myths across many cultures have stories telling how matriarchal systems were destroyed by a new order led by a dominant male God. The radical change in world-view has been put down to a biological shift from the right side of the brain (imagination, wholeness) to the left side (order, reason, logic).

The move to patriarchal power needed justification in the form of reading Genesis 2 and 3 in a way that emphasised the primacy of Eve's fault and the justness of the most aggressive of the three punishments, hers. She's punished with the pains of childbirth and, in a much discussed passage, with a future in which 'your desire will be for your husband, and he will rule over you'. This was and is taken to mean that women's desire is not hers to dispose on herself but a desire only real in the sense that it's subject and subservient to male desire.

Chaucer's 'Knight's Tale' has a moment that's very pertinent here, especially as his women are generally more sensible and practical than his men. I'm not sure if its unpleasantness has been recognised very widely. This is when Emily, who wants to remain a virgin for her entire life rather than be anyone's mistress or wife, but now faced with two men who confidently expect her hand, asks the goddess Diana to turn their hearts away from her so that the fire of their violent loves will 'be queynte' (quenched) and her 'maydenhede' be preserved. And Diana's response? The two fires on her altar behave in a very 'queynte' (curious) way. One of them 'queynte' (quenched) and then 'quiked' (started up) again while immediately the other 'was queynte and all agon; / And as it queynte, it made a whistelinge' followed by the running of many drops apparently of blood.

The terrified Emily has no idea what this means. It means that one suitor will be defeated but survive ('quiked'), and one bloodily won't, but those five intrusively obvious repetitions of 'queynte' (curious; quenched) can't but be read as an ironic reply to her wish to stay a maiden all her life (and why shouldn't she?) with the love of both men 'queynte' (quenched) – but also as very aggressively punning on a third sense, which Chaucer uses elsewhere, 'queynte' as female genitals ('grabbed her by the queynte' in 'The

Miller's Tale' – this worried me very much when I was a fifteen-year-old at school – and as later in Marvell's 'your quaint honour' in his 'Coy Mistress' poem which I'm sure many of you know). So Diana's reply to Emily's wish to conserve her maidenhead is, in effect: sorry, no – men are going to take your virginity, whether you like it or not. And the blood would also signify her ruptured hymen. This still shocks me; I'm sure it does you.

Women's desire being subservient to men's is also the issue at stake in the Gnostic history of Adam's first wife Lilith, who insisted on being on top during sex and was (of course, therefore) not at all right for original manly Adam who asked God for a more submissively compliant model; and so Lilith was ejected from Eden to become the mother of all witches. Lilith in turn lies behind textual representations of the self-pleasuring woman and thus the Victorian treatment of 'hysterical' and of 'fallen' women, whose story is obsessive-compulsively narrated in the Victorian novel, as I will explore in a later lecture, at the centre of this book.

The myth of the Fall and the early church's misogynistic reading of it is largely due to multiple instances of male envy – of women's ultimate creativity in childbirth, of their certain knowledge of true parenthood (men never know for sure) and, I think crucially, of the female orgasm and the clitoris itself. The male organ 'falls' in detumescence and the dread of that knowledge would be enough in itself to make woman the 'author' of the Fall.

Along with misogyny the early Christian church displayed a hatred and fear of sex itself, and of the body itself, and this too led to readings of the Fall in which, for instance, Adam's unruly member becomes a sign of how all men must be on permanent alert against the evil of sexual desire for woman which is death. Augustine insisted that man propagates death in sex, in what he called the unclean motion of the generative parts, and that both death and desire are the punishment that have been bequeathed to us all. Despite the Christian dogma of marriage Augustine declared that there was no essential difference between a man having sex with his wife and a man having sex with a prostitute, for both were equally sinful.

Most tellingly of all, there's nothing in Genesis about the serpent being Satan or about original sin. These are the inventions of early Christian church fathers, notably again Augustine. (Equivalently, according to a new and well-received study by John Barton, there are only two references to the key Christian notion of the Trinity in the entire Bible, both added to the gospels by later scribes). The early church needed to make the death of Jesus into the ultimately meaningful event so the notion of Redemption was created and 'read back' into Genesis 3. If Jesus died to redeem original human sin then Adam and Eve's Fall must have been much more serious than we thought. And if original sin is to be imported into Genesis 3 then it needs an agency more momentous than a serpent. So (in effect) it was decided that the serpent was Satan and, to give his agency yet more momentous motivation, the quite separate story of Satan's Fall, following his rebellion and the war in heaven, was attached in readings of the Fall. What that also conveniently achieved was to make Satan's Fall into a type or prototype of (particularly) Eve's. The association of Satan and Eve, as if their Falls are one Fall, affects social and literary culture in predictable ways, with the convenient male fiction that Eve is equivalent to Satan. Augustine had insisted that every woman is Eve the temptress. Pope Gregory the Great, two hundred years after Augustine, took it further by declaring that Eve herself is actually Satan. A cleric in the Pullman trilogy dutifully refers to Eve as the cause of all sin. Making Satan's Fall a prototype of the human Fall further underlines the required significance of our Fall and of the extraordinary doctrine of original sin – which Elaine Pagels suspects only survived because people preferred to feel guilty rather than helpless.

The impact of these early church readings and teachings has been incalculable in their capacity to inflict self-loathing, guilt, unhappiness, sexual violence, and an enfeebled sense of our own potential for power and freedom.

As evidence of the coercive durability of this doctrine, and on the simplest level, we can glance at the fact that some older Catholic women even today talk about periods as the Curse. Or we might glance at 'A Meditation to be Said of Women with Child', a touching little poem by the Elizabethan poet William Hunnis, written by this man but to be recited by women in labour who are to address God like this: 'Although by sin / deserved I have right well / Such pain as this, / yea, more than tongue can tell: / Yet ah, my God, / turn not away thy face, / Nor me forsake, / in this so sharp a case.' This is a poem designed to be used in a practical way: to help women by allowing them to express their genuine belief that their suffering is their fault, because of Eve. Or we might ponder the sexual habits of a very remarkable community which typifies the issue sharply.

This community numbers some 350 people, grouped in 59 families which share thirteen surnames. Marriages are arranged for economic reasons. The average family has seven children. Men associate with men, women with women both before and after marriage. Many women seldom leave their cottages. The religion is Christian but the community also believes in spirits, demons and witches. The religious leaders exercise full social control and there is a universal fear of damnation. Children are brought up in total sexual ignorance. Women are unaware of the biology of menstruation and menopause. The latter is considered a sign of impending madness. Men believe that sex is debilitating and that women are dangerous to men at menstruation and after childbirth. The female orgasm is virtually unknown. Marital sex is carried out without foreplay and with underclothes. Men exclusively instigate sex and always lie on top.

Children are sexually segregated from the outset and at school, at church and in social life generally. Bodily contact between the sexes is unknown. Some girls refuse to dance because that might involve having to touch a boy's hand or arm. Nudity is horrifying to the community. Children and adults wash only their faces, necks, arms and legs. Nobody learns to swim because to do so would be to partially bare their bodies. Sermons from the pulpit and lessons in school reinforce the sexual orthodoxy and there is an extensive use of informers so the religious leaders can police the details of everyone's life. Sexual morality is also reinforced through religious journals, found in every home. Children are severely punished for any sexual expression such as masturbation, mutual exploration or the use of any words relating to sex.

An extreme early 17th-century New England Puritan sect? No. A mid-20th-century Catholic community on a small island off the west coast of Ireland which the anthropologist who studied the community there for a decade called Inis Beag (Messenger 1969).

As the early church grew in influence and power a wholly new way of reading emerged, one that had the effect of closing off any wholesale scepticism about issues of Biblical truth. This is called typological reading and its methodology is nicely summarised by Frye. 'How do we know that the Gospel story is true? Because it confirms the prophesies of the Old Testament. But how do we know that the Old Testament prophesies are true? Because they are confirmed by the Gospel story'. Frye adds that the so-called evidence is like the bouncing of a ball between the two testaments (Frye 1982: 78).

To assess the sheer weight of oppressiveness in the orthodox story with which radical writers like Milton, Blake and Pullman are wrestling we'll look at C. S. Lewis' creation-and-Fall novel in his 1950s Narnia cycle. This is *The Magician's Nephew*. As we'll see this is his Old Testament complement to *The Lion, the Witch and the Wardrobe* which is his (New Testament) version of the betrayal, crucifixion and resurrection. Lewis' strategy, in retelling the Fall to children in the form of a Narnian adventure, is to tell it in multiple ways, to split it into a series of Falls, as if obsessively, or as if to cover every eventuality. The first Fall, as in Genesis, is Eve's. This happens when the children Polly and Digory accidentally get into Uncle Andrew's study. (He needs two humans to confirm his discovery of the means to travel to other universes, by magic rings.) Flattering Polly with courtly extravagance ('such a very attractive young lady'), as Milton's Satan flatters Eve, she's tempted to touch the rings. These are yellow and green (apple coloured) and, if Polly had been a bit younger, 'she would have wanted to put one in her mouth' (Chapter 1). She's tempted, Digory tries to stop her but she touches and falls. This Eve falls through infantile orality and vanity.

Digory's Fall, once he's been sent to bring Polly back, takes place in Charn where Digory is tempted to strike a bell with a hammer rather than suffer from not knowing 'what would have followed' if he hadn't. Polly tries to stop him but, man-handling her aggressively (hurting her 'quite fairly badly'), he succumbs and strikes the bell. If her Fall was a regression to baby-girl wanting to suck (staying with mummy, at her breast), his is a violent man dragging down his Eve as he falls himself. That is, they fall separately, ignoring each other's advice, and in aggression not mutuality. (In sharpest contrast, and as we'll see at the end of this book, Milton's Adam chooses to fall with Eve because of his love for her.)

Digory's Fall is incomparably the more momentous of the two in so far as striking the bell awakens the Witch/Queen Jadis who, to summarise, is thus brought into Narnia just at the moment of its creation. In a typical Lewis joke, when Digory grabs Polly's wrist and strikes the bell, it's said that 'he was very sorry for it afterwards (and so were a good many other people)' (Chapter 4). Good many other people? Only, in effect, the whole human race.

Back home Digory's mother is dying of an incurable disease. Approaching Aslan to ask for some magic fruit to make her well, Digory has instead to undergo a humiliating inquisition in front of Narnia's first leaders ('this is the Boy who did it'). Aslan forces him to explain how and why 'evil' has already entered this new world, 'waked and brought hither by this son of Adam'. The source of the guilt, he's forced to admit, is that 'I wanted to know what would happen if I struck a bell'.

I wanted to know. Within less than a page of Digory's confession Aslan is addressing his chosen first King of Narnia, saying to him 'I have known you long. Do you know me?', receiving his reply 'I feel ... we've met before' (meaning that this London cabby is a Christian), at which Aslan continues: 'You know better than you think you know, and you shall live to know me better yet'. The coercive, regressive idea could hardly be clearer or more depressing. The only fit object of human knowledge is the knowledge of God. Knowledge beyond that object, as Digory's wanting to know, is, disastrously, to invite evil into the world. (To eat from the tree of knowledge of good and evil.) And this demonisation of the drive to knowledge connects tellingly with the fact that to know a woman, in the Old Testament, is to have sex with her.

Aslan promises that the worst of the evil that will ensue will fall upon himself (that is, on the cross) and Digory is given the chance to 'undo the wrong' (Chapter 12) by finding the means of protecting this new Eden from enemies like Jadis, at least for a time. For this, Digory has to journey to an Eden within an Eden, a garden on a hill where he must pluck an apple from a tree and bring it to Aslan. Perhaps, incidentally, Lewis is thinking of Marvell's poem 'The Garden', as is made clear when Digory sees an exotic bird preening itself in the tree. The bird is Marvell's and Digory's soul or conscience. Marvell, like his friend Milton, was instinctively sceptical about the Fall, even presenting it, as in that wonderful poem, as comic, with sexy fruits pressing themselves on the enraptured speaker who just topples into the grass.

> What wondrous life in this I lead!
> Ripe apples drop about my head,
> The luscious clusters of the vine
> Upon my mouth do crush their wine,
> The nectarine and curious peach
> Into my hands themselves do reach,
> Stumbling on melons, as I pass,
> Ensnared with flowers, I fall on grass.

The scene in Lewis' Eden within an Eden is one in which Digory, about to 'undo' his Fall by plucking an apple, must undergo another temptation to Fall. To his horror, he sees Jadis in the garden and she has already eaten one of the special apples and recognised its power. (In the enchanting illustrations, the tree in the enclosed garden is like a sinuous and willowy woman, and Jadis, having eaten her apple, is standing close to it, her body insinuatingly fluid – hand on waist, knee crooked – in an equivalently erotic and duplicating way. This is woman as whore (Lilith), garden as woman's body.) So Jadis (with Satanic persuasiveness) tempts Digory with another 'Fall', the lovely idea that he can use the apple he's taken for Aslan to return to his world and cure his mother instead. He successfully resists, takes the apple to Aslan who plants it and from it grows another tree from which Aslan lets Digory take an apple. He takes that apple home and it cures his mother.

He later plants that apple's core and yet another tree grows, one that bears particularly delicious apples. And when that tree blows down in a storm, Digory, now an old man, makes the wardrobe out of its wood. Thus the Narnian magic in the wardrobe. Lewis has in effect read his own Narnian cycle typologically, like the early church fathers who insisted, for instance, that Jesus' cross was the same wood as Adam's tree. The typological purpose is to close the circle of meaning and 'truth' and lock it tight. Or the novel could be described as simultaneously playing the role of two myths – a myth to explain, relieve anxiety about and justify the biblical myth of the Fall (Lewis himself said he wanted his Narnia books to steal past children's inhibitions about faith) and to justify (etc.) the myth of *The Lion, the Witch and the Wardrobe*, the two novels being the 'evidence' bouncing back and forth between old and new testaments.

The repeated actions outlined above in effect present the Fall five times, three times as 'bad' – Polly's baby-girl innocent Fall, Digory's at the bell, the witch 'stealing' one of Aslan's apples – and twice as 'good' – Digory taking the apple and resisting a Fall and Digory taking an apple because he resisted that Fall. At no point do Polly and Digory act together or in mutuality in this sequence of critical actions. (Polly senses that she can't even enter the garden within the garden.) Three apples; two trees; two temptations; two father-gods (bad Andrew, good Aslan); two mothers, the sick one back home and Jadis who, in turn, is both Eve with her apple and serpent/Satan tempting Digory.

The fairy-tale formula of splitting parents into good/bad mothers and fathers is duplicated in the distinction Aslan makes between motives for taking the apple. To take in obedience to others is good. To take for self and knowledge is bad: the 'fruit is good but they loathe it ever after' (Chapter 14). For this Lewis might have been thinking of Shakespeare's Sonnet 129 in which sex is 'enjoyed no sooner but despised straight'. There's a very telling detail about the witch's mouth after eating her stolen apple. 'The juice was darker than you would expect and had made a horrid stain around her mouth' (Chapter 13).

After Digory's mother is cured she 'had such games with Digory and Polly' that it's said of her that she's 'the biggest baby of the three'. Her cure in effect cancels her ever having been an adult, sexualised woman at all. The desexualised mother is Hamlet's most longed-for desire. The suggestion is that adult sexuality, even adulthood, is something we need to be cured of. The two mothers correspond to dirty (horridly staining) and clean (mother's 'pretty pale blue' bedclothes) (Chapter 15). Good mothers are pale and pretty; witches have darkly flowing, staining juices and steal their auto-erotic self-pleasures guiltily. The idea that adult sexuality, and even adulthood, is something we need to be cured of is what drives the most notorious feature of the whole Narnian cycle, the 'resolution' of the final volume, *The Last Battle*, and it's the starting point for Philip Pullman's very public antagonism towards what Lewis is really up to in the Narnia books. It's also one of the formative influences behind his own great trilogy in which (in sharp opposition to Lewis) the Fall, as in *Paradise Lost* (which I'll be lecturing on in the final lecture in this book), is recuperated and re-written as the source and celebration of all that is creative and ennobling about human beings as they grow up and love each other. Let me very briefly indicate what Pullman is up to in his wonderful *His Dark Materials*.

The first angels were made from a coalescing of Dust (sub-atomic particles that perpetuate themselves out of love for consciousness and self-understanding) and one of those angels, who called himself the Authority, God, and other names in other worlds, propagated the lie that he was the creator of everything that happened to follow his own creation. One female angel discovered the lie and led a war against the Authority in which the rebellious angels lacked the resources to succeed and were banished.

Thirty-five thousand years before the events of the trilogy the rebellious angels exact revenge by intervening in the evolutionary processes in all worlds by massively amplifying Dust in the conscious beings in all these worlds, bringing knowledge, creativity, critical awareness, ambition and enterprise into the worlds. And in each of them a narrative, a myth, emerges to account for (relieve anxiety about) this evolutionary development. In our world, which is Will's world, that narrative is of course the Christian Fall, told and then retold and reshaped by an oppressive Church as a story of punishment for a disaster. In Lyra's world there's the added detail in the myth that the Fall was the moment when children's daemons (their visible

souls, as an animal) settle into their final form. In the much more benevolent and co-operative world of the Mulefa the narrative tells of how a
serpent (nice touch) passes on the knowledge that brings the wisdom and
maturity to connect the creatures to their trees and the trees' oil in a mutually enhancing eco-system. (It's this benevolent and wisdom-imparting serpent that Mary is told to duplicate by playing the serpent for Lyra and Will.)

In Lyra's world the Church mobilises an enormously elaborated counter-
revenge, setting up networks of oppression devoted to the task of min-
imising the effects of Dust and experimenting in ways of eliminating it
entirely – experiments in cutting away daemons from children at the outset of adolescence (in effect castration and FGM). As part of the counter-
revenge the Church invents and propagates the fiction of heaven and sets up
what one rebel-angel rightly describes as a prison-camp for the dead. And
it's during the centuries long struggle between the beneficial effects of Dust
and the Church's campaigns to stifle or eliminate it, for the sake of their
own continuing powers to oppress, that a prophecy emerges among the
witches that a child will be born whose destiny is to be the second Eve and
who, if she is allowed to fall, and if the Church fails to stop her, will mark
the triumph of Dust and the end of the tyranny of the Church – but at an
enormous personal cost. And I'll stop short of describing that cost and what
happens at the end. I was inconsolable.

Let's return to Lewis and the end of the final Narnia volume, *The Last
Battle*: the English children from the novels, apart from one, Susan, find
themselves (after what they thought might have been a railway accident in
England) as Kings and Queens in Narnia just as Aslan is closing that world
down (and separating sheep from goats etc.). When a Narnian asks where
Susan is Peter says 'gravely' that she's 'no longer a friend of Narnia' and then
we hear that she's only interested in 'nylons and lipsticks and invitations'
(Chapter 12). (I'll just add here that Lewis' high valuation of children is rather
selective, as shown in the casual reference in *Prince Caspian* to a classful of
'dumpy' girls who run away in terror when they see Aslan.) Anyway, on the
(admittedly moving) last page of *The Last Battle* Aslan explains that 'There
was a real railway accident ... Your father and mother and all of you are – as
you used to call it in the Shadow-Lands – dead. The term is over: the holidays
have begun. The dream is ended: this is the morning.' Lewis adds: 'And as
He spoke He no longer looked to them like a lion; but the things that began
to happen after that were so great and beautiful that I cannot write them'
(Chapter 16). Moving, yes (though not remotely so compared to the end of
the Pullman), but what appals Pullman and others is the clear and coercive
notion that the best thing to happen to children, to stop them becoming
sexualised adolescents like Susan (and what sort of life for her now, losing
her entire family? Is this a kind of punishment for liking lipstick? Mind you,
Hamlet gets all hysterical when he thinks about women's make-up) – the best
thing to stop children becoming sexualised is for them to die.

Or for someone to catch them before they fall, which is of course
my cue to turn to Salinger's fascinatingly analogous 1951 iconic classic

The Catcher in the Rye. Why must Holden Caulfield be the catcher in the rye, the catcher of children when they threaten to fall over the cliff, out of the garden, into adulthood and loss? One answer is that he doesn't actually want that but its opposite, to be caught as he falls, to be held, as he never has been. His psychic history has been scarred by the fear of being let down and letting down others. He punishes himself, wish-fulfillingly, for being the dumb one in the family by failing at school after school, thus letting his parents down, to forestall any further letting down of himself. For he has been most crucially let down by the one person whom he most crucially let down himself – his dead brother Allie, who let him down by dying, whom he couldn't catch. So he has to catch all other children, not allow them to get let down by, among other things, what he, another Hamlet, perceives as the dirt of sexuality (the explicit graffiti on the children's school wall, which he typically assumes was done by an adult not a child).

'I *really* fouled that up', he says (Chapter 9), after failing to arrange an encounter with a good-time girl, but he made himself fail that test of adulthood for fear of the sullying (Hamlet's word) or fouling (sleeping with an adult) it would have entailed. The prostitute scene is equivalently impossible once Holden sees the girl as a girl, a child. It's crippling fear of the growing-up process that makes him adopt his worldly-wise cynicism, fear of change (where do the ducks go after the fall?), of being hurt (even being given presents or wished good luck hurts, even bad films hurt so he has to mock them savagely), again or anymore, after the original wounding fall of Allie, off the cliff, out of their garden.

Catching and falling persist from the outset. Holden can't start his novel (leave his school) till he can feel a goodbye and so he remembers a moment of time suspended, a moment equivalent to Tennessee Williams' Brick and Skipper (in *Cat on a Hot Tin Roof*) tossing high passes to each other in endless summer-adolescence, only stoppable by time in the form of Maggie, like Hermione in *The Winter's Tale*, saying that it's now or never. Three boys chucking a ball around between them, keeping on catching, not letting the ball fall, while everything outside the charmed moment of held time is darkening, the day falling into nightfall.

> It was getting pretty dark out, but we kept chucking the ball around anyway. It kept getting darker and darker, and we could hardly see the ball any more, but we didn't want to stop doing what we were doing. Finally we had to.
>
> (Chapter 1)

The nicely named Mr Zambesi (the authority-name at the end of the alphabet-world, as Allie is its beginning, its golden age) stops the game (Maggie, according to Brick, laid down the law when insisting on marriage) and calls them in.

The effect is a brutal version of Marvell's wistful-gentle 'let's in', the kindly reasonable return to the attritions of living, at the close of his

Appleton House, and it's that brutal stoppage – Mr Zambesi, perhaps inevitably, teaches biology – that allows Holden to get to the next stage of
substitute-mourning. For, like Hamlet, he has never completed the mourning for Allie, and he has to hold the memory in suspension, like the way he
imagines and wants the world of childhood, and the Museum of Natural
History, to be (where everything always stays where it should be), and all
the ducks accounted for.

There's another child-boy, apart from Allie, whom Holden failed to catch,
the rather pointedly named James Castle (J.C. suggests Jesus – Holden is
typically cross with the disciples for letting Jesus down) who threw himself
out of a window when faced with the brutalities of bullying. Holden's sister
Phoebe challenges him to name something he really likes. He likes nothing
really apart from Phoebe herself and his brother(s) and Jane Gallagher – but
big brother D.B. is now lost to the movies which is why Holden purports to
hate movies, D.B. having left the nest – and, having lost the other two, he
can't bring himself to contact Jane in case she's changed from the child-girl
he loved, so he has no answer, apart from to think of James Castle, who fell
and finished it all.

This falling out of it all is frighteningly materialised later for Holden
but there's a more consoling instance when Holden watches a family on
Broadway. The kid is singing the novel's title song (which turns out to be the
most moving of false memories: the song actually has 'meet a body' coming
through the rye, not catch), singing next to the kerb and walking calmly on
while Broadway roars around him. It's a moment of suspended time again.
The kid's parents pay him no attention, allowing Holden to get closer and
hear the song. This positions Holden precisely in the between-world which
is so painfully his throughout (he has streaks of premature grey hair). It's as
if he's invisible to the child; only as invisible can he truly inhabit and return
to that garden. The effect is like the invisible-disguises Carroll wears in
Wonderland and Looking-glass worlds; in Alice's space, those gardens, he
has no place as his troubled self; he has to keep performing in role, being
invisible.

The novel presents a number of gardens as Edens and this pervasive sense
of garden (and falling) is clearly something to do with Holden wanting to
be mother to all children, his own mother being a tellingly muted figure in
the novel, subject to nerves (after Allie's death), perceived vaguely as threatening. The only thing Holden writes about in his History essay quoted at
the novel's outset is mummification; at the end he takes two kids to see
the mummies in the museum. Crucial to the novel's psychic-topography is
Central Park, a very real centre but a persistently lost presence, the source
of memories of Allie and his own childhood, but now a garden where he
doesn't belong.

Thus the force of the two moments towards the end, in one of which
Holden helps a child with her skate (so that she doesn't fall), and in the other
of which, seeing tiny kids on a see-saw, he tries to even up the weight (to

stop a potential falling off again) but then realises they didn't really want him there. He's there, but as if invisible, again. As if disappearing – which is exactly what he fears and feels walking up Fifth Avenue later.

> Every time I came to the end of a block and stepped off the goddam kerb, I had this feeling that I'd never get to the other side of the street. I thought I'd just go down, down, down, and nobody'd ever see me again.

This is a literalising of the fall that Mr Antolini forecast for Holden – a fall that keeps falling – and only using Allie as a kind of totem ('Allie, don't let me disappear. Please, Allie!') can keep Holden from that Fall (Chapter 25).

Other intimated gardens include his plan to escape and live rough with Sally in Vermont (where it's especially beautiful in the fall), and the later plan to hitchhike west, to act deaf-mute, possibly marry an actual and beautiful deaf-mute, have children and hide them, and to live the rest of his life in a cabin 'right near the woods, but not right in them, because I'd want it to be sunny as hell all the time' (Chapter 25). The prostitute's name, as unlucky in her name as Beckett's Lucky, is Sunny. Beckett's Estragon wants to go far away west, to wander in the Pyrenees. West is where Gabriel Conway in Joyce's 'The Dead' recognises at last he must go. It's towards nightfall. It's *Twelfth Night*'s 'there lies your way, due west ... Then westward ho!' (Act 3, Scene 1).

The most intently realised sacred space, the Edenic garden within the garden, is the carousel in the park, where the novel's most moving scene, nearly its last, is enacted. The rain is falling – returning the reader to the rain on another sacred space, the novel's anti-type garden, Allie's grave (as the snow on Michael Furey's grave in 'The Dead') – but, unlike the visitors at Allie's grave who run to their cars, and unlike 'all the parents and mothers and everybody' in this scene, who stand close to their offspring under the carousel, Holden stays sitting on his bench alone and out-of-it. Neither parent or mother (or anybody?), not physically with Phoebe, Holden is conscious at last that 'the thing with kids is... if they fall off, they fall off'. He's soaked by the rain as if cleansed, but now at last 'so damn happy' (the novel's rarest word) just to see Phoebe ('she looked so damn nice') riding but not for a fall, going round and round and never falling (Chapter 25).

But it's not the last page. Turning to find that, it's a shock to hear, after this moment of passionate and unguarded sentiment, the wintry tone, as in the opening of the novel but much more chillingly dismissive (of the reader, particularly), with which, from his psychiatric ward, Holden tells us that he doesn't feel like telling us which school he's going to next. He's missing everybody. The poet Robert Lowell, home after three months in *his* psychiatric ward (eight years after *Catcher*), looked at tulips fallen horizontal and wondered whether they (that is, he) can take another year. For Holden there's only the question of where he'll be 'next fall' (Chapter 26).

Holden's mother is a troubling absence. More usually, despite the intensity of desire between them, Mother has to let the infant fall. When Peter Rabbit's mother, in Potter's 1902 story, issues the single prohibition ('don't go into Mr McGregor's garden') she is in effect telling him to do just that, to exercise his inquisitive 'human' nature (all his sisters have rabbity names) and to transgress. She's also in effect activating Peter's oedipal impulse to compete with his father (who was 'put in a pie') and to avenge him like Hamlet. Entering the forbidden garden, Peter eats till sated and thus calls down the presence of Mr McGregor, the punitive God. Peter has now 'forgotten the way back', loses his shoes and has to run 'on four legs', an Adam reverting to the animality from which he was raised. (The Fall might be connected with the evolutionary moment at which humans first stood up, thus exposing our genitalia to view, an evolutionary development that is associated with a move from the primacy of smell to that of sight: so that being 'raised' becomes available to be read as a kind of fall.) Peter 'gave himself up for lost' and can only 'wander about' in a world from which he is now alienated (the other animals can't now communicate with him).

'Mother' sends the child on an equivalent mission in Wordsworth's poem 'Nutting'. This poem recounts an intensely sexualised Edenic rapture and falling. The mother-figure sends the young boy, one Edenic day ('one of those heavenly days that cannot die'), dressed as if for some rite of passage (like Red Riding Hood), to go nutting in 'some far-distant wood'. He forces his way through 'matted' and 'tangled' vegetation, reaching the 'virgin' scene. It's a 'dear nook / Unvisited' where 'the hazels rose / Tall and erect, with tempting clusters hung'. Once there he gets what can only be described as intense auto-erotic foreplay as, 'voluptuous, fearless of a rival', he 'eyed / The banquet'. He's in a 'bower' which is Milton's word for Adam and Eve's love-nest (the poem is full of anxious echoes of the Edenic scenes in *Paradise Lost*).

The violence of what follows is conveyed through the suddenness of its telling. The boy 'rose' and 'dragged to earth both branch and bough, with crash / And merciless ravage' and the nook and bower 'deformed and sullied, patiently gave up / Their quiet being'. The bower is now 'mutilated' as he leaves 'rich beyond the wealth of kings' but with a new 'sense of pain', an alone-ness in a world where the sky is now always 'intruding'.

In the Edenic space the boy brings the garden down, felling it and himself in the process. He's also discovering the sullying of sexuality (Hamlet feels that his flesh is 'sullied' by his mother's sexual behaviour), its self-punishingly empty fulfilments and its resulting exclusion from happiness. 'Nutting' is a story of intense sexual anticipation turning to equally intense sexual destructiveness. It's a story of a boy getting his nuts. It's a story in which the mother releases the boy to learn the aching vacancies of the intruding sky.

Or let's think about Ridley Scott's 1979 film *Alien*. I saw this with a friend in Paris, shortly after it came out. It upset me very much and it took me some days to work out why. It activated a memory but one that was on the edge of recognition, wanting to be both remembered and forgotten, throbbing away, again. Here's what eventually fell into place, the obsession appeased. (Feel free to consider what follows as a more than usually personal reading of a text: I know it is, but you might accept it at least partially.)

The film begins with a remarkable emblem of pre-sexualised humanity, the crew of a spaceship in deep sleep, as if waiting to be born or made real, men and women innocently and gently together. The ship is called the Nostromo, an obvious nod at Conrad but also notre/nos home, our common Eden. They wake up to investigate a mystery-planet, impelled by their own curiosity but actually, and unknown to them, by the deep plans of their employer (the Company), its agent disguised on board and the ship's computer. They enter a nightmare-landscape where an egg-like, fruit-like object attaches itself to the face of a crew-member, ingesting itself into him. Against company-policy rules, but actually let in by its agent, the affected man is brought into the ship where, in time, the ingested object explodes out of his body, gestates rapidly and devours in turn all but one of the crew.

That exploding out of the body is an intensely realised moment of rich iconographic significance, tapping down into many root-anxieties. On first sighting the alien is sexuality rampant and polymorphous (the mobile phallus, the vagina-dentata on a stalk) but it's also the infant at parturition (it screams on emerging) and it's the Eden-serpent's long neck and head. (I was also very worried by the visual resemblance to one of Francis Bacon's screaming-lamenting female-furies 'at the base of a crucifixion'.) Sexuality has entered the garden and destroys everything (the alien caresses one of its female victims before devouring her). The agent on board is in effect Satan disguised as a serpent (when its head is hacked off, its tubular body and innards are exposed) and is carrying out the Company's malign economic-political hidden agenda, to use the alien as a global weapon system. The Company is the God who intends the Fall to happen and places the serpent-agent there to effect it. And in the sharpest twist to the formula, the on-board computer that is secretly orchestrating the crew's actions, forcing them to the Company's will, has a nickname: Mother.

The mother releases us into aching vacancy and there's plenty of that in Beckett's *Waiting for Godot* (first published in English in 1954), more than the first audiences could handle. Many walked out. *Godot*, the most richly complex and the closest to myth of Beckett's plays, represents falling and the Fall in ways that typically intensify the archetypes. (A lecture on *Godot* follows quite soon in this book.) Beckett's wondrously peopled world keeps reverting to Eden. There are a number of doubtfully benevolent deity-fathers in Beckett's universe (Youdi, Mr Knott, Godot) who are bemaddeningly absent and always, but with impenetrable vagueness, threatening retribution for which forgiveness (but for what?) seems to be required. (One of my opening questions about the Fall: what am I being punished for?). Beckett also explores the frustrated longings to re-find the mother, the little matter of the Eden lost.

When Estragon dreams he dreams of falling. 'I was falling – ', 'I was on top of a – ' (Act 2), but Vladimir never lets him remember or tell him in more detail. It's the forbidden subject, the play's one taboo. It mustn't be spoken of. To speak of falling would be to admit how precariously positioned they are, how each day makes their precariousness more anguished, their dialogue more difficult to sustain while silence threatens to take over. And what keeps them from falling is not only the illusion that there's a reason to be there but each other. When they're separated at night Estragon is or claims to be beaten and when Estragon is asleep Vladimir is or claims to be unhappy. They seem curiously ageless, touchingly immune to the time that ravages Pozzo and Lucky. When the four protagonists fall into a heap in Act 2 Estragon and Vladimir get up again when they choose and without difficulty ('child's play'); Pozzo has to be supported and keeps falling back. Estragon and Vladimir, together and only together, are the Edenic couple, as perhaps are all comedy double-acts, unfallen man, though their garden is worryingly closer to Calvary and Gethsemane (tree; mound) than to a conventionalised Eden. They are every, any couple in their mutually sustaining illusions. But it's precarious, and though they have each other, that's all they've got. Pozzo and Lucky, conversely, are falling/fallen man, falling in terrible slow-motion as we watch, falling down a slope that seems specifically invented for Pozzo's own punishment. Defining himself by his possessions, his apparently inflexible schedule, his insights, and the thinking-aloud of his prophet, he is promptly stripped of each in turn, his watch, vaporiser, pipe and, in Act 2, of his sight ('so don't count on me to enlighten you'), of his notion of time itself, and of Lucky's voice. The bags that we took to be full of his material goods and wealth turn out to be full of sand. It's running out for both of them, fast.

But the expulsion from the Edenic nest finds, I think, its purest and most desolating literary expression in a rather surprising place. That's the end of Swift's *Gulliver's Travels* (1726).

In Houyhnhnm-land Gulliver had 'settled my little economy to my own heart's content'. (By economy he means everything about his way of life.) 'I enjoyed perfect health of body and tranquillity of mind.' The horses treat him as an indulged child and that's exactly how he wants to be treated. An adult, he has achieved the universal dream of a return to Edenic infancy. Gulliver is a blissfully happy Adam, with his idealised horses as his patrons, protectors, parents. Gulliver has his Eden. Then he loses it.

'In the midst of all this happiness, and when I looked upon myself to be fully settled for life', Gulliver's Houyhnhnm 'master' relays the assembly's decision to eject this Adam from this Eden. 'Struck with the utmost grief and despair … and unable to support the agonies I was under, I fell into a swoon at his feet.' It's the randomness of the expulsion, apart from its unjustness, that carries such an elemental charge. This is because it evokes so vividly the child's sense of random unjustness when he is expelled from the bed or the nest. Gulliver, when he comes out of his swoon, says that he 'could not blame' the assembly's decision and that too carries a sharp force (Book 4, Chapter 10). The worst thing about the child being expelled from its Eden-nest is the sense the child internalises that the loss is somehow something that he or she is being punished for (but why and for what?), that it's somehow his or her fault.

Which is where I started and where I now end. Thank you.

Further Reading

John Barton, *A History of the Bible: The Book and Its Faiths* (Allen Lane: 2019).

Samuel Beckett, *Waiting for Godot* (Faber and Faber: 2006).

Northrop Frye, *The Great Code: The Bible and Literature* (Routledge and Kegan Paul: 1982).

Stephen Greenblatt, *The Rise and Fall of Adam and Eve* (Bodley Head: 2017).

C.S. Lewis, *The Magician's Nephew* and *The Last Battle* (HarperCollins: 2009).

John C. Messenger, *Inis Beag, Isle of Ireland* (Holt, Rinehart & Winston: 1969).

Elaine Pagels, *Adam, Eve and the Serpent* (Vintage: 1989).

Philip Pullman, *His Dark Materials* (Scholastic: 2000).

J.D. Salinger, *The Catcher in the Rye* (Penguin: 2010).

Jonathan Swift, *Gulliver's Travels*, ed. Albert J. Rivero (Norton: 2002).

2 Claribel's Story

A Few Thoughts on Gender, Race and Colonialism in *The Tempest*

Claribel? Who's she? Don't worry too much if that's your first response to my title. Claribel doesn't get widely discussed in criticism of and commentary on *The Tempest*. One reason for that is that the play itself passes over her, and her story, in a rather perfunctory way. But I think she has important things to say about the play. Claribel is one of a number of women who are both in and not in the play. That is, like Sycorax and Mrs Prospero, as Carol Ann Duffy would call her, Claribel is talked about but doesn't appear on stage. (Isn't *The Tempest* the only Shakespeare play to feature just one woman in the stage-action?) All three of these absent but talked-about women, incidentally, do actually appear in Peter Greenaway's remarkable film *Prospero's Books* and Mrs Prospero even gets allocated a name (but I've forgotten it).

Claribel's story is told in Act 2 Scene 1 when Gonzalo tries gamely, and much to the contemptuous amusement of Antonio and Sebastian, to cheer up Alonso. Gonzalo is struck by the odd fact that, despite being 'drenched in the sea' during the shipwreck, all their garments are 'as fresh as when we put them on first in Afric, at the marriage of the King's fair daughter Claribel to the King of Tunis'. After three attempts to draw Alonso's attention to this fact, he gets this suddenly angry response:

> You cram these words into my ears against
> The stomach of my sense. Would I had never
> Married my daughter there! for, coming thence,
> My son is lost and, in my rate, she too,
> Who is so far from Italy removed
> I ne'er again shall see her.

Alonso is certain that he's lost Ferdinand to the seas, a wound into which Sebastian then pours some rather unbrotherly salt.

> Sir, you may thank yourself for this great loss,
> That would not bless our Europe with your daughter,
> But rather loose her to an African …

You were kneeled to and importuned otherwise
By all of us, and the fair soul herself
Weighed between loathness and obedience, at
Which end o' the beam should bow.

Later in the scene, after Ariel has put the rest of the court party to sleep, Antonio tempts Sebastian with his assassination plot on the grounds that Claribel, after Ferdinand the next heir of Naples, now 'dwells / Ten leagues beyond man's life' (an amazing phrase that I've long wanted to steal for a poem and have instead smuggled into your *Twelfth Night* lecture) and therefore can't possibly pose any threat to their plans.

And that's the Claribel story. She's only mentioned once more, in the play's last moments, when Gonzalo remarks on the marvel that, in one voyage, 'Did Claribel her husband find at Tunis, / And Ferdinand, her brother, found a wife / Where he himself was lost' (Act 5, Sc. 1).

What do we make of this? One point to start with is that Claribel's marriage is a forced marriage. It's made quite clear that it was only her 'obedience' to her father that outweighed her 'loathness', her dislike of the marriage and the husband. This is the tyrannical father imposing his will on his daughter, as threatened (but not fulfilled) in *A Midsummer Night's Dream*. The next point is that everyone else in the court of Naples objected to the marriage as well, though not it seems out of sensitivity to Claribel's feelings: the Neapolitans' objections were racist, opposed to Alonso's plans to 'loose her to an African' rather than to a European. I'm very struck by the word 'loose', and I'm sure you are as well. Before Frank Kermode's Arden edition the word was usually printed in student editions as 'lose' (as it appears in the original Folio but that is their usual spelling of 'loose': I've amended my public domain text above to 'loose'). It means 'mate her with' and the brutal image is of the mechanics of animal breeding, so here it's as if Claribel is being seen as a bit of sweet white meat to be tossed to a wild black animal. There's also the obvious pun on 'lose' (Alonso loses daughter as well as son). Polonius uses the word in an equivalently brutal and, as her father, almost unbelievably unfeeling way, when planning to use Ophelia as decoy or bait with Hamlet: he tells Claudius that when Hamlet is next seen reading in the lobby 'at such a time I'll loose my daughter to him' (Act 2, Sc. 2). That is even more shocking and I recall my shock as a schoolboy who rather fancied himself as a Hamlet.

So why does the marriage happen at all? The play is silent on this but the answer is clear: Claribel is forced into a marriage with the King of Tunis for reasons of geo-politics and/or trade. Claribel is the commodity or prize (or bait) in an act of commercial-colonial calculation over Africa. And the reason the Neapolitan court party is now on Prospero's island is that they were on their way back to Naples after the marriage in Tunis. Even Alonso himself, faced with the presumed death of his son, seems to regret his actions with his daughter, who is now 'so far from Italy removed / I ne'er again shall see her' (Act 2, Sc. 1). And it's very remarkable that Gonzalo forces us to think again about Claribel's situation at the very end of the play. Yes, 'in one voyage / Did Claribel her husband find at Tunis' (Act 5, Sc. 1). But is that a happy ending, for her?

Why is all this important? One answer is that, in this very highly patterned play, we're being invited, if only part consciously, to see Claribel as a version of Miranda. At first the differences seem clear: Miranda loves Ferdinand and Ferdinand is Italian and the marriage is not forced. But it is nonetheless an arranged marriage – Prospero very deliberately manipulates his daughter into making it possible – and it's also an important dynastic marriage that politically consolidates the relations between two Italian city-states, though with the odd effect, as critics have pointed out, of consolidating and extending the power of Naples over Milan.

The Claribel story, then, gives a muted ironic edge to the Miranda story, making us uneasily recognise that Miranda too is a commodity. It also has an effect on the way we perceive Caliban. If the King of Tunis is the unwelcome black suitor whom the white bride tries to resist, then that's the Caliban story told in a different way as well. Miranda is able to resist Caliban successfully and her father stigmatises and punishes the transgressor; Claribel is not able to resist and her father delivers his daughter into the black embrace. The King of Tunis becomes the son-in-law; Caliban is the son that Prospero can only unwillingly 'acknowledge mine' (Act 5, Sc. 1).

The Claribel story both sharpens the racist representation of 'loathsome' Africa, home to Sycorax and Caliban, and also underlines the questionable morality of Prospero's European colonising power over Caliban, equivalent to Alonso's ambitions with Tunis. Another pattern positions Claribel as one of three virtuous white women – Miranda, Claribel and Mrs Prospero, the latter described as a 'piece of virtue' ('piece' means masterpiece) – who collectively thus further demonise Sycorax as the 'dark' or 'other' woman and mother. One other effect of the Claribel story is very strange. It undermines Prospero's authority and stage-management. In the second scene he explains to Miranda that 'by accident most strange, bountiful Fortune ... hath mine enemies / Brought to this shore' (Act 1, Sc. 2). But it's not an accident at all: it's Alonso's decision to impose the King of Tunis on his daughter that has brought Prospero's enemies to this shore. Moreover, Prospero, who apparently knows everything, shows no awareness or knowledge of the Claribel story. The effect of this is to strike another ironic note, one that makes Prospero, in this matter at least, less all-powerful authority and more victim of circumstance.

And it's that way of thinking about Prospero that I find most helpful. For all his stage-management he's the victim of one crucial circumstance above all: the fact that his daughter has grown up and he has to lose/loose her to another man. And he can't do anything about it. His ignorance of the Claribel story is an emblem of that inability. The play explores most subtly in the area of father and daughter and that's why the Claribel story is so important. From among the play's earliest moments – and twice in one speech – we can hear a father trying to tell his daughter that she must now at last know him properly, now before it's too late. In what I take to be a very poignant oral/aural pun (perhaps an early modern Warwickshire accent would help here), though I don't think I've seen it commented on elsewhere, Prospero says 'Tis time / I should inform thee farther' and, ten lines later, 'Sit down; / For thou must now know farther' (Act 1, Sc. 2).

The need for her to know (find out) things 'further' is to know her 'father' properly, at last – at the moment when he has to lose her. As Gonzalo says, it's finding and losing at the same time. I suppose most fathers have to go through this.

Thanks for listening.

**

This short lecture first appeared as an article in emagazine Issue 28, April 2005. Reproduced by kind permission of the English and Media Centre.

Further Reading

Kate Aughterson, *Shakespeare: The Late Plays* (Palgrave: 2013).

Jonathan Dollimore and Alan Sinfield edd., *Political Shakespeare: Essays in Cultural Materialism* (Cornell U.P.: 1985).

John Drakakis ed., *Alternative Shakespeares* (Methuen: 1985).

Stephen Greenblatt, *Learning to Curse: Essays in Early Modern Culture* (Routledge: 1990).

Sean McEvoy, *Shakespeare: The Basics* (3rd ed., Routledge: 2012).

Kiernan Ryan, *Shakespeare* (Palgrave: 2001)

William Shakespeare, *The Tempest*, ed. Stephen Orgel (Oxford U.P.: 1987).

Valerie Traub ed., *The Oxford Handbook of Shakespeare and Embodiment: Gender, Sexuality and Race* (Oxford U.P.: 2018).

3 *Wuthering Heights*
Myth and the Wounds of Loss

As ever in these lectures on very well-known texts, but perhaps especially so with this novel above all texts, I can hardly claim much in the way of originality in what I'm going to say, though there may be a few re-inflections of the critical tradition in what follows. But to attempt at least something in the way of a fresh approach to *Wuthering Heights* let me say that the lecture deals first, and in general terms that then become more specific, with the novel as myth, in four senses; then with some straightforward remarks on the novel's highly unusual opening, explored in contrast to the opening of *Jane Eyre*; and then (the heart of the lecture) with a close look at the unfolding psycho-sexual drama (my fourth sense of myth) that constitutes the Cathy-Heathcliff relationship – and this will mean a focus on the first part of the novel with my having little or nothing to say about the second-generation story. I apologise in advance for that: I'm very aware that the Lawrence Olivier/Vivien Leigh film from 1939 notoriously stopped at the end of the first-generation story, as in effect I do as well. Actually, I'm going to (more or less) stop before the film does, before Cathy's death, and I hope that makes for something in the way of a different kind of lecture on this novel.

Myth in four senses. First, and at the outer frame of the novel, is the Bronte mythology or Bronte industry which is not exactly a helpful way into the text. For that reason, I'll say little about it but will just point to the well-upholstered Bronte/Haworth tourist industry, the familiar mythology or fairy-tale of the three sisters with Emily the silent, private and hidden one at the centre, barely straying from the home like her later namesake Emily Dickinson, but (like her) the most profoundly gifted of the family, dying of consumption, like Keats whose poetry she echoes in her own and who died even younger than she. It's the biography as fairy-tale that I suppose F. R. Leavis was reacting against when he refused the novel entrance to his austerely restrictive 'great tradition' of the 19th-century novel (George Eliot, Conrad and Henry James – er, that's it), dismissing it as a freak.

This leads to my second use of myth, the myth of the novel being unplanned, wild, emerging straight from the head of the child-genius Emily, unread and untaught, a freak of nature, not really a 'proper' novel at all.

Sister Charlotte, to be fair, set this one running and she needed to after the poor reception given to the novel's first edition. So in her 'biographical notice' and 'preface' to the 1850 edition Charlotte, though clearly sympathetic to the novel, defended it against its first readers by calling Emily's powers 'immature' and claiming that, having formed her characters, 'she did not know what she had done'.

The third point is this: the myth, as we might call it, of *Wuthering Heights* being the greatest love-story of all time. This notion, perhaps, lay behind the extraordinary decision made, not that many years ago, by one of the world's most famous popstars, then in his late fifties, to act the teenage Heathcliff in a musical version of the novel which calls Heathcliff a misunderstood man. This is the Heathcliff who (it is strongly suggested) sexually tortures his wife Isabella (a premonitory clue to this is his hanging her pet-dog, aptly named Fanny), mentally tortures his son Linton, and with calculated coolness savagely slaps the younger Catherine seated meekly on his lap. Anyway, the greatest love-story? Is it a love-story at all? The notion that Cathy and Heathcliff 'fall in love' with each other (surely a prerequisite of great love-stories?) is absurd. Mind you, I still teach the novel from the battered old Penguin edition I used as a teenager and I still have my teenage notes from class. Scenes like the savage slapping of the younger Catherine, which I've just mentioned, have my scribbled notes (scribbled down from what my teacher must have said) that excuse Heathcliff's savagery on the grounds that 'he's in love'. Oh dear.

But my last point about myth is serious: in a profound sense the novel is closer to myth (and myths have a more profound relationship with reality than 'realism') than realist novels like *Jane Eyre* (about which more later) or *Great Expectations* (which I'll be lecturing on later – when we'll note its uncharacteristic debt to Emily Bronte). We can see a tendency in critics of the novel to read it mythically – from David Cecil's 1934 account of a mythic conflict between children of calm and children of storm (this old chestnut still pops up in my students' assignments) to Terry Eagleton's 1975 mythic-Marxist account of economic systems (feudal and capitalist) in conflict – and Eagleton, in a later study of the novel, added the more specifically cultural-materialist point that the infant Heathcliff found on the docks at Liverpool might have been abandoned by poor Irish parents escaping famine, immigrants like those whom Emily's brother Branwell may have seen in Liverpool and told his sister about, the wayward brother thereby appropriately providing Emily with the most disruptive element of the novel (Eagleton 1998: 380). Perhaps most influential of these mythic readings has been Dorothy Van Ghent's description of Cathy and Heathcliff's 'mythological romance', a love belonging to the 'realm of the imagination where myths are created' (in Kettle 1972: 111).

This matches what I feel about the novel: that at its centre (though as I argue later it's a kind of absent centre) is the primitively elemental myth of the Cathy-Heathcliff relationship, not a love-story in any conventional sense but love felt and lived at its most mythic-psychic and raw level, not love as sexual desire but love as loss, love as constituted in and structured by loss, loss as the heart of love (even its deliberate heart if we think of Cathy deliberately choosing to marry Edgar, choosing the obstacle to love rather than its goal, and I'll return to this later), their relationship only understandable as a wounding series of separations and loss. It's this psycho-sexual drama, so close to what we saw in the first lecture, on the impact of the Fall, as Lacan's reading of infantile ego development, that I will trace later in this lecture. But just two quick points for now: infantile development is an inescapably relevant idea when we consider (which the absurd musical version clearly didn't) that Cathy and Heathcliff are in effect children. She's 12 when taken into Thrushcross Grange, 15 when Heathcliff walks out of her life for three years, 17 when she marries and 18 when she dies. He's one year older. And in *Great Expectations* (a lecture soon) we have Joe Gargery's lovely comment to Pip in London, that life is 'so many partings welded together' (Chapter 27).

Let me now turn to the myth of the unplanned, wild and disorganised novel somehow managed by the unread girl who didn't know what she was doing. The unread point is simply answered: though Emily Bronte may not have read as widely as Dickens she certainly read (like Emily Dickinson, also sometimes assumed to be unread) more deeply. We can think of Milton and *Paradise Lost* (the subject of the last lecture in this book). There's one local, admittedly pointed reference to the epic's final lines, as we'll see, at the end of the first part of *Great Expectations*, but Milton's poem is structured into the fabric of *Wuthering Heights*, with notions of being in heaven or in hell, dreams of falling out of heaven, and both Cathy and (comically) Lockwood figured as the fallen Satan. There's *King Lear* for the dispossessed son scheming to take possession of the family property/title. There's the Gothic tradition, Walter Scott, Byron and much else. As for the notion of the novel being unplanned it was as early as 1926 that C. P. Sanger's now famous family-tree showed the amazingly symmetrical structuring of the families and, even more so, the uncanny way Sanger was able to date, just from apparently casually dropped internal evidence, so many crucial family events, even to the month or day. There's also the novel's intricate and closely-informed knowledge of complex inheritance laws (which I can never get my head round).

In terms of the novel's alleged disorganisation, the opposite is the truth. Is there a more brilliantly organised 19th-century novel with multiple narrators more brilliantly interwoven than we have here? Here's a list of the narrators as the novel unfolds, moving forwards as well as back in flashbacks, some stretches of narrative of course occupying many chapters at a time, others (like Cathy's diary) just a few paragraphs. (This makes the Chinese-boxes framed narratives of *Frankenstein* seem elementary.) Lockwood; Cathy; Ellen; Heathcliff; Lockwood; Ellen; Isabella; Ellen; Lockwood; Ellen; Isabella; Ellen; [12-year gap in the story, equivalent to that, incidentally, in the middle of Shakespeare's *The Winter's Tale*]; Ellen; Catherine; Lockwood; Heathcliff; Zilla (of course you know who she is); Ellen; Lockwood; Ellen; Heathcliff; Lockwood. A consequent feature of the novel (we'll see this also in *Madame Bovary* in a later lecture on the fallen woman, though that novel at least deploys the regular omniscient narrator) is the absence of an authorial, authoritative moral commenting voice, and that led, predictably, to early reviews finding the novel deeply immoral – one American reviewer's advice was to read *Jane Eyre* and burn *Wuthering Heights* – and the effect of the narrative complexity and multiplicity is to dramatise the destabilising, de-centring effect of competing and contrasting points of view.

A nice example of this (and I'm not sure if this has received much or any critical attention) is the sequence of events in the novel that is actually narrated twice, though it would be quite understandable if you hadn't noticed this as the two versions are so completely different. They're also about 110 pages apart (in Chapters 17 and 29). The first is in Isabella's narrative to Ellen, having escaped from the Heights, and it's an eight-page account of the evening Hindley, armed with gun and knife, and she lock Heathcliff out of the house. You'll recall the appalling and bloody violence involved as Heathcliff attacks Hindley after forcing his way in. The scene extends to the next morning when he attacks Isabella.

> The charge exploded, and the knife, in springing back, closed into its owner's wrist. Heathcliff pulled it away by main force, slitting up the flesh as it passed on ... His adversary had fallen senseless with excessive pain, and the flow of blood that gushed from an artery or a large vein. [Heathcliff] kicked and trampled on him, and dashed his head repeatedly against the flags ... He exerted preter-human self-denial in abstaining from finishing him completely; but getting out of breath, he finally desisted ... Instead of endeavouring to reach me he snatched a dinner knife from the table, and flung it at my head. It struck beneath my ear ... but pulling it out, I sprang to the door ... The last glimpse I caught of him was a furious rush on his part, checked by the embrace of his host [Hindley]; and both fell locked together on the hearth.
>
> (Chapter 17)

Twelve full chapters later Heathcliff is musingly describing to Ellen his memory of the scene we all know in which he starts digging up Cathy's grave and then feels her 'sigh' and her warm presence as-if summoning him back to the Heights. So he rushes back. This, astonishingly, is his narrative 'take' on what we heard just now from Isabella.

> Having reached the Heights, I rushed eagerly to the door. It was fastened; and, I remember, that accursed Earnshaw and my wife opposed my entrance. I remember stopping to kick the breath out of him, and then

> hurrying upstairs, to my room, and hers – I looked round impatiently –
> I felt her by me – I could *almost* see her, and yet I *could not*!

> (Chapter 29)

So that appallingly violent attack on Hindley was as it were a momentary and inconvenient obstacle (ten words) to get past on his rush to the room where the novel starts, haunted. And there's no further mention of Isabella and her escape. I really can't think of another 19th-century novel where versions of the same event are narrated to such brilliantly divergent effect. The effect, I would add, is an irony attendant on such fictively strategic narrative devices – and I will call this strategy modernist as opposed to realist.

Of the multiple narrators identified just now, of course Lockwood and Ellen are the principal ones and it's the startling difference between them as well as the way they are complementarily unreliable and not wholly sympathetic (to the reader but also, in Ellen's case, to Cathy) that is so unusual. (I'll say a little more about the two of them a little later.) Lockwood at the outer frame of the novel is a particularly destabilising figure, and a largely comic figure – though, for me, he understands his own absurdity, especially when it comes to young women, rather better than most of his critics, so the comedy also carries pathos. Lockwood's comic-pathetic inability with young women at the outer frame is a subtle ironic commentary or counterpart to the love-as-loss at the novel's aching and wounded centre. And his urbane and civilised normality (well, what he would consider normal) is the ironic commentary to the extremities traversed by the novel. These come together in one marvellous moment (perhaps, again, not widely discussed by critics) where the anguished desire to be haunted clashes with the mechanics of household routine. As Heathcliff is about to try desperately to gain contact with Cathy ('Come in! come in!') after hearing of Lockwood's apparent encounter with her, Lockwood is surprised by how little of the night has passed and says 'we must surely have retired to rest at eight!'. Heathcliff's reply (as if from an automaton) is 'Always at nine in winter, and always rise at four' (Chapter 3), making him sound like a bed-and-breakfast landlady rigidly laying down the house-rules.

Let me move to two more aspects of the novel's brilliantly planned artfulness, examples of rich and subtle patterning, before I end this first section. The first point is the emblematic and suggestive dates and names at the outset, seemingly blank of significance for the reader and for Lockwood, as-if empty signifiers. The first word of the novel is not a word but a date followed by a stop and a dash: '1801. – ' On the next page is another date '1500' and a name 'Hareton Earnshaw', both just readable above the 'principal door' of the Heights (Chapter 1). Then at the start of Chapter 3, scratched into the paint on the ledge by the bed he's in (Cathy's), Lockwood reads the names *Catherine Earnshaw*, *Catherine Heathcliff* and *Catherine Linton*. The names and the dates set up patterns of ownership, possession, shifting and unstable identities and liminality (boundaries or edges).

The three scratched names, as has been often pointed out (I forget where I first saw this brilliant idea), can be read both forwards, to predict the first generation story (for Cathy) and, backwards, for the second generation story (for Catherine). The dates are beginnings and endings of centuries and novels and the name on the house, its 16th-century founder, is also the name of its owner at the close, to be happily married on another liminal occasion, New Year's day, after we close the novel.

The larger point is also about liminality. Cathy's 'ghost' (is it?) crying to Lockwood 'Let me in!' and Heathcliff's ensuing 'Come in!' (Chapter 3) are the start of a richly patterned motif about being let in or out. As J. Hillis Miller argues in a typically excellent account, this request to be let in is also what the reader and Lockwood (whom Miller calls our 'delegate', though he fulfils that role not exactly competently) are obliged to ask, to be let into the text, into its inner secrets, to 'penetrate' further and further in (Miller 1982: 43, 70). The novel repeatedly images liminal objects like thresholds, doors, windows and latches: when Heathcliff returns after three years his fingers are seen holding the latch at Thrushcross Grange 'as if intending to open [it] for himself' (Chapter 10), the latch itself imaging Cathy's sexual body. Let me in and let me out: the first motif suggests sexual possession, the return home, the return to the mother/the womb, into the bed, into the coffin (for Lockwood Cathy's bed is a kind of coffin); and let me out – of the locked room (and of myself, Lock-wood), the grave, out of heaven (where Cathy dreams she doesn't belong), out of the prisons of bourgeois marriage and patriarchy, out of the suffocating space into the air where Cathy, hallucinating, says of the wind from the moor 'let me have one breath' (Chapter 12). As at the end of *King Lear* (a lecture follows later in this book) the motif – let me in, let me out – is ultimately reduceable to the simple request to be able to breathe.

**

Let me say something about the highly unusual opening of the novel in relation to the opening of the much more conventional *Jane Eyre*, published in the same year. In terms of their narrative strategies – the ways by which narrative works on the reader to create senses of identity and consciousness – these openings, though both in the first person, could hardly be more different. If the narrative opening in *Jane Eyre* works to consolidate Jane's identity in a way that comforts and flatters the reader, that in *Wuthering Heights* has the opposite effect of confusing and even alienating the reader with Lockwood's awkwardly intrusive (and indeed confused) narrative presence, to the point where some readers, perhaps some of you, might even have given up reading. To describe this difference, we might call *Jane Eyre* a classic-realist text, where the reader is comfortably positioned and by and large passively consuming explicit meaning, while *Wuthering Heights* might be called an interrogative text, even proto-modernist, where the reader is forced to answer challenging questions and has to actively negotiate through largely implicit or deferred meanings, filling in the 'gaps'. This is the difference between what Roland Barthes famously called 'readerly' and 'writerly' texts (Barthes 1990: v).

In a strategically planned narrative process of information being made available to the reader, by stages and not too much at once, the opening chapter of *Jane Eyre* establishes that we're in a comfortable country house environment but one not comfortable to Jane whose identity is subtly accumulated out of perceived and felt differences. She is positioned as both part of but not part of the family group. The 'we' in the second sentence ('we had been wandering ... in the leafless shrubbery') seamlessly slips into the 'I' of the second paragraph whose 'dreadful' sense of physical pain in turn seamlessly moves to emotional pain, her heart both 'saddened' by being chided by Bessie and 'humbled' by her 'physical inferiority to Eliza, John, and Georgiana Reed'.

Jane's difference constitutes her identity and is why we (treasuring our own sense of being different) find it easy to relate to. With the title in front of us and the narrator addressed by name just after we've heard of Eliza, John and Georgiana Reed, Jane is identifiable as not a 'natural' member of the family (Mrs Reed wants Jane to be more 'natural'). This is enough to suggest (to Victorian readers certainly) that she's an orphan, but one whose consciousness of 'physical inferiority' to the other children suggests an unspoken awareness of her superiority to those children (intellectual, moral), which is underlined by their only being named collectively, further isolating Jane's uniqueness. And more differences accumulate and cluster around Jane. While the Reed children are characterised, again collectively, as 'darlings... for the time neither quarrelling or crying', Jane's one spoken line of dialogue ('What does Bessie say I have done?') has a calm, reasonable and indeed adult air, and a simplicity compared to Mrs Reed's petulance towards her. And as a narrator Jane has a nice touch of (again adult) irony and humour, as in her seeing those 'darlings... clustered round their mama'.

When Jane is then isolated in the breakfast room, wrapped against the cold in the curtain in the window-seat, she is 'shrined in double retirement' (a nice ironic use of shrine): she's at the centre of a series of enclosed spaces, reading about birds in an intensity of imaginative projection, in her own sense of being 'solitary', like in the 'haunts of sea-fowl', and in her need to be as free as they, 'happy at least in my way'. And what is particularly comforting and flattering to the reader is that we are positioned by the narrative as duplicating what Jane is doing. Like her, we are reading a book, her book, probably comfortable and perhaps wrapped warm, in a chair or in bed. The effect is that we are locked closely into Jane's consciousness and identity, enjoying our sense of specialness like Jane, to whom for that reason we feel even closer.

Wuthering Heights is a much more complex novel than *Jane Eyre*, not least, as I've already indicated, in its narrative complexity and multiple narrators, the first and last of whom, Lockwood, is bewilderingly (and comically) at odds with the rest of the novel. There is a modernist lack of fit between Lockwood and the novel over which he notionally has narrative control. One bewildering question is what exactly Lockwood's narrative is and who it's addressed to. Why does Lockwood start the novel, as we've seen, with '1801. -'? Is this a diary? But what kind of diary would have this: '(N.B. I dine between twelve and one o'clock.)' (Chapter 2.) What kind of novel reader needs to be told that? Or, indeed, what kind of narrator addressing what kind of reader needs to launch into the random and embarrassing anecdote that Lockwood feels the need to tell about his falling in love with a girl at the seaside and then, as soon as she gave a look of reciprocated feeling, 'icily' withdrawing from her? (Chapter 1). So what's that about? Nothing – until we realise that it may serve (however absurdly) as a narrative premonition of Cathy withdrawing from Heathcliff in the full knowledge of their reciprocated love.

The presiding sense in the early chapters is that Lockwood is not only a deeply unreliable narrator but an inappropriate one, comically so, misunderstanding everything he sees at the Heights. He absurdly assumes that Heathcliff is just like him – he quite wrongly claims he has 'a sympathetic chord' that makes him able to read people on sight. He is blandly certain of his magnetic ability to attract any and every young woman, warning himself to take care lest he cause Catherine 'to regret her choice' because he knew 'through experience, that I was tolerably attractive' (Chapter 2). Later he seriously considers eloping with her to London – though the seaside anecdote suggests he wouldn't have dared. This is a young man estranged from everyone else, even for most readers. So his difference, unlike Jane's, is awkward and embarrassing and not, as with her, the source of the reader's intimate affection.

But, as I've said, I do find Lockwood a sadder and more self-knowing character than often portrayed by critics. His bluster about young women and his rather self-regarding literary vocabulary (he's fond of words like penetralium) mask a more vulnerable and inadequate figure. He's seemingly unaffected by the encounter with the ghost of Cathy (if that's what it is), just as at the end of the novel he shows no sign of being affected by anything he's heard from Ellen and is only interested in catching one more (pathetic) glimpse of Catherine. In effect Lockwood, the narrator at the outer frame of the novel, and in his own self-deluding belief a potentially crucial romantic player in the last stages of its plot, is peripheral to any plot, ignorant of the novel's significances, and sadly half-aware of that. Lockwood is superfluous to what some readers take from the novel (which is why he's simply dropped from most film versions), and yet he is so subtly characterised on its margins.

Ellen as principal narrator starts her story three pages into Chapter 4. Though central to the events unlike Lockwood, she too is not wholly reliable. She is wilfully unwilling to understand or sometimes even to listen to the young Cathy in her emotional confusions, as we'll see very soon. But the start of Ellen's narrative brings up another generically intriguing issue, to put alongside the way Lockwood's narrative seems comically to belong to quite a different kind of novel. Ellen's narrative starts: 'One fine summer morning … Mr Earnshaw, the old master, came downstairs, dressed for a journey.' He asks his children what gifts they want him to bring them from Liverpool. Hindley asks for a fiddle and Cathy chooses a whip.

This, generically, is not classic-realist fiction but fairy-tale (though with the gifts in reversed gender associations) and serves as a reminder that this extraordinary novel is closer in terms of narrative ancestry to myth and fairy-tale than the much more realist *Jane Eyre*. The challenge is to adjust to the demands of such a mythic text in the middle of the realist 19th century. And it was with myth that this lecture began. So let me now move to the last section.

**

Here we do something that as students you will have been told not to do, on pain of being ticked off in the name of literary theory. Ignoring (largely) the brilliantly structured artfulness of the novel's moving back and forward in time, and treating its characters as if they were 'real' people rather than textual constructs, we will try to trace the Cathy-Heathcliff relationship through its phases and moments as if in 'real' and 'chronological' time, to see if we can read its psycho-sexual stages.

We start with Heathcliff's arrival in the Earnshaw household (in 1771) – as I've just mentioned, this is the fairy-tale opening (again like *King Lear*) to Ellen's narrative in Chapter 4, with the father going off on his journey and the symbolic gifts he promises to his children on his return – and the telling detail emerges that because of the strange orphaned child the gifts are lost or ruined. Hindley's 'fiddle' is 'crushed to morsels' in the father's greatcoat, crushed by the pressure of the child's body, and Cathy's whip is lost. This pre-figures Heathcliff's later crushing or emasculating of Hindley (the 14-year-old 'blubbered' like a baby seeing the crushed fiddle: we'll later see the adult Edgar behaving like a baby on Heathcliff's return, after Cathy 'crushed' Edgar's fingers into Heathcliff's hand) and it also prefigures his struggle over emotional power (the 'whip-hand') with Cathy. Even more telling is the family decision (clearly, the father's) to call the stranger Heathcliff: 'it was the name of a son who died in childhood' (Chapter 4). Over many years of teaching the novel, I've noticed students have always assumed that this lost son was the first-born. I wonder if you felt the same. For the father there is the need to replace what was the original heir, to salve that wound to his male vanity; for the mother the new arrival is a persistent reminder of the suffering she wishes to forget: explaining both her hatred and his affection. The child is a replacement for a lost-object, an emblem of loss. (And that Heathcliff ends up as, in effect, old Earnshaw's heir is particularly piquant.)

The next phase is again about loss, Cathy and Heathcliff's loss of the father (the mother is now dead, and Hindley sent away to college). This is the short Chapter 5 with its highly unusual domestic-interior scene, the novel's sole representation of 'ordinary' domestic-family life at the Heights (even Joseph is being friendly), the kind of scene favoured by many a Victorian sentimental painter. One detail, just before the death, again very telling: Cathy 'leant against her father's knee, and Heathcliff was lying on the floor with his head in her lap'. This unbroken chain of physical intimacy between a father and his two children is touching because unique in the novel, especially touching as (despite popular conceptions of their relationship) Cathy and Heathcliff are virtually never seen physically bonded (and, of course, certainly not sexually so). The scene immediately following the father's death – the children discovering their 'loss' – has Ellen noticing them 'comforting each other' in their bedroom and in terms of physical intimacy between them, that's more or less it for the whole novel – until the ravening intensities of their final embraces (inadequate word) before her death.

Next in terms of chronology means leafing back in the novel to Chapter 3 and Lockwood reading Cathy's diary before his encounter with her 'ghost'. Hindley (aged 20) is back and is acting the tyrant-father, the 'bad' father of fairy-tale, replacing the 'good' dead father, or, to put it another way, acting the old-Testament prohibiting (thou-shalt-not) and punitive God. Cathy (aged 12) puts it like this: 'Poor Heathcliff! Hindley calls him a vagabond, and won't let him sit with us, nor eat with us anymore; and, he says, he and I must not play together, and threatens to turn him out of the house if we break his orders'.

I'm going to play the psycho-analyst here and claim, though I recognise the absurdity of doing this with a novel, that that list of the father-Hindley's prohibitions – Cathy and Heathcliff can't sit together, eat together or play together – has one item missing and it's missing because it was too traumatic for the young Cathy to record in her diary. The evidence is a hundred pages later, in Chapter 12, as Cathy is slipping in and out of hallucinations in her sickness. She says to Ellen that she thought she was back in her 'oak-panelled bed' at the Heights: 'I was a child; my father was just buried, and my misery arose from the separation that Hindley had ordered between me, and Heathcliff – I was laid alone, for the first time, and rousing from a dismal dose after a night of weeping...' So the imposed separation that mattered most was that Heathcliff is banished from the bed the two of them shared (Cathy in the passage just quoted says that she now feels that at 12 she was as if 'wrenched' from the Heights and from 'my all in all, as Heathcliff was at that time' and made 'at a stroke, into Mrs Linton ... an exile and outcast') and the really crucial words here are 'I was laid alone, for the first time'. This, inescapably, is the term used for a child separated for the first time from the mother's bed and that, of course, establishes Heathcliff as Cathy's as-if mother (or rather they are each other's mother, real mothers being conspicuously absent in the novel: the absent-mother motif in the novel has been regularly written about, and of course I'm not the first to claim that the two of them are each other's mother). So this first crucial separation (as mentioned earlier we will be reading their love as a series of wounding separations) imposed by Hindley also establishes him as the Oedipal father banishing the son from the Oedipal mother (in effect the *Hamlet* story, as I touched on in the first lecture) – and also laying-down the incest-taboo, that forbidding intercourse between mother and child and between siblings, for Cathy and Heathcliff, even more than mother-child, are brother-sister. Eagleton speculates that Heathcliff may well have been Mr Earnshaw's illegitimate son – but adds, in one of his better jokes, 'just as he may well have passed his two-year absence living in Tunbridge Wells' (Eagleton 1998: 55).

More evidence for this comes a little later in Chapter 3 (back in 1801) as Lockwood struggles with the haunting or nightmare appearance of Cathy's 'child's face' at the window. Here the crucial words the child says, after 'Let me in – let me in!', are 'It's twenty years ... twenty years, I've been a waif for twenty years!'. A waif is an orphaned and abandoned child. A little simple maths shows us that twenty years before 1801 takes us (almost) exactly to Cathy at 15 – when Heathcliff walked out of her life after hearing that marriage with him would 'degrade' her. (This is the third separation to which I'll return.) So Cathy has been in effect a mother-less orphan since Heathcliff, again her as-if mother, left her at 15. A psychological corollary might suggest that Heathcliff, the abandoned waif-orphan at Liverpool, then as-if exerts a repetitive process of being the orphaning-agent for Cathy, willingly as here or earlier in the first separation by compulsion, in ways we've been tracing. Just to add that Cathy's hallucinating scene later, as we've seen, includes her insight that marriage at 18 made her feel 'an exile and outcast' – and she says she feels 'burning' and in 'a hell of tumult' as she talks to Ellen in that scene, establishing her as the fallen Satan – and Satan was the favoured child before his fall. (I'll return to this as well.)

Let's now go to the second separation, back to Cathy at 12. This is in Heathcliff's narrative to Ellen about how the two of them looked in through the windows at Thrushcross Grange (a kind of 'heaven') and how Cathy was then seized by the 'devil' of the bull-dog Skulker. Then: 'the dog was throttled off, his huge, purple tongue hanging half a foot out of his mouth, and his pendant lips streaming with bloody slaver [= saliva]' (Chapter 6). Cathy is taken into the Grange where she stays five weeks and then returns to the Heights sort-of a 'lady'.

The conventional reading of this passage is that Cathy is here inducted into puberty, into adult and bourgeois ladyhood, the process and transition marked by what is imaged as a bloody rape. The phrasing of the dog-attack can indeed easily (if queasily) be read as hymen-breaking rape but the rest of the reading might be queried. For a start Cathy's induction into ladyhood is only partial and temporary: she soon reverts (at least for a time) to preferring Heathcliff's company. But 12 is too young for puberty at this period which for girls was more typically 15 (and for boys 16) – I'll come back to that. In any case this does mark the second separation – the partially successful attempt to wrest Cathy away from Heathcliff in terms of class.

The third separation is the most divisive and also decisive in terms of plot. I've already talked about it as it marked the twenty years of being an orphaned waif that the 'ghost' speaks of. And earlier in the scene is the account of Cathy's dream (which, as later, Ellen tries to stop her talking about) of being unhappy in heaven and 'flung' out for that reason – figuring her, as mentioned and as we saw later in her hallucinating, as Satan. This separation is Heathcliff (as-if her mother) walking out of Cathy's life for three years after hearing how marrying him would degrade her – leaving before he could hear the ensuing and famous 'I *am* Heathcliff' speech. He not hearing it when he might have done so easily and, in terms of plot, very decisively, adds a pathos which is compounded by Ellen's complete lack of sympathy. The speech, for many readers the purest expression of 'romantic' love, is a kind of impossibility or absent centre – and it is about the absent centre that constitutes their love. It is as-if spoken to nobody (Ellen crossly calls it 'nonsense') and it ends with the words 'so, don't talk of our separation again – it is impracticable; and – ' which is a particularly sharp irony as Heathcliff has just, and very practicably, separated himself from her (Chapter 9). Two more things to add about the speech. On, again, a very practicable level, Cathy's choice to marry Edgar and not Heathcliff makes the kind of perfectly understandable economic sense that would have applied to very many young women at the time (we need only think of Charlotte and Mr Collins in *Pride and Prejudice*). But more psychologically interesting is the notion (mentioned briefly earlier), that Denis de Rougement explains in his *Love in the Western World*, that love thrives on and seeks out obstacles rather than the ostensible goal, and that what it seeks at its heart is death. Cathy's 'reasoning' can be read as a very pure example of this. And a simple point is that the words 'I *am* Heathcliff' paradoxically deny both the self and the loved-other existences as separate human entities, in effect acts of willed self-cancellation and obliteration of the other.

Realising that he's gone Cathy rushes into a storm that (again as in *King Lear*) is as much symbolic as real, a storm from which she catches the fever that gets passed to the Linton parents who nurse her and die from it. Cathy is 15. If Emily Bronte is subtle enough, as I certainly thinks she is, to image the onset of puberty in the process we've been tracing, then this symbolic storm (the storm in her body, her emotional confusions) may be it – and how appropriate that her puberty marks the death of the other parents left in the novel, the parents of her husband-to-be. This third separation, then, not only marks what her 'ghost' later images as her being orphaned (Heathcliff as mother) but also the deaths of her as-if parents. And puberty is figured as being flung out of heaven and 'into the middle of the heath' (/ cliff) for not being happy (enough). Or looked at another way, Heathcliff (by walking out) kills his rival's parents. (His original arrival as-if kills his 'mother'. These parents all – apart from old Earnshaw – die as it were in parentheses.)

The marriage is three years later, and those three years are Heathcliff's extended absence, another aching vacancy, ended by the marriage (Heathcliff hears about it, as we'll see) which is the fourth separation. Ellen describes the first months of the marriage in a telling phrase about Cathy: 'the gunpowder lay as harmless as sand, because no fire came near to explode it'. When Heathcliff then returns Cathy sarcastically asks the unimpressed Edgar (whose fingers she is about to 'crush' into Heathcliff's hand, as mentioned earlier) if he'd rather have two tables set, one for the 'gentry' (him and Isabella) and one for 'the lower orders' (Heathcliff and herself). She adds 'Or must I have a fire lighted elsewhere?'

The two images of fire can be taken together and looked at in the light of what happens that night, after the awkward meeting over tea in which (again, as mentioned earlier) Edgar, like a fractious child, makes 'a slop in his saucer'. Heathcliff leaves the house and the excited Cathy comes to Ellen to complain of Edgar being, again infantilised, 'sulky... pettish, silly' and inclined 'to cry', but says eventually that she, in her joy at Heathcliff's return, will now return to Edgar and make her peace with him – and Ellen adds that next day seems to have proved the peace-making a success as husband and wife are ordinarily happy with each other (Chapter 10). You'll forgive me for being literal and explicit with this subtly intimated material – and also forgive me if I just say the words 'c'mon baby, light my fire' – but the clear inference is that during this night Cathy at last makes love with Edgar (or perhaps for the first time 'properly') and that she's only able to do so because her fire has been 'lighted elsewhere', that she's able to make love only because of Heathcliff. And what adds even more piquancy is that we can date the conception of Catherine from this event, making Heathcliff the as-if father of her child.

If the marriage is the fourth separation, the fifth and last is of course Cathy's death. But the plot could have gone another way with the fifth and last separation being not her death but his. Let me move towards the end of this lecture by speaking briefly about this, as it's a very strange aspect of the novel that generally receives little attention. It's in the same scene over tea we were just looking at, with Edgar reduced to a baby making a slop in his saucer. Heathcliff, in an extraordinary speech to Cathy, a speech 'murmured' but obviously audible to Edgar (if it's audible to Ellen), says this.

> I heard of your marriage, Cathy, not long since; and, while waiting in the yard below, I meditated this plan – just to have one glimpse of your face – a stare of surprise, perhaps, and pretended pleasure; afterwards settle my score with Hindley; and then prevent the law by doing execution on myself. Your welcome has put these ideas out of my mind; but beware of meeting me with another aspect next time ...
>
> (Chapter 10)

So he's telling Cathy what was going to be his Plan A: murder her brother, kill himself – and then the novel, rather shorter, would presumably end. Her warm welcome changes his plans, as, more significantly, does Isabella's crush on him from which he gradually evolves Plan B, the strategy to acquire both houses. Plan A would of course be more melodramatic but perhaps not necessarily more so than the male-male struggle with Edgar that occupies the chapters before Cathy's death – a struggle that is helpfully illuminated by the critical work of Eve Sedgwick. Her 1985 book crucially identifies the male-male relations (from violent rivalry through to homo-erotic bonding) that structure the economy of desire behind the hetero-normative plots of classic fictions, male-male desire in which the woman is reduced to an exchange-commodity or bargaining-chip. There is certainly something excessive about the Heathcliff-Edgar dynamic. In the scene of threatened and then actual violence in front of Cathy we read that Edgar 'sprang erect, and struck [Heathcliff] full on the throat a blow that would have levelled a slighter man' (Chapter 11) – 'erect' and the attack on the Adam's apple is equivalent to kicking him (if I can lift a joke from Beckett) among the testicles. And also excessive is the Heathcliff-Hindley dynamic, as we've seen: and Cathy, in both cases, is in effect a kind of part-object in the energies released in those dynamics.

And that's a rather muted way for me to draw this discussion of the Cathy-Heathcliff relationship, and this lecture, to a close. I've tried to trace their relationship and their love as capable of being conceptualised only as a series of wounding separations and losses, based on a kind of mother-loss, a compulsive repetition of that loss. 'I *am* Heathcliff' is, after all, the expressing of the Lacanian idea that for the infant the entire world is one undifferentiated unity of infant-plus-mother. It's in that sense that Cathy and Heathcliff are an undifferentiated unity of pre-socialised infant-hood. In the hallucinating scene (Chapter 12) and just before the key phrase 'I was laid alone for the first time' – the clue to the trauma of the first separation in our sequence – we hear from Ellen that the exhausted Cathy, desperate to breathe the air from the moor, 'was no better than a wailing child!' This, quite brilliantly (and again characteristic of the novel's intricate internal architecture) takes us to the wailing child, the orphaned waif that appears to Lockwood in 1801 – and the link is confirmed within a page when Ellen, unable to stop Cathy opening the window herself, says that she 'bent out, careless of the frosty air that cut about her shoulders as keen as a knife' (Lockwood pulled the child's 'wrist on to the broken pane, and rubbed it to and fro till the blood ran down').

The wailing child and the orphaned waif in these scenes, and the first trauma of being laid alone for the first time (from Heathcliff as mother) – this is essentially the only Cathy we have, the purest expression of her need and her lack, the need to return to the undifferentiated unity of infant-plus-mother and the wounding scar (bleeding) of that permanent lack.

Heathcliff's expression of the equivalent comes at the end of the novel (in Chapter 33). Musing on how everybody and everything recalls Cathy to his imagination ('what is not connected with her to me? and what does not recall her?') he utters the words that for me haunt the entire enterprise of the hetero-normative 19th-century realist novel, and come out of the purest expression of the infant's undifferentiated universe that we have in our literature. 'The entire world is a dreadful collection of memoranda that she did exist, and that I have lost her!'

Thank you for listening.

**

Part of this lecture first appeared as an article in emagazine Issue 77, September 2017. Reproduced by kind permission of the English and Media Centre.

Further Reading

Roland Barthes, *S/Z*, trs. Richard Miller (Blackwell: 1990).

Ian Brinton, *Bronte's Wuthering Heights* (Continuum: 2010).

Emily Bronte, *Wuthering Heights*, ed. Richard J. Dunn (Norton: 2003).

Emily Bronte, *Wuthering Heights*, ed. Heather Glen (Routledge: 1988).

Terry Eagleton, *The Eagleton Reader*, ed. Stephen Regan (Blackwell: 1998).

Heather Glen ed., *The Cambridge Companion to the Brontes* (Cambridge U.P.: 2006).

Arnold Kettle ed., *The Nineteenth Century Novel: Critical Essays and Documents* (Heinemann: 1972).

J. Hillis Miller, *Fiction and Repetition* (Harvard U.P.: 1982).

Raymond Williams, *The English Novel from Dickens to Lawrence* (Chatto and Windus: 1970).

4 Beckett's *Waiting for Godot*
Transforming Lives

I spoke about *Godot* in the first lecture in this series, on the impact of the myth of the Fall, and I return to the play now. It has been very important to me over the years so let me start with a bit of personal history that I hope you don't mind me sharing with you.

It's a dreary November afternoon and it's raining. A 16-year-old boy in a private boarding-school is trying to kill time before school supper. He sits alone, not very happy and rather lonely, in the study of an older boy who has befriended him. He glances at the bookshelf. His friend (considered rather 'arty' and 'intellectual') has a large collection of 'literature' books. The spine of a Faber paperback catches his eye because of its strange rust-mud colour. There's still an hour before supper and it's still raining. He yanks the book out, yawns and starts to read.

An hour later he realises he has become certain of three things. First, he knows he has to act in and direct the play he's been reading, as soon as he can. Second, he knows he won't talk about the book with his usual cigarette-smoking companions. He's rather frightened of them, anyway. Third, he knows he feels different and that the world feels different too – odd and rather worrying feelings.

Yes, that was how *Godot* entered my life. And I also knew I had to be Estragon: it never occurred to me to act any other part. (Failed poet? Needy child?) We all know the cliché about texts changing lives, but *Godot* does just that. There are numerous testimonies to its strange and transformative power. You may know that, just at the time when it was puzzling and antagonising audiences round the world, it was performed in front of prisoners in San Quentin jail in the States. The reception was electrifyingly responsive; they knew, after all, about waiting and about deferred hopes. Their uncomplicated response fits well with Beckett's nice exasperation with the more refined of critics who, as he knew, could only complicate simple things, like his play. I like to think that at 16 the play was speaking to me with the transformative directness that electrified the San Quentin prisoners. Or perhaps at 16, and without knowing it, I considered myself condemned to a life-sentence of trying to give myself the impression I existed. I doubt I actually thought of anything like that as I turned the pages. But what I do remember thinking then was not how gloomy the play was – I've never felt that – but rather how funny it was and how its humour was of a kind I'd never met elsewhere. It was encouraging to discover much later that Beckett wrote *Godot* (first in French), not out of deep despair but as a means of re-laxation when grappling with the composition of his great trilogy of novels, *Molloy, Malone Dies* and *The Unnameable*.

I've started on a personal note because I've found that people feel very personally possessive about *Godot*. It takes over and changes. (One San Quentin prisoner, when released, devoted his life to performing Beckett's plays.) And change, of course, is also a pressing concern within the play itself. Estragon and Vladimir desperately want their lives to be taken over and changed by Godot – if he comes 'we'll be saved' (Act 2) – but find that, instead, 'they all change. Only we can't' (Act 1). Pozzo and Lucky are transformed bodily in front of our eyes: the tree randomly grows leaves; but Estragon and Vladimir seem suspended from time's processes, at least when they're with each other.

This may make sense if we consider the four protagonists as patterned in pairs. Estragon's ruined-poet and stubborn neediness is neatly offset by Vladimir's parental but unimaginative practicality, and the complementary nature of their inter-dependency speaks of a bonded mutuality that keeps the ravages of time at bay. I spoke in the lecture on the myth of the Fall about Estragon and Vladimir so I'll just add that the other pairing, Pozzo and Lucky, is of course one based on power, control and ownership – and thus the two pairings are themselves opposing ways of conceptualising human relationships (communitarian love versus master-slave oppression), with consequent results in the opposite effects of time: Pozzo and Lucky are ravaged by time and the effect is painfully clear in Act 2. This is why the two Acts (Beckett said that one would have been too few and three too many) are crucially both the same and different. Dialogue between them becomes more difficult (pauses in Act 1 become silences in Act 2) but for Estragon and Vladimir Act 2 complements Act 1: for Pozzo and Lucky it undoes and ravages it. Unfallen man/men; fallen man/men.

I'm reading the play, as I did in the first lecture, as a wry, ironic and poign-ant revisiting of the biblical story of the Fall (a thread that runs through this book of lectures). You will have noticed multiple references to Chris-tian ideas through the play, from Vladimir's worried interest in the two thieves at Calvary at the start, to his response ('Christ have mercy on us!') to the boy's news, at the end, that Godot's beard, or so he thinks, is white (Act 2). And their Fall would be to admit to the desperate pointlessness of their precarious position 'on top of a –' (Act 2). Vladimir's protectiveness and Estragon's stubborn forgetfulness together ensure that by and large the truth of their position is kept out of sight, the dreams of falling are not discussed, but in the play's most painful moment, at the end of Act 1, after angrily interrogating the boy, Estragon's face is contorted in unhappiness at a recognition that he's been evading for the rest of the play.

VLADIMIR: What's the matter with you?
ESTRAGON: I'm unhappy.
VLADIMIR: Not really! Since when?
ESTRAGON: I'd forgotten.
VLADIMIR: Extraordinary the tricks that memory plays!

Estragon tries to speak but gives it up. 'I'd forgotten.' This is the only time he expresses or half-expresses the recognition that, yes, he does know and has always known the terrible truth of their empty lives, their empty futures, that Godot won't come, and that it has all happened before. But Vladimir, characteristically, doesn't understand him ('Extraordinary the tricks that memory plays!'); and Estragon gives up the effort to say any more.

Pozzo in Act 1 suggests the related sense that the world itself is running down, falling away. The world's supplies of tears and laughter, according to his bleak logic, are always constant in quantity – and yet 'it is true the population has increased'. That's less emotion to go around, a wearing out. The universe of the play is already glimpsing the apocalypse of Lucky's speech, the stones and the skull. Pozzo is on his way, as he now realises, to the apocalyptic Judgement, 'the place known as the Board' (I'm sure this is a pun on 'the bored', suggesting Purgatory, and also the boards of the ultimately absurd theatre). The others haven't heard of it.

Estragon and Vladimir's precarious hold on this world may be difficult but it is maintained. They have each other. They'll be there tomorrow. At least I thought so all those years ago on a rainy November afternoon. Age transforms most things and I suppose I'm less sure now.

We started with the play's power to transform audiences. We've now looked at the way the play anxiously and poignantly dramatises issues of personal transformation and change. A third transformation to consider is the impact the play had on Western theatre. Overnight, and to the dismay of some audiences and critics, *Godot* tore up the rule-book that had governed plays from the mid-19th century onwards, the tradition of naturalist realism, and it restored theatre to its true traditions in ritual and myth, symbolic performative action on an explicitly theatricalised bare stage and in the charged patterns of rhythmic language and silence. This return to the more radical theatre (radical means its roots) of, for instance, Greek tragedy, medieval morality plays, later Shakespeare (especially *King Lear*: I'll be talking about this aspect of *Lear* in a later lecture in this book when I contrast it with *Hamlet*) and others in the anti-illusionist tradition had a transforming and liberating effect on later playwrights throughout the world. But I would add that Peter Hall's 1955 London production that introduced British audiences to *Godot* lumbered the text with 'realist' stage-baggage, over-gestured and over-elaborated stage-directions and, unbelievably, bits of music, presumably to fill those anti-naturalist silences. The result was protractedly slow. Beckett sat in the audience and made audible comments about the production doing it all wrong.

A last word about the play in history and today. *Godot*, as I've suggested, may have the universality of myth and ritual but it's just as true that it's a mid-20th-century response to very mid-20th-century anxieties, stemming from the experiences of war, in which Beckett himself played a brave but typically quiet role in occupied France. (Critics have read the play in the light of that history.) And today those anxieties – issues of exile, refugees, displaced people, lives cast adrift and without purpose – are, if anything, even more pressing.

Godot is still the most urgently contemporary of plays.

⁎ ⁎

This short lecture first appeared as an article in emagazine Issue 20, April 2003. Reproduced by kind permission of the English and Media Centre.

Further Reading

Samuel Beckett, *Waiting for Godot* (Faber and Faber: 2006).

Peter Boxall, *Samuel Beckett – Waiting for Godot/Endgame: A Reader's Guide to Essential Criticism* (Macmillan: 2000).

Ruby Cohn ed., *Beckett: Waiting for Godot (Casebook Series)* (Palgrave: 1987).

Steven Connor ed., *Waiting for Godot and Endgame (New Casebook)* (Palgrave: 1992).

Anthony Cronin, *Samuel Beckett: The Last Modernist* (HarperCollins: 1996).

Hugh Kenner, *A Reader's Guide to Samuel Beckett* (Thames and Hudson: 1973).

David Pattie, *The Complete Critical Guide to Samuel Beckett* (Routledge: 2000).

Dirk Van Hulle ed., *The New Cambridge Companion to Samuel Beckett* (Cambridge U.P.: 2015).

5 *Great Expectations*
Intertextualities, Endings and Life after Plot

Great Expectations had to be good, very good. This is because at the end of the 1850s Dickens was going through an uncharacteristically difficult time, and on a number of fronts. His journal *Household Words* (which had serialised *Hard Times*) was closed down after Dickens fell out with its publishers. In typical defiance he started a new journal *All The Year Round* before the earlier one had even closed and took a gamble by serialising in it *A Tale of Two Cities*, a rather schematic novel (well, so is *Hard Times*) which didn't go down that well with the reviewers. Dickens was also very aware that his 'brand' of novel was facing competition from the new and fashionable 'sensation novel', like Wilkie Collins' *Woman in White*. Most pressing of all, and indeed the reason for the break-up with the publishers of *Household Words*, was the awkward fact that Dickens had been carrying on a secret affair with the teenage actress Ellen Ternan (he was 45 and she was 18 when they met), and in then separating from his wife he was stung by hitherto loyal supporters (like publishers) who took her side. His response was to write public letters claiming that the separation was perfectly amicable (it wasn't for his wife and his many children) and strongly denying any of the unspecified rumours about his private life. He simply couldn't afford to lose his enormous fan-base, founded as it was on the notion of his being the purest and most patriotic upholder of Victorian family values as evidenced in the novels. But he wasn't. The Ellen Ternan story is excellently told in Claire Tomalin's *The Invisible Woman*. (He set her up, invisibly, in an alternative 'establishment' and might even have died there in her arms – with his body then secretly conveyed at night back to his official home to be, officially, found and declared dead.)

So the pressure was on (and some male friends weren't best pleased with having to keep quiet about Ellen) and he had to prove he could deliver. The choice of novel to do just that was characteristically bold – a novel drawing, like the much-loved earlier *David Copperfield*, on his autobiographical experiences (more congenial territory for Dickens than the politics of *Hard Times* and *A Tale of Two Cities*, both of which betray only limited political sympathies with the kind of radical ideas which we might expect a liberal writer with his history to have supported), though the challenge was not to go over the ground too closely again. The need to avoid repeating himself gets neatly displaced in *Great Expectations* and thematised (here as elsewhere I draw on Peter Brooks' discussion in his great book *Reading for the Plot*) in the novel's as-if compulsive obsession with questions of return and repetition. The new taste for sensation gets rich treatment in the form of Miss Havisham (another woman in white – the Collins novel came out a year earlier in 1860) in the characteristic Gothic setting and with the secret back history (here neatly deployed as one secret back story misrecognised as its 'other' – the Miss Havisham/Magwitch stories, about which more soon).

But the most telling sign of Dickens' determination to plug this novel directly into its moment was its subtle response to the extensive debates (aired not least in journals like *All the Year Round* and read as if intertextually along with the novel) sparked off by another and very far-reaching text that came out in 1859, just a couple of years before *Great Expectations* (though its ideas date back some twenty years) – Darwin's *Origin of Species*. The anxieties over natural selection and the debate we've come to know as nature versus nurture (to say nothing of Dickens' own anxiety over his as-if secret origins) connect, as Brooks emphasises, with the most durable and myth-like of the classic 19th-century narratives, the hero's self-making struggle to realise his ambitions and aspirations, through accumulation and class mobility – a narrative given added piquancy when the hero is an orphan and thus without hereditary baggage, and a narrative that crucially duplicates what the newly powerful Victorian middle-classes wanted to read – in effect, about their own struggles to succeed against a demonised underclass and an effete and degenerate aristocracy. Degeneracy debates were no less fraught than, and were intimately tied up with, the Darwinian story.

Great Expectations intervenes in a complex, or one might say conflicted, way in these debates. Pip's status as orphan allows the novel the space to suggest that his self-making is a way of refuting the Darwinian emphasis on the primacy of the hereditary in the formation of the self, but the countertendency in the novel is to suggest that Pip's roots in the forge – to which he later both wants to and doesn't want to return – exert more force, call into question whether he makes anything much of his self, and account for the mixed and very muted ending to the novel – mixed and also multiple, as we'll see later when we turn to the novel's alternative endings. The conflicted and unresolved nature of the novel's take on Darwinism is most sharply focused in the famous moment in Chapter 44 when Pip, exasperated with Estella's unreceptive and cold responses to his love, says to her 'surely it is not in Nature'. (Capital N, the natural state in 'human nature'.) Her brilliantly chilling reply is: 'It is in *my* nature.' (Lower case n, Estella suggesting that her nature is merely the consequence of her nurture at Miss Havisham's hands, consequences which have outweighed 'Nature' – though again the end of the novel may soften this.)

I've spoken so far of the way the novel is at pains to respond to its moment in cultural history and to Dickens' own personal circumstances. It had to be good. It was. To explore its qualities, some of which are unusual for Dickens, I'm keen to emphasise its remarkable intricacies: its highly patterned form, skilful and rich deployment of othering and doubles as well as its varieties of making and self-making, and its unusual intertextualities. To these I will now turn, before closing with some thoughts about closure and endings.

**

The patterns of the novel may be traced first through its interest in fathers and mothers, the search for parents, for origins – for authority or authorship, in effect to authorise one's narrative. This is to see Pip (like David Copperfield) as a novelist in search of his story – and in a later lecture we'll see Jane Austen's Emma as a proxy novelist as well. (To make another connection, it's not entirely absurd to see Pip as a precursor of Proust's Marcel. That is my plea for you to all to read Proust and the greatest novel ever written, please, one day. I'll make a more elaborate plea in the form of an entire lecture much later in this book.)

The search for the father is activated, and alarmingly so, from the novel's opening gestures, from Pip reflecting on the 'authority of his [father's] tombstone' just before Magwitch 'start[s] up from among the graves' (narratives in novels start up from graves – from absences and loss), as the pseudo-father returning from the dead (more on *Hamlet* soon) and, literally, turning Pip (and his life) upside down (Chapter 1). It's not long before another pseudo-father, in another moment of man-on-boy violence, Jaggers, exercising his jabbing forefinger on Pip, 'turned up my face' (Chapter 11). Joe behaves as Pip's father, though as what Pip calls a 'larger species of child' (Chapter 2), Pip is in effect his father – and later, with Biddy, his Oedipal rival. When Magwitch returns into Pip's life the unknown footstep reminds Pip of 'the footstep of my dead sister', the idea again of the parent returning from the grave, in order in Magwitch's case for him to assert, in the ironic climax of the search for the father, that Pip is 'more to me nor any son' (Chapter 39). Also 'like a ghost' from the dead, and described as such, the pseudo-father (old Hamlet) Compeyson menacingly sits behind Pip in the theatre (Chapter 47) and, in a subtle weaving of parental ideas, Compeyson as Miss Havisham's as-if husband is therefore Estella's as-if father – as Jaggers is as well, being, in effect, the guardian-father who took her from her real mother (Molly) and placed her with her pseudo-mother. So both Jaggers and Magwitch are as-if or real fathers to both Pip and Estella (and Miss Havisham is both of their as-if mothers): all of which points to the sharp irony of Pip and Estella being as-if incestuous brother and sister.

If that reminds you of *Wuthering Heights*, another connection is that in this novel as well there is a conspicuous absence of mothers. Pip's anguish early in the novel is largely his unrealised sense of having no maternal love, Mrs Joe being closer to the sadistic stepmother of fairy-tale to the extent that Pip is said to be 'nursing' his sense of injustice (Chapter 8), as if obliged to be his own maternally nursing figure. Miss Havisham's devouring nurturing of Estella is a bitter parody of maternal nurturing and, in a pattern that has some perhaps fearful misogyny on Dickens' part, she and Mrs Joe both become what Molly, under Jaggers, has become, the 'wild beast tamed' (Chapter 48; Mrs Joe by Orlick's attack, Miss Havisham by the fire). There's the suggestion that women for Dickens are intrinsically wild and need to be tamed. But it is touching that, in another pattern, Pip witnesses or hears of Mrs Joe's one word 'pardon' (Chapter 35) and Miss Havisham's one word 'forgive' (Chapter 49).

The patterning in the novel of doubles and others is no less intricate though I'll be suggesting in one case possibly not so convincingly managed. We've already noticed Magwitch and Jaggers as doubles (real or pseudo-fathers to both Pip and Estella) and of course the novel turns on the Miss Havisham/Magwitch parental/benefactor misrecognition plot (in fairy-tale terms I'd call them the bad father who turns out to be the good [Mag]witch and the fairy godmother who turns out to be the bad-Witch). There's also the murderous violence between the doubled or othered Magwitch and Compeyson, as between the literally murderous Molly and her rival (when they fight over Magwitch), a violence comically rehearsed early in the novel between the young Pip and the then unknown Herbert when they fight (as-if over Estella who is watching and, with a 'bright flush' (Chapter 11), perhaps even sexually enjoying it: a muted and rather coercive link to her real mother Molly's sexual violence) and – to return to fairy-tale – there's the bad sister Mrs Joe and the sort-of good sister Estella, and (to steal an idea from my friend and ex-student Chloe Murphy) Biddy (who becomes literally the 'other' Mrs Joe) as good sister to Estella's bad sister.

Perhaps most interesting in terms of othering is the one that, again perhaps, doesn't quite work and that's the Pip/Orlick doubling. Orlick acts out what the repressed, furious side of Pip wants to but fears to do – assault/murder Mrs Joe, rob and humiliate Pumblechook – and these are ironically and neatly anticipated early in the novel when the young Pip fears that he'll be arrested for stealing and murdering. It's also appropriate that later Pip blames himself for the attack on Mrs Joe – and thus also, though less plausibly, Orlick's point that in effect Pip *did* kill Mrs Joe. If this all sounds familiar I think it is; so I'll say (of course this is just speculation) that I think Dickens is consciously imitating the Jane/Bertha othering in *Jane Eyre* and, indeed, and this is more plausible, the Frankenstein/Creature othering in that novel. Bertha and the creature act out what their alter egos won't or can't. If I'm right about *Jane Eyre* then Dickens saw what was going on a hundred years or so before it was elaborated in *The Madwoman in the Attic*. But does it work in the case of Orlick and Pip? You decide. More on intertextuality soon.

My last category for intricacy of formal design is the topic already mentioned: the novel's subtly patterned interest in notions of human making and self-making. We saw that Pip's self-making is the novel's notional narrative trajectory but of course it is embedded in a more complex story of people making each other – the Frankenstein story (about which more below). A bald list would include the following – and the point is that the more the examples accumulate the more they provide together an ironic commentary on the standard Victorian formula of self-making.

Miss Havisham makes Estella into her 'Creature'. Pip thinks Miss Havisham makes him – and makes him for Estella (which 'makes' them as-if siblings). Magwitch makes Pip – though not in quite the way he thinks he does – not so much making him into the intended gentleman as humanising or gentling Pip's feelings – not least towards him. Pip makes Herbert (a success: as Magwitch wants him to). Molly (in her trial) makes Jaggers (a success) – and Jaggers then makes/remakes Molly (as his tamed servant). Jaggers makes Estella (by rescuing her as 'orphan'). Compeyson makes Estella (in the form of Miss Havisham's vengeance on him). Joe makes Pip (by nurturing him and then, ironically, by marrying Biddy).

Before turning to intertextuality, I want to say a little more about incest and (to swerve to another controversial phrase in the Freudian lexicon) a word about what I would call the novel's 'primal scene'. The patterns explored above establish a way of thinking about Pip and Estella as siblings and I've already mentioned Cathy and Heathcliff – and in another later lecture we'll look at Emma and Mr Knightley (in their case it's father/daughter as well as brother/sister). There are of course other examples in 19th-century novels, notably George Eliot's Daniel Deronda and his eventual wife Mira (whom he rescues from drowning and through whom he discovers his Jewish roots, in effect becoming her as-if brother). But incestuous ideas seem unusually structured into *Great Expectations*. Dickens goes out of his way to allow Magwitch to say that Pip reminds him of his (apparently) lost daughter of the same age. But it's not just Pip and Estella; it's their 'parents' as well. Miss Havisham's devouring love for her as-if daughter takes the form of (for instance) ornamenting her with jewels in her breasts, to attract Pip – and the male reader – and this is worryingly suggestive of a mother erotically acting out her desire for her daughter. This is duplicated (again, patterned) by the more muted and less worrying but still notably erotic affection Magwitch displays for his 'dear boy' Pip on his return – and wish to see him as-if ornamented in poses of (for instance) reading foreign languages aloud. These are two 'parents' living through erotically displaced desires for their 'children'. This is very unusual for Dickens and has the effect of complicating the very nature of desire in the novel.

This leads me to the crucial importance for the novel of what I will call its primal scene. I think this has not received as much critical attention as it deserves. The scene I mean is in the novel's back story – Molly's murder of her rival, the woman/woman struggle over 'a certain man called Abel'

(Chapter 50) as it's described to us (of course, this is later revealed as Magwitch). I call this scene primal as it has an as-if mythic power and reach, determining as it does the entire novel ahead (the sequence that includes Estella becoming Miss Havisham's ward). To signal that mythic power (I can't be the first to notice this) the man that precipitates the murder is called Abel, evoking of course the world's first murder, Cain's murder of Abel (which incidentally is pointedly referred to in *Hamlet*). So Molly's murder of her rival is positioned in the novel's mythic substructure as the original act, the primal scene. And as we've seen, the ensuing trial of Molly was what 'made' Jaggers' reputation – and this means that his performance in court, persuading the jury of what he knew to be a lie, freeing Molly (to become his 'made' object), is the unsolved crime at the heart of the novel – and that too is very unusual. At the start of the novel's action is an unsolved murder and a lie that ensures it remains unsolved. And even more sharply ironic is the fact that Jaggers' romantic desire to use Estella as 'the one pretty little child out of the heap who could be saved' (Chapter 51) is deeply subverted by what actually ensues: Estella, the child to be saved, becoming calculatedly not saved but (in effect) lost, abandoned and irrevocably damaged – by the treatment of Miss Havisham as mother and then Drummle as husband. This is, compared to Dickens' other novels, a profound and troubling thread below the surface of the novel.

**

With intertextuality I need to say first that I'm using the term rather too loosely (as others do), to include explicit reference and quotation, and conscious imitation. (The term more properly is about unconscious ways in which texts or parts of texts are caught up in other texts.) *Hamlet*, as already indicated, is subtly deployed throughout. To choose just some of the links, Magwitch among the graves is the father's return from the dead (the return of the repressed; the uncanny); the absurdities of Wopsle's performance as Hamlet has its more ominous afterword of Pip's dream of playing Hamlet to Miss Havisham's ghost (itself a nice patterning between Miss Havisham and Magwitch); Magwitch's arrival in Pip's apartments has the clock striking (as with old Hamlet's ghost) and the eerie appearance of Compeyson behind Pip in the pantomime is, as we saw, like a ghost. A muted connection is Pip's conversation with the pub landlord before his crisis with Orlick, their exchange a subtle and witty variation of Hamlet's with the gravedigger in Act 5 (I think this connection hasn't been much or at all noticed), and this is subtle because Pip is very close to being on the way to his own grave. *Hamlet*'s relevance is of course the notion of the father placing the pressing and impossible burden on the son.

Another classic landmark of Western literature is directly referenced at the end of the novel's first part, as Pip leaves the forge for London. In words that neatly prefigure the novel's last sentence, we read that 'the mists had all solemnly risen now; and the world lay spread before me' (Chapter 19). This is a close echo of the end of *Paradise Lost* and raises some sharp and ambivalent questions about whether Pip is losing Eden (despite his treatment at the forge) or is about to find it. It's worth reflecting on why (again uncharacteristically) Dickens evokes two of the world's greatest literary monuments in this way: it might take us back to where we started, the ambitious scope and nature of this novel, its need to stake out the highest literary claims.

But even more unusual is the novel's explicit evocation of a text published not long before it, *Frankenstein* (originally 1818 but I think it more likely that Dickens read the more easily available 1831 edition). I've mentioned above the close relevance of Mary Shelley's novel to the network of ideas we saw around people making other people (Estella being positioned by the novel equivalently to the Creature) and the explicit reference is about Magwitch when Pip reflects on his new place in his life: 'the imaginary student [= Frankenstein] pursued by the misshapen creature he had impiously made, was not more wretched than I, pursued by the creature who had made me' (Chapter 40): and this very cleverly turns and turns about as the sentence unfolds in terms of 'making' – at first positioning Pip as making Magwitch and then Magwitch as making Pip. All this is clear but I'd add that less noticed is Magwitch's long retrospective narrative about his life duplicating the Creature's equivalent autobiographical narrative and I think this too is deliberate imitation on Dickens' part. The details are striking, with both narratives marking key stages like the discovery of language, truth and identity (becoming 'aware of myself'), and then of people catching 'fright' of the narrator and driving him off (Chapter 42). In both cases these are narratives that also mirror or mimic the story of human evolution (both crucially feature the use of fire) which, returning us to Darwin, seems to me decisive in arguing for Dickens drawing on Shelley. The effect is that Magwitch, again, gathers a kind of myth-like or origin-like status, as we saw with his name Abel and what I called the novel's primal scene.

There are two other and even more recent novels (both from 1847) that Dickens stirs into the mix and these may be less conscious on his part. One I've already mentioned when I speculated that the Pip/Orlick doubling may have its base in the Jane/Bertha doubling in *Jane Eyre* and there's some family resemblance in the way both novels, in their painful evocation of childhood, stress the cruelties and injustices of the child isolated in the family structures. But I'd like to offer another speculative suggestion and that is about Pip's love for Estella and particularly his impassioned outburst to her just after the 'not in Nature / It is in *my* nature' exchange which we looked at much earlier. Here are some extracts.

> You are part of my existence, part of myself. You have been in every line I have ever read, since I first came here... You have been in every prospect I have ever seen since – on the river, on the sails of the ships,

on the marshes, in the clouds, in the light, in the darkness, in the wind, in the woods, in the sea, in the streets ... The stones of which the strongest London buildings are made are not more real ... than your presence and influence have been to me, there and everywhere, and will be. Estella, to the last hour of my life, you cannot choose but remain part of my character, part of the little good in me, part of the evil ...

(Chapter 44)

Sounds familiar? Students regularly recognise this (so I'm sure you do as well) as close to the famous 'I am Heathcliff' speech (Chapter 9) that Cathy voices to the uncomprehending Ellen ('my great thought in living is himself ... My love for Heathcliff resembles the eternal rocks beneath ... not as a pleasure, any more than I am always a pleasure to myself – but as my own being ...') – and, though rather less regularly, students also connect Pip here with a less well-known but even more closely echoed speech at the end of *Wuthering Heights* where Heathcliff muses to Ellen about how Hareton always makes him think of Cathy. The end of this speech is (as I suggested in the earlier lecture) perhaps the most anguished evocation in the Victorian novel of the knot always tied between love and loss.

[But] what is not connected with [Cathy] to me? And what does not recall her? I cannot look down to this floor, but her features are shaped on the flags! In every cloud, in every tree – filling the air at night, and caught by glimpses in every object, by day I am surrounded with her image! The most ordinary faces of men, and women – my own features mock me with a resemblance. The entire world is a dreadful collection of memoranda that she did exist, and that I have lost her!

(Chapter 33)

Consciously or not on Dickens' part, Pip's speech seems like a weaving together of these iconic moments in a novel that (as with *Jane Eyre*) we can be pretty certain that Dickens read and it makes us wonder what kind of claims are being made (consciously or not is unimportant) for Pip's love here in relation to the Cathy/Heathcliff archetype (which you'll recall I explored in terms of myth and psychoanalysis in the earlier lecture). Students regularly object to thinking that Pip's love for Estella is in that kind of 'league' and they wonder if Dickens is drawing on similar language to artificially inflate it beyond its true capacity or nature – but, perhaps as a romantic and naïve reader, I'd want to add that the unrequited nature of Pip's admittedly idealised love for an idealised woman makes it no less 'real' and no less painful than something more obviously equal. (Or perhaps I'm just writing about myself, as usual.) As always, I urge you to think about where you are personally with these ideas.

**

Let's move to endings for the last phase of this lecture. There's been quite a lot of critical work done in this area, focused especially on the two 'actual' alternative endings that we'll look at soon, but I wanted to take a different angle first and suggest that, again unusually, the novel teases us with potential endings as if in a kind of radical scepticism towards exactly the kind of romantic endings of more typical Dickens novels.

The first of these is at Magwitch's death in the prison hospital. It's a moving scene (though a Biblical final paragraph rather spoils it for at least this reader). Pip gets the dying Magwitch to confirm that he had a child 'whom you loved and lost'. Then Pip says to him: 'She lived and found powerful friends. She is living now. She is a lady and very beautiful. And I love her!' (Chapter 56). Magwitch then dies at peace ('his head dropped quietly on his breast') and it can't just be romantic readers like me who thought, at first reading, that (however tortuously the plot would take to get there – there's the small matter of Drummle in the way) we were in for a Pip/Estella marriage and happy ending. But, of course, no. And the same is true for the next potential happy ending. If not Estella, then how about – yes, go for it! – Biddy? Ten pages later Pip outlines in his head what he will say to persuade Biddy that he is now at last worthy of her love (there's rather a gap in his thinking when it comes to his feelings for her which is a little worrying, but hey, it will all be ok when we get there): but on arrival at the forge Pip finds her just married to Joe so it's, of course, no again.

The third potential ending is more muted (after these romantic let-downs) and again it's just a few pages on. Pip parts from Joe and Biddy, sells up and joins Herbert's business in the East. The little secret of how Herbert was funded gets explained and, in fairy-tale idiom, Pip ends (potentially) living 'happily with Herbert and his wife' (Chapter 58), in effect happily (sort of) ever after, though there's something a little comic and more than a little sad about this bachelor moving into middle-age in someone else's family home. But ...

The ending we have all read and know, the one in your books, has often been described as very open to interpretation, deliberately so, as to exactly how likely it suggests an eventual union between Pip and Estella. What complicates things further is that there's one tiny but perhaps momentous change that Dickens made between the first bound edition and the revised 1868 version. The first edition has this: 'the evening mists were rising now, and in all the broad expanse of tranquil light they showed to me, I saw the shadow of no parting from her'. In 1868 and all subsequent and modern editions this becomes '... I saw no shadow of another parting from her' (Chapter 59). I won't pretend I've got my head round how those differ in their implications for Pip and Estella's future together or apart, for my head hurts when I try. In seminar discussions students come up with a range of possibilities. (Or perhaps Dickens was just clarifying the syntax.) You decide. Or not.

But I've left till last the earlier ending that Dickens was persuaded to drop and re-write (by his friend Bulwer Lytton). And I've left it till last for a reason.

It was much shorter and it's just a few words and a paragraph with nothing of the later final chapter at Satis House. Here it is, a little abridged.

> It was two years more, before I saw herself. I had heard of her as leading a most unhappy life, and as being separated from her husband who had used her with great cruelty ... I had heard of the death of her husband ... and of her being married again to a Shropshire doctor ... I was in England again – in London, and walking along Piccadilly with little Pip – when a servant came running after me to ask would I step back to a lady in a carriage who wished to speak to me. It was a little pony carriage, which the lady was driving; and the lady and I looked sadly enough on one another. 'I am greatly changed, I know; but I thought you would like to shake hands with Estella too, Pip. Lift up that pretty child and let me kiss it!' (She supposed the child, I think, to be my child.) I was very glad afterwards to have had the interview; for, in her face and in her voice, and in her touch, she gave me the assurance that suffering had been stronger than Miss Havisham's teaching, and had given her a heart to understand what my heart used to be.
>
> (In Angus Calder, ed., Appendix A)

The reason I want to end (sort-of) with that is that I think it much more moving and much more appropriate to the novel's tone (even the slightly injured and selfish note struck in the last words) than the ending that replaced it. Many students over the years have agreed and I wonder if you do. Particularly moving is the muted line in brackets about Estella thinking the child was Pip's – Estella left for the rest of her life with the idea that Pip has achieved the normative happy-ending of marriage and fatherhood. In a novel that hinges on mis-recognitions, this last one carries quiet and very poignant force.

Another ending, to this lecture, and a return to Peter Brooks. He makes the point that in a sense the choice between these ending matters little, as Pip has – again this is very unlike normal Dickens – moved beyond plot. Brooks' word is that Pip, and the novel, and in effect the reader, are all 'cured' of plot (Brooks 1984: 138). Once Pip has realised his fundamental mis-recognition (the source of his wealth) that realisation gets displaced onto his detective-like drive to prove Estella's parentage. There's an element of Oedipal rivalry here in the sense that this detective-work out-does that of his pseudo-father Jaggers. And it is this that makes, again, Pip (as we'll see with Jane Austen's Emma, though in a very different way) into a proxy-novelist, as he was on the first page, in search of the author/authority.

But Brooks' point is that having at last discovered Estella's true parents he can't put the information to any use. In a more typical Dickens novel the uncovering of that truth would allow the protagonist the power to change lives, his own and Estella's, ideally by marrying her. But the knowledge remains, though so hard-won, in effect redundant, an empty category of knowledge. Brooks calls it 'radically unusable ... offer[ing] no comfort and no true illumination to the detective himself ... It produces no authority for the plot of life' (135). He adds: 'at the start of the novel we had the impression of a life not yet subject to plot ... So at the end we have the impression of a life that has outlived plot ...: life that is left over' (138).

Actually, though Brooks says the choice doesn't really matter, I think that is why the original ending is so much more moving and appropriate and why I choose it and why I wish editors would print it in preference. Pip, and Estella, and Estella misrecognising the child as Pip's, is life that is left over.

Thank you.

Further Reading

Peter Brooks, *Reading for the Plot: Design and Intention in Narrative* (Harvard UP: 1992).

Charles Dickens, *Great Expectations*, ed. Angus Calder (Penguin: 1968).

Charles Dickens, *Great Expectations*, ed. Edgar Rosenberg (Norton: 1999).

John Mee, *The Cambridge Introduction to Charles Dickens* (Cambridge UP: 2010).

Andrew Sanders, *Charles Dickens, Authors in Context* (Penguin: 2003).

Claire Tomalin, *Charles Dickens; A Life* (Penguin: 2012).

Claire Tomalin, *The Invisible Woman* (Viking: 1990).

Nicholas Tredell, *Great Expectations* (Icon Books: 1998).

6 Emily Dickinson
'And Then the Windows Failed'

When I did my postgraduate teacher training the course-organisers decided, I now realise rather kindly, that the school where I should do my placement should be a private boarding-school, very similar to the one I'd been at myself. They must have realised, with good reason, that I'd be eaten alive at any state day-school. So I had a rather congenial time in the Berkshire countryside with schoolboys, and staff, at least some of whom were rather like myself (callow and rather snobbish). One day I set my class of 15-year-olds their regular weekly homework for English.

'We've been looking at Romantic poetry. Write a poem yourselves tonight, as romantic as you like!'

When I got the homework in, I was very taken with one poem by a boy who had hitherto been silent and even sullen, and apparently quite uninterested in anything I'd thrown at the class. Thinking, in the way callow student-teachers would, that this sudden flowering of poetic talent was, of course, the direct result of my teaching, I returned it with extravagant praise, copied it out and, as it was now the half-term break, took it up to Oxford to show to a few friends. One of them (who after university became A Famous Actor and we'll meet him again in the lecture on *Hamlet* and *Lear*, later in this book) read it carefully and looked at me. I gabbled 'isn't it amazingly good for a 15-year-old?' and his reply was a cool 'yes, Richard, it is good. But then it should be, it's by Emily Dickinson'.

Ah well, at least I recognised the quality of the poem. (I was too embarrassed and ashamed to say anything to the boy once term started again. I dare say some colleagues at that school would have applauded or at least indulgently smiled at his enterprising spirit.)

I came to Dickinson myself later than most of the writers who moved me at school and university. It may just be me but she's the clearest example that I know of a poet whose 'voice' can take a long time to tune into before readers – well, in this case me – can 'hear' her. In my case it was more or less suddenly, in my later twenties, that I 'heard' her, or 'got' her. I guess I'd been just reading her badly before then, reading her with the inappropriate expectations of what a 'proper' poem should look and sound like. Or, to make a connection with Kate Chopin's *The Awakening* (about which more in a later lecture where I connect it with Gilman's story 'The Yellow Wall-paper'), perhaps I was, like Edna, not yet 'ready', in mind and body, my 'being' not yet 'tempered to take an impress of the abiding truth', the truth-fulness of an apparently estranging poetry that changes lives, as Edna's life is changed by music that suddenly speaks to her body, as Dickinson's poetry, above all others, speaks to the body (and, as we'll see, of and from the body).

And a larger cultural point (in my defence) is this. Dickinson is one of those poets who start off by being the deviant outsider to the mainstream, considered eccentric, odd or even mad, but who (though much later) end up as redefining by enlarging what that mainstream is. Blake is the closest example I can think of and his poetry has much in common with hers, though it's almost impossible that she could have read him. It took until the 1950s and 1960s (urged on by the counter-cultural movements of the latter: the '60s rock-band The Doors got their name, via Aldous Huxley, from Blake's 'If the doors of perception were cleansed everything would appear to man as it is, infinite') for Blake to be understood as the re-defining figure of European Romanticism. In Dickinson's case it took (as it happens, more or less coincidentally with Blake) until the 1950s (though in a later lecture we'll see that Jean Rhys read and understood her in the 1930s), when the first full and properly scrupulous edition suddenly made her the re-defining voice of mid/late 19th-century American poetry. And, as with Blake, her influence over later poets, many of whom acknowledged her lasting effect on their work, has been profound, in Dickinson's case on poets as different as William Carlos Williams (he called her his patron saint) and Sylvia Plath.

I need to add before we go on that all the quotations from Dickinson's poems below are from the Little, Brown edition of 1926 put together by Dickinson's niece (a couple of intrusive commas have been removed). See Further Reading below.

**

We know little about Dickinson's early life but one fact stands out: aged 17 she left Mount Holyoke Female Seminary after only a year there. This was what we would call a college of further or higher education and had only been founded about ten years earlier, with a relatively innovative cur-riculum for young women, including science and physical exercise. There's been much speculation about why Dickinson left. A few relevant points are that she was rather younger at 16 than most of the other 230 students when she started there but that many students also only attended for a year, with the cultural expectation that marriage, motherhood and domes-tic life beckoned. So leaving at 17 was unusually young. And we also know that the seminary (here and above I draw gratefully on material from the Dickinson museum) organised students into three Christian groups in its orthodox Protestant way: those who professed, those who hoped to, and those without hope of professing. (I'll be speaking about the importance of the Puritan/Protestant inheritance in American culture in the Chopin and Gilman lecture.) Dickinson was in the third category at the start of her year (with eighty others) and also at the end of her year – with now less than thirty others: and this suggests an admirably firm response to the pressure to conform, despite being labelled hopeless.

What may seem like decisive evidence in this matter of her leaving is that, despite local revivalist movements around her and her (Calvinist) family, she never professed or joined a church and, from her thirties, never attended church ceremonies. Her father, a leading lawyer, seems, in his rather distant way, not to have minded and her mother was someone (like Edna Pontellier's mother in Chopin's novel) whom Dickinson once said she'd never really had. And, of course, we have the simple fact that marriage, motherhood and domestic life may have beckoned for most of these New England young women, curtailing their further education, but emphatically didn't for Emily Dickinson. If you explore in her poetry and letters you'll very soon notice a radical scepticism about orthodox Christian ideas and even an anger about a distant and unsympathetic God (as well as a need for a secular God-like substitute in her own life: the mysterious 'master' to whom she addressed a few very striking letters) but also a lingering desire for the comfort of faith, to believe in something rather than nothing. In one poem she writes about her 'lack of heaven' but not of God's heaven.

**

In April 1862 Dickinson wrote to the man who became her leading poetic advocate and adviser, Thomas Higginson, enclosing four poems and asking him whether they were living things. I find it telling that she didn't ask him if they were any good, as the Dickinson I'll be speaking more about is a woman who knew what she was up to and knew that she wrote good poetry. When, years later, she realised that the chances of more than a handful being published were minimal she, in effect, gave up that game and chose, strategically, to 'publish' on her own terms, sending poems as love-gifts, in and as letters to loved friends. Among these friends was Sue (Susan Gilbert, later her sister-in-law), whom she loved above all others in an intensely charged way: she once said she'd rather have Sue in her life than the chance of heaven; I guess she had Sue in mind when writing 'Parting is all we know of heaven / And all we need of hell'. The signs are that Sue reciprocated her love but her letters to Emily don't survive, perhaps destroyed by the Dickinson family. (The later feud between two sides of the family had a bad-tempered effect on the publishing of the poems; this is well-described in a chapter in the Cambridge Companion called 'The Dickinson Wars'.) And Emily stitched poems into little hand-written books, to be discovered in her bedroom after her death by her sister. (The current tally of poems stands at an astonishing 1,775.) She compared publication to slave-auctions and called fame a 'fickle food', and she starts a poem, with cool wit and quite without bitterness, regret or self-pity, saying 'This is my letter to the world / That never wrote to me'.

This is a poet who calls herself (in a brilliantly subversive poem) 'no-body', who (in another poem), whenever she hears the word 'escape', says that 'I tug childish at my bars – / Only to fail again' (the woman in 'The Yellow Wallpaper' sees a figure trapped – in effect like Bronte's Bertha – behind bars and tugging at them; Beckett has 'fail again, fail better') and who elsewhere puns marvellously when thinking of how she could die in a noteless way: making no sound (like a dead singing-bird); leaving nothing written; unnoticed and unnoticeable; leaving nothing worthy of note. In that poem Dickinson is, as ever, strategic: she is or was playing at being the whimsical and even scatty figure, silently controlled by patriarchy. And she wittily notes in another poem that being out of order, labelled mad, is really the 'divinest sense' because what passes for sanity is only uncomplainingly agreeing with conventions while those who (wisely) disagree are labelled 'dangerous / And handled with a chain', very like Bertha.

Everything she did was strategic or performative. Refusing to be the typical church-going, home-visitors receiving, married and child-raising woman, she turned herself into her own myth, as she was literally called by locals, wearing white (like a kind of benevolent Miss Havisham or, at least, as a kind of parody of desirable virginity), only rarely leaving her house or even her room. She mythologised herself in order to be herself, on her own terms, and to write, on her own terms.

Those terms were centred on difference and transgression. (Here I draw on Helen McNeil, the subtlest of Dickinson critics.) One poem sharply notes that 'internal difference' is 'Where the meanings are'. Acutely aware of her difference from other women and other poets (poets both male and female), and strategically exploiting those differences, she chose an opposi-tional identity, writing as a nobody, a prisoner, mad, a witch, the smallest in the house – not a proper adult. In a poem that seems to poke fun at Poe's Gothic she writes of the self 'behind ourself concealed' (where we might expect the self behind the mask): suggesting the self as multiple selves in se-rial displacement, as presented in 1970s post-structuralist theory. And she chose silence and invisibility, mistrusting language and speech themselves, always aware that the inexpressible is where the deepest feelings lie, that eloquence can be and often is falsehood, and that truth can only be told in oblique ways.

In sharp opposition to conventional and Wordsworthian Romantic and post-Romantic notions of the poetry of presence, inclusion, the achieved expression of the self, she is the poet of absence, exclusion, silence and loss, intimating also that those are the woman's terms within patriarchy. In one poem she is 'wrecked, solitary, here'. (The earlier Romantic poet John Clare, whom I don't think she could have read, has 'the vast shipwreck of my life's esteems'. In the same poem he says 'I am the self-consumer of my woes'. 'A solitary soul' was the working title of Chopin's *The Awakening*; 'solitary' ends *Paradise Lost* and this book of lectures.) The refusal to title her poems and the brilliantly subversive dashes within and even at the end of them suggest that silence is her default 'language' and that silence surrounds the expressed words in the poems and threatens to swallow those words. The dashes are like explosions of silence.

The poetry is subversive in so many ways. Avoiding (like Blake) prestigiously 'literary' conventions like the iambic pentameter and the long, ruminative or narrative poems of the period, hers are minute flashes of intensity in what we call common-metre, closer (again like Blake) to folk forms like child's rhymes, simple hymns, proverbs and riddles. She also avoids conventionally decorative adjectives and adverbs, aiming for a bare, stripped-back language of the essential. She, in effect, invents half-rhyme (I recall being taught at school that Wilfred Owen invented it – so that's forty or fifty years after she did?) and these, at the ends of poems, leave a sense of the unfinished, the unsaid, the impossibility of full-closure, especially when followed, as often, by a finally transgressive dash.

And she's very funny. This needs emphasis because her subject matter, considered in the abstract, can lead readers to assume a gloomily depressed and self-centredly morbid poetry. (We'll see in a later and closely connected lecture on Chopin and Gilman, two other and later transgressive American women, that more than one early reviewer of *The Awakening* accused Chopin of being morbid.) Hers is the opposite. Saying, as mentioned earlier, that she's 'nobody' she adds 'How dreary to be somebody!' as all that means is being 'like a frog' absurdly pronouncing its name all day 'To an admiring bog'. In a lovely joke she turns received wisdom on its head by saying she walks through life 'with that precarious gait / Some call experience'. She deconstructs (to use a word that used to be more modish than now) culturally revered myths, as in a wonderfully witty stage-by-stage dismantling of the myth of Jason and the golden fleece, which ends denying that there was any fleece or even any Jason. She gets a particularly humorous effect (this hasn't received much critical attention) by slipping in incongruous Latinate words into her usual simple Anglo-Saxon vocabulary. In one of her very best poems, one of a few that brilliantly and subversively imagine her own death, 'I heard a fly buzz when I died', she makes a nice joke about making a will, signing away 'What portion of me' could be 'assignable' and adds that then 'There interposed a fly'. Interposed! (That poem then gives us the amazing words 'And then the windows failed': the title of the book on Dickinson I've never got around to writing.) Even better is what I offer to you as the best of all her jokes, in another poem on her death, one drawing on Keats (whom, unlike Wordsworth whom she thought much less of, she very properly admired). This poem starts 'I died for beauty' and adds that she then 'was scarce / Adjusted in the tomb'. Adjusted! Now, I'll just make myself comfy in my coffin.

Dickinson was committed to a project of knowing the world and herself as intensely as possible (McNeil notes that the word 'know' and its cognates are pervasive: I'd add that she would have been aware that 'knowing' is biblical language for sex), especially when it came to a fiercely but coolly analytic understanding of her own suffering and pain, and in her calm, scrupulous anatomy of the aftermath of pain. One poem allegorises life as the inevitable journey from the heart asking for 'pleasure first' and then, as if immediately, for 'excuse from pain'. Elsewhere she notes that 'Pain has an element of blank' and 'no future but itself', the future that, in another poem, she knows will just be presented to her 'in the Act –', making both preparation and escape impossible. She also knew that suffering, despite the cliché about time assuaging ('Time never did assuage'), strengthens over time, 'As sinews do, with age'. Dickinson's drive to knowledge is centred on her body, as if a hyper-sensitised instrument where each sense is at its most intense pitch, and it's a transgressively realised body. (We'll see the same is true of Chopin's Edna Pontellier; and the struggle in Gilman's 'The Yellow Wallpaper' between husband and wife is, in effect literally, over her body.) Dickinson knew that the poem she happened to be reading was a real poem when it made her body feel too cold for fire to warm or when it felt like someone had taken off the top of her head. Once she saw a circus pass by her window: it felt like she was literally tasting its vivid colours.

Dickinson encountered life with a permanently erotised body: McNeil notes that the poems repeatedly figure the sexualised body as jewels, flowers entered, crowns, volcanoes. One poem starts 'I like a look of agony / Because I know it's true'. In another poem, one that remarkably anticipates the key scene of Edna suddenly being able to swim in *The Awakening*, she speaks of the 'exultation' of going to sea, 'the divine intoxication / Of the first league out from land': the passage in Chopin uses 'exultation' and 'intoxicated' and both texts are sexually evocative. A poem talks of the sea threatening to 'eat me up / As wholly as a dew / upon a dandelion's sleeve –'. A group of poems (pointedly excluded from Ted Hughes' selection for Faber but thankfully in McNeil's rival and much better Everyman selection), probably about Sue, explore what seems to be a polymorphous sexuality. One starts 'Come slowly, Eden!' and speaks of the 'fainting bee' that reaches 'his flower', then 'Counts his nectars – enters, / And is lost in balms'. I'll end with perhaps the most startling and best of these poems (which as in the poem just quoted seems to figure orgasm as Eden in a way that reminds me of Proust's Albertine – we will meet her towards the end of this book of lectures – who reportedly and at the relevant time sighs 'oh, I'm in heaven!') and I hope this will usefully prefigure what I'll say in the later lecture about the sexualised body in Gilman and Chopin. Here is the poem.

Wild nights! Wild nights!
Were I with thee

> Wild nights should be
> Our luxury!
>
> Futile the winds
> To a heart in port –
> Done with the compass
> Done with the chart!
>
> Rowing in Eden!
> Ah! the sea!
> Might I but moor
> To-night in thee!

'Ah! the sea!' Poems – a single line in a poem – only very occasionally dare to use language like that.

Thank you. I very much hope that your lives are as intensely enriched by the poems of Emily Dickinson as mine has been.

Further Reading

Sandra Gilbert and Susan Gubar, *The Madwoman in the Attic* (Yale U.P., 1979).

Emily Dickinson, *The Complete Poems*, ed. Thomas H. Johnson (Faber and Faber: 2016).

Emily Dickinson, *Selected Poems*, ed. Helen McNeil (Everyman Poetry: 1997).

Margaret Homans, *Women Writers and Poetic Identity: Dorothy Wordsworth, Emily Bronte and Emily Dickinson*, new ed. (Princeton U.P.: 2014).

Wendy Martin ed., *The Cambridge Companion to Emily Dickinson* (Cambridge U.P.: 2002).

Helen McNeil, *Emily Dickinson* (Virago: 1986).

Martha Nell Smith, *Rowing in Eden: Rereading Emily Dickinson* (University of Texas Press: 1992).

7   *Emma*

Rhetoric, Irony and the Reader's Assault Course

Jane Austen's *Emma* deploys, with a kind of casual or even whimsical bravado, a sophisticated, and for the reader morally challenging, range of rhetorical and ironic techniques. And this is more so than with the other great 19th-century European novels – and that it's also the first of them (by almost fifty years) is one of its other incidental ironies. Wayne Booth, who famously wrote about the novel in his *Rhetoric of Fiction*, could just as appropriately have addressed it instead in his later book *Rhetoric of Irony*. But let's start where he does, to remind ourselves of what we mean by rhetoric in fiction. It's all about strategies. These are the strategies by which the author seeks to persuade the reader of her views – which, Booth adds, may be ideological, unconscious or contradictory. Later in this lecture, when I bring *Emma* into (I hope ironic) conjunction with a near-contemporary novel by a very different kind of female writer (so you've got plenty of time to start guessing which novel), we'll see the way this novel (like the other one) is conflicted between political and social impulses which are indeed ideological, unconscious (or partly so) and contradictory, and that conflict gets played out in terms of politics, class and especially gender. (Let me just add that conflicted texts is a thread that connects some of the chapters in this book.)

Two of the novel's key rhetorical strategies may be identified as under the general categories of style and structure. The most far-reaching rhetorical technique in terms of style is Jane Austen's invention (the word is not too strong) of what was later called (at first in French) free indirect style and applied later especially to Flaubert's *Madame Bovary*, which I'll be lecturing on later. There may be – well, there are – more profound and wider-ranging 19th-century English and European novels, but *Emma* and *Bovary* are for me the most formally perfect of all. Flaubert's deployment of free indirect style is indeed brilliant and unsettling but Jane Austen's use of it in *Emma* is no less brilliant. The term refers to narrative where the narrating voice is in standard third person but adopting the vocabulary, thoughts and feelings of a particular character: it's as if floating between third and first person and thereby always an ironic challenge to the reader. Is this what Jane Austen thinks, feels, knows or is it Emma? Readers always face falling into the trap of mistaking one for the other.

I'll give an extended example in a moment but let me just say that free indirect style in *Emma* is particularly acute and challenging for the reader because Emma is, paradoxically, on the one hand, like Jane Austen, a kind of novelist, and, on the other hand, not (to put it mildly) always a very like-able person. When Jane Austen famously said that she was going to take a heroine that only she would like, she really meant (as her subtlest modern critic D. A. Miller argues) that no reader would like Emma as much as Jane Austen does – because Emma is (unlike all other Austen heroines) a proxy-novelist, an imaginative fantasist. Her match-making is like a series of not very good novel-plots (the Jane/Dixon one is an especially bad one) in which she alone, or so she thinks, has no novelistic end in sight – because, like her father, she hates change, is (I'd add) frightened of it, preferring pseudo-lesbian friendship with Harriet (infatuation is Mr Knightley's word) to a sexualised love ('I never have been in love; it is not my way, or my nature' (Volume 1, Chapter 10)) – a love where she could lose the con-trol she always needs to exert, and lose it to a man. It's not her 'way' to be in love because she's frightened of that. But the novel is, as we'll see, quietly pushing her into hetero-normative closure.

As to Emma's dubious likeability we will all have our 'favourite' exam-ples of Emma at her worst – well, apart from her savage and very public humiliation of Miss Bates at Box Hill, which must be the leading candidate for the cruellest thing anyone says to anyone else in the 19th-century novel. This terrible moment has been neatly pre-figured in another subtle struc-tural point: the first words of the novel call Emma 'handsome, clever and rich' (Volume 1, Chapter 1) and when we later hear about Miss Bates for the first time she's described as 'neither young, handsome, rich nor mar-ried' (Volume 1, Chapter 3): something, later, will clearly light that fuse. My own choice of Emma at her worst (apart from Box Hill) is actually something Harriet says, as it's a blazing and awful proof of how Emma has subtly moulded this sweet tempered and innocent girl into thinking along brutally snobbish class lines. Of Jane Fairfax's piano-playing skills (about which Emma is jealous) Harriet says this: 'besides, if [Jane] does play so very well, you know, it is no more than she is obliged to do, because she will have to teach' (Volume 2, Chapter 9). Emma has the grace not to reply.

Here's free indirect style at work. Here Jane Austen gives us Emma on Harriet, having just got to know her. (Two passages are here edited and stitched together).

> [Harriet] was a very pretty girl and her beauty happened to be of a sort which Emma particularly admired ... She found her altogether very en-gaging ... showing so proper and becoming a deference ... that she must have good sense and deserve encouragement. Encouragement should be given. Those soft blue eyes and all those natural graces should not be wasted on the inferior society of Highbury ... The acquaintance she had already formed were unworthy of her ... though very good sort of

people [they] must be doing her harm ... [They resided] in the parish of Donwell – very creditably she believed – she knew Mr Knightley thought highly of them – but they must be coarse and unpolished and very unfit to be the intimates of a girl who wanted only a little more elegance and polish to be quite perfect ... [Harriet's] early attachment to [Emma] was very amiable and her inclination for good company, and power of appreciating what was elegant and clever, showed that there was no want of taste, though strength of understanding must not be expected. Altogether, she was quite convinced of Harriet being exactly the young friend she wanted – exactly the something that her home required.

(Volume 1, Chapters 3–4)

I used to teach that passage to students who hadn't read the novel and we would analyse and discuss the details, noting for instance those give-away 'must's ('they must be doing her harm', Harriet 'must not be expected' to be intelligent – a nice cover for what Emma really means which is that she wants her to be stupid), being gobsmacked at Harriet being described as 'the something that her home required' (from IKEA) and looking at the way the sentence construction registers her need to respect Mr Knightley's judgment but her more pressing need to prefer her own to his – and I was regularly amazed that those students then, in effect, knew Emma better than she knows herself, a rich source of the irony without which we wouldn't like her (feel sorry for her) as much as we do. Let me add a side-note on style and sentence construction. From the very first paragraphs of the novel we need to be alert to the ironies of the Jane Austen sentence: with Miss Taylor (just as we've seen with Mr Knightley) Emma got used to 'doing just what she liked: highly esteeming Miss Taylor's judgement, but directed chiefly by her own'. A few lines later, on this first page, after the delicate understatements about Emma's 'power of having rather too much her own way, and a disposition to think a little too well of herself', it's added that these potential dangers were 'at present so unperceived, that they did not by any means rank as misfortunes, with her' (Volume 1, Chapter 1). Confession: I added the comma before the last two words. As I would before the last four words in another lovely sentence: 'Mr Woodhouse was fond of society, in his own way' (Volume 1, Chapter 3).

To restrict free indirect style to Emma herself (whereas Flaubert bewilderingly disperses it through the main characters) is particularly daring of Jane Austen. With a couple of exceptions all the chapters in the novel are restricted to Emma's point of view. And she's not only not always very likeable, she's of course often, crucially and painfully wrong. This is where we can re-join Booth whose essay on *Emma* is called 'Control of Distance'. Free indirect style, and restricting point of view to Emma who gets things wrong, obliges Jane Austen to get the very difficult balance exactly right between mystification (keeping the reader in the dark, letting the reader fall into the same errors) and irony (allowing the reader the space to read correctly and thus at an ironic distance from Emma). The control is over our distance from Emma, allowing for a kind of doubled vision or doubled reading. Of course, re-reading the novel (and no other 19th-century novel absolutely demands re-reading) alters the balance and distance – unless you're such a preternaturally brilliant reader to see all of Emma's mistakes first-time round, to read completely with irony and without mystification. As a 17-year-old schoolboy (at boarding school, fondly thinking I knew all about everyone else's romances when I actually knew nothing) I was the opposite. I got absolutely everything wrong, falling into every single trap that Emma was in. At the end I felt that I'd been through a particularly galling and shaming moral assault course, a series of crises of interpretation, at all of which I'd failed. I'd just add that, quite brilliantly, these crises of interpretation, or crises of reading, are mirrored or patterned in the novel in a textualised web of word-games, charades, riddles, anagrams. After the assault, and with schoolboy pretentiousness, I would say 'this book is about me. And it hurts'.

Having said that I'd add, to excuse my early naivety at least in part, that I think Jane Austen 'cheats', once, in this matter of control of distance. See what you think. It's at the end of Chapter 10 (in the first volume) where Emma contrives (with the pseudo-broken shoelace) to get Harriet into the vicarage and leaves her with Mr Elton, expecting him to use this rare opportunity (yes, I was naive enough to think this too) to declare his love. At last Emma can't put off entering the room any longer. The narrative (after a conventional, non-free indirect style paragraph) then has this: 'The lovers were standing together at one of the windows'. I suppose we could say that the phrase 'the lovers' is a sudden and tiny moment of free indirect style (what Emma thinks) but really that would be stretching it. I'd call it cheating.

Structure. The highly patterned structure of the novel carries considerable rhetorical force. The plot can be (and has been by critics) mapped, diagrammatically, as a series of ironic triangles (the first of which is Emma, Harriet, Mr Elton) and these come to a head at the end in the way Emma and Mr Knightley realise their love for each other. This can be seen in the light of what the French theorist Rene Girard said about desire being imitative and triangulated, that imitation of another's desire precedes the identification of one's own desire. I'll say more about this a little later but here's another structural point. The last of Emma's mistakes is to think that Harriet has fallen for Frank because he rescues her from the gypsies. This only 'works' as both plausible and a mistake because Jane Austen plays the rhetorical and rather sly trick of positioning the gypsies scene immediately after Mr Knightley 'rescues' Harriet from her cruel treatment by the Eltons at the ball. The structural patterning of the two rescues allows for both Harriet and Emma to be 'right' when talking, in a properly veiled way, about the rescue that for each of them means something different. Mind you, a more sceptical reading might say that the gypsies scene is only in the novel at all as a decoy to deflect attention from the 'real' rescue that Harriet means. Further scepticism would add that this, in terms of class and politics, is manipulatively patronising about gypsies.

The structure of the novel also deploys an intricate series of mirrors, doubles and others, again I think more subtly so than in any 19th-century novel. In a way that reminds me of Hamlet (who keeps bumping into versions of himself in other characters: you'll find I discuss this in a later lecture) Emma herself is mirrored or othered through the novel – most obviously by Mrs Elton whose snobbery, arrogance and blindly patronising and manipulative treatment of Jane Fairfax are all grotesquely inflated versions of Emma herself and her treatment of Harriet. We may prefer to distinguish sharply between Emma and Mrs Elton, as Emma herself of course does, but rhetorically we can't do so and we have to recognise that the source of Emma's intense dislike (in what psychologists call projection) is an uneasy and unconscious self-recognition. The opposite is true about Jane. She is an idealised version of everything Emma would like to be but isn't – which is precisely why Emma dislikes her even more irrationally than she dislikes Mrs Elton.

More subtle still is Frank as Emma's double or other. His secret engagement to Jane and his treatment of Jane and of Emma is positioned as the equivalent in its capacity to cause pain (especially to Jane) as Emma's as-if secret and manipulative plans for Harriet – and brilliantly they come together, causing or potentially causing most pain, at Box Hill. You won't need reminding, though Emma – who seems oblivious to it – does, that by flirting with Frank she is potentially hurting Harriet (potentially, because Harriet is not in love with him though Emma thinks she is, so it's just as bad of Emma), as much as Frank is actually hurting Jane. That is a very subtle patterning. What Mr Knightley says of Frank's conduct (below we'll see the force of what Emma says) – 'always deceived by his own wishes … his own mind full of intrigue' (Volume 3, Chapter 15) – is what he (and the novel) say, rather more kindly, about Emma. Emma's sharpest humiliation is the recognition that rather than Frank being part of her game, object to her subject, he has used her as his pawn, object to his subject.

I said earlier that *Emma* can be very productively brought together with a very different but nearly exactly contemporary novel by a very different woman writer. You've all guessed which novel by now so let's go there now. The two novels are startlingly different but share submerged structural anxieties: of course, they are *Emma* and *Frankenstein*.

Marilyn Butler, back in 1975, described the political war of ideas in Jane Austen's novels (this book radicalised Austen studies, in effect overnight – I was a postgraduate student at Oxford and remember the excitement) and we can see in both these novels conservative and revolutionary elements in rhetorical conflict. Butler sees the connection between Jane Austen and the radical William Godwin, Mary Shelley's father, and there's even a possible sly gesture towards Mary Wollstonecraft, her mother (and to Thomas Paine), when the narrator in *Emma* jokes that 'a private dance, without sitting down to supper, was pronounced an infamous fraud upon the rights of men and women' (Volume 2, Chapter 11). Butler pertinently refers to a Victorian critic of 1870 who noted that virtue, for Austen, was a matter of struggle and conquest – and that is the revolutionary vocabulary of social progress.

Chris Baldick in his fine 1987 book argues that *Frankenstein* stages an equivalent war of ideas, reflecting conflicted ways of 'reading' the French revolution, as in conservative and radical pamphlets at the time, and that these affect the presentation of the Creature, revealing Shelley's own uneasy mix of revulsion and sympathy for him. (I'd put the sympathy higher than the revulsion and I've found that students do as well.) Both novels betray what is also perhaps conflicted anxiety about the dangers of playing God (Emma as-if creates Harriet; Harriet then turns on her by 'aspiring' too high – and aspire is a Miltonic word appropriate to *Frankenstein*) and about hierarchies of class and gender (the Creature can be very plausibly read as any 19th-century woman, the as-if only partially-made species). But politically it comes as something of a shock for readers of *Emma* – and I wonder if you felt this – to discover (if I can here quote myself, from a recent book on teaching narrative):

> that Frank Churchill, that great opener of windows and fierce advocate of the class-dissolving opportunities of balls, is rewarded (especially after he treats her at Box Hill with such callow cruelty) with the most desirable and "perfect" of all Austen's young women, Jane Fairfax, in sharp contrast with how Jane Austen handles those other deceptive charmers in her novels like Willoughby, Wickham and Henry Crawford.
> (Jacobs 2018: 7)

Some of you will agree with Mr Knightley that Frank simply doesn't deserve Jane. The more reflective part of Frank thinks so too.

Austen, as Butler shows, was at least in part sceptical about the landed conservatism that early critics claimed she supported, like the early 20th-century critic Lord David Cecil who said that if you didn't like Jane Austen you didn't like sunshine or unselfishness. For critics like Cecil (and my teacher at school), what the narrator says about the Donwell estate is a clear endorsement of the allegedly transparent values of landed conservatism: 'It was just what it ought to be, and it looked what it was' (Volume 3, Chapter 6). The 'Janeites' were nicely mocked by Henry James who wrote about the 'pleasant twaddle' of 'their dear, our dear, everyone's dear Jane'. But the Janeites at least liked her work – Charlotte Bronte, who didn't, famously claimed of the 'rather insensible' Jane Austen that 'the passions are perfectly unknown to her' (both in Lodge 1991: 17, 50–51). I hope some of you agree that there's at least as much passion in *Emma* as in *Jane Eyre*.

Austen's sympathies go partly out to characters like Frank (and the Crawfords in *Mansfield Park*) and this is reflected in the vein of waspish exasperation with the comfortable and complacent middle-England which she exposes in all her mature novels, as in these sharp words in *Emma* about schools 'where young ladies for enormous pay might be screwed out of health and into vanity' (Volume 1, Chapter 3) or the evocation of this tightly closed society where (this is about Emma, Harriet and Mr Elton, after the debacle) it seems more like a prison (or, say, a boarding-school) than a prosperous village:

> Their being so fixed, so absolutely fixed, in the same places was bad for each, for all three. Not one of them had the power of removal or of effecting any material change of society. They must encounter each other, and make the best of it
>
> (Volume 1, Chapter 17)

– and this is again, at least potentially, the language of social change.

That sense of claustrophobia, being locked into an airless and changeless space, is powerfully evoked in the two great carriage-scenes in the novel, as often subtly patterned against each other. In the first, with the carriage moving through the snow at agonisingly slow pace (on Mr Woodhouse's orders – so it's as if the father, selfishly as usual, is responsible for the protracted pain of what now happens), Emma and Mr Elton have to endure each other's presence alone in that box after his clumsy love-making and her angry rebuttal. In a few particularly sharply phrased words the narrator says that 'their straightforward emotions left no room for the little zig-zags of embarrassment' (Volume 1, Chapter 15). In the other passage, at the end of the Box Hill scene and following Mr Knightley's very stern rebuking of Emma for her cruel treatment of Miss Bates, it's now the carriage that is moving too quickly and it's all too late. I need to share this with you, the novel's most moving moment – and I can still recall my reaction as a 17-year-old. I'd never read anything like this. This moved me, well, upset me is the better word, more than anything in, say, *Hamlet* or *King Lear*.

> While they talked, they were advancing towards the carriage; it was ready; and, before she could speak again, he had handed her in. He had misinterpreted the feelings which kept her face averted, and her tongue motionless. They were combined only of anger against herself, mortification, and deep concern. She had not been able to speak; and, on entering the carriage, sunk back for a moment overcome – then reproaching herself for having taken no leave, making no acknowledgement, parting in apparent sullenness, she looked out with voice and hand eager to show a difference; but it was just too late. He had turned away, and the horses were in motion. She continued to look back, but in

vain; and soon, with what appeared unusual speed, they were half way down the hill, and everything left far behind ... It was not necessary to speak. There was only Harriet, who seemed not in spirits herself... and very willing to be silent; and Emma felt the tears running down her cheeks almost all the way home, without being at any trouble to check them, extraordinary as they were.

(Volume 3, Chapter 7)

Let's turn to Emma's response to the truth about Frank. She describes him, with unusual severity, as deploying 'espionage and treachery – to come among us with professions of openness and simplicity' (Volume 3, Chapter 10). (The word 'espionage' is used nowhere else in Austen and had only recently came into the language, from French. The suggestion is that Frank has French-revolutionary sympathies.) But the Frank/Jane relationship, though emphatically not what it ought to be and very much not looking like what it was, has a 'romantic', even a proto-Victorian feel about it, very different to typical relationships in Jane Austen. How did you find it? I've found in class discussions that students respond to the Frank/Jane romance more powerfully than they do the Emma/Mr Knightley one.

What we might call the official and conservative side of the novel privileges Emma and Mr Knightley's love at the novel's centre and, in effect, puts into question the scandalous nature of the Frank/Jane story, hidden in its margins. I mentioned earlier Rene Girard's ideas about imitative and triangular desire, and these give a kind of psychological plausibility to the Emma/Mr Knightley love: their love only becomes manifest to each of them when faced with the hidden jealousies revealed by the plot. Their love for each other is unwittingly activated by Frank and Harriet. And there's a particularly touching paralleling of incidents, widely separated in the novel and thus not easily noticed, in relation to Frank and Mr Knightley as 'rivals'. Early in the novel, Frank is about to confess his love for Jane to Emma and she thinks he's about to express his love for her – but something stops him. This is structurally mirrored at the end when Mr Knightley is about to confess his love to Emma, but she stops him – because she thinks he's about to confess his love of Harriet to her.

Earlier in the novel we read of Mr Knightley returning to the 'coolness and solitude' of Donwell (Volume 3, Chapter 5). I find that use of 'solitude' very difficult to read. Does he enjoy it or not? The meaning is provocatively hovering between, say, Marvell's 'delicious solitude' and Edward Thomas' 'since I was born into this solitude'. (We'll be looking, at the end of this book of lectures, at the word 'solitary' in the last lines of *Paradise Lost*.) But it's a solitude that seems more self-knowing than Emma's. Nonetheless, hovering over the end of the novel and their coming together in what I earlier called hetero-normative closure, and in the at least sceptical absurdity of their living chastely and for ever in Mr Woodhouse's house, is the question as to whether solitude is the 'natural' state for both of them.

There are other potentially sceptical aspects of the Emma/Mr Knightley relationship. They joke about being brother and sister but not about it being closer to father and daughter with that 16-year age gap (much more than any other in Jane Austen). But he does joke at the end about being in love with Emma since she was – er – 13, when he was about 30. (A man in his thirties and a 13-year-old girl. Now, what's that mid-20th-century American novel that comes to mind? Ah yes, that one.) And do we really think Emma will be a 'different' person as Mrs Knightley? Readers will argue over this. What do you think? We're conditioned by our novel-reading (by the rhetorical conventions of closure in happily-ending classic-realist novels) to assume that a 'corrected' Emma will ensure happiness and heteronormative fulfilment but some of us might wonder about how emotionally and sexually 'correctable' Emma is – but indeed why should she be? What's with all this 'correcting'? Older male critics and editors – sadly including Wayne Booth – come over all correctional and punitive with Emma (versions of 'what Emma has to be educated into after her grave errors is [etc.]') but I can't help, at the end, thinking back to the passage we mentioned earlier when she says to Harriet that being in love is 'not my way, or my nature'. A few moments later, projecting forward to her life as an older woman, she comes out with the funniest words in the novel – 'If I know myself, Harriet' – and the passage ends with, correspondingly, the most terrifying words in the novel: 'My nephews and nieces! – I shall often have a niece with me' (Volume 1, Chapter 10). I think we might, with a little justification, worry on behalf of that niece – and at least agree that the prospects for the Frank and Jane relationship are, let's say, more straightforward. These ways of reading the differences between the Emma/Mr Knightley and the Frank/Jane relationships can be simply described, in terms of rhetoric, as Jane Austen being conflicted between contradictory ideas that she's persuading us about.

We can call this strategy the rhetoric of difference (whichever reading of the relationships we ourselves prefer) and we can add to that by returning to style and making the point that the novel – as in Jane Austen generally – activates a differentiated hierarchy of languages. By this I mean that for all the brilliantly and colourfully realised and individualised languages for each of the characters (Miss Bates' long speeches must be the most amazingly sustained and verbalised streams of nonsense-consciousness in the English novel) there's a privileged language in the novel that I would describe as white, neutral or as-if transparent (as-if because of course no fictional language can be transparent). Marilyn Butler makes a related point when she notes that one of the most eloquent aspects of the novel is the complete silence of the most simply strong-feeling character in the novel – Robert Martin, who loves Harriet. Mr Knightley says, in surprisingly post-Romantic language, that he's 'desperately in love' (Volume 1, Chapter 8). I'd add that the silences of the heroines in the two most under-rated of the Austen novels, Fanny Price in *Mansfield Park* and Anne Elliot in

Persuasion, carry the same emotional and strategic weight. (When Fanny speaks accidentally 'out' by asking an innocent question about the slave-trade that funded Mansfield Park itself there's a famously shattering silence that the wonderful Edward Said pointed to.) This privileged language in *Emma* that I'm talking about is as it were non-socialised, un-mediated by the societal conventions to which Jane Austen is so finely attuned.

It's just one exchange in the Weston dinner party scene (and of course many critics have looked at this) when there's consternation about the snow that's falling – Mr Woodhouse being particularly alarmed about getting home. The exchange is between Mr Knightley and Emma; there's nothing like it elsewhere; and on the page it even looks unlike anything else in its bare, 'white' form. The exchange is introduced very unusually too, with 'thus - ':

> Mr Knightley and Emma settled it in a few brief sentences: thus –
> 'Your father will not be easy; why do not you go?'
> 'I am ready if the others are.'
> 'Shall I ring the bell?'
> 'Yes, do.'
>
> (Volume 1, Chapter 15)

This, rhetorically, does more than anything else to establish in the reader's mind, perhaps only unconsciously, the notion that these are two people (to whom, of course, we alone, in this social gathering, are privileged to listen) who don't need to use social conventions, emotional gestures, even tonal colourings to communicate: this is communication reduced almost to telepathy. The rhetorical message (not easy to resist) is that these are two people 'meant' for each other. I remember being very moved by it at school. Whether this is enough to counterbalance the more sceptical ideas we ex-plored above is, of course, up to each reader, up to you – and so it's now over to you; and thank you.

Further Reading

Jane Austen, *Emma*, ed. George Justice, new ed. (Norton: 2011).
Chris Baldick, *In Frankenstein's Shadow: Myth, Monstrosity, and Nineteenth-Century Writing* (Oxford U.P.: 1987).
Wayne Booth, *The Rhetoric of Fiction*, new ed. (University of Chicago Press: 1983).
Marilyn Butler, *Jane Austen and the War of Ideas* (Oxford U.P.: 1975).
Richard Jacobs, *Teaching Narrative* (Palgrave: 2018).
David Lodge ed., *Jane Austen: Emma* (Casebook series, new ed.) (Palgrave: 1991).
D.A. Miller, *The Novel and Its Discontents* (Princeton U.P.: 1981).
David Monaghan ed., *Emma* (New Casebooks) (Palgrave: 1992).
Edward Said, *Culture and Imperialism* (Knopf: 1993).
Janet Todd, *The Cambridge Introduction to Jane Austen*, 2nd ed. (Cambridge U.P.: 2015).

8 *Dorian Gray*

'Queering' the Text

A queer reading of *The Picture of Dorian Gray* would, I'm sure you're thinking, seem a rather superfluous thing to do as it's pretty clear to us all that this is a gay text with a network of – at least – homoerotic feelings flowing between Lord Henry, Basil and Dorian as well as clear suggestions of Dorian's gay influence over aristocratic young men and his manipulation of Alan Campbell's gay secret life. Edward Carson, in Wilde's first trial, certainly used the novel to advance his case that it was advocating 'improper feeling' and 'unnatural vice' (in Gillespie 2007: 384, 386).

But is it clear at all that the novel is a gay text? For reasons that don't need much elaboration, we can really only argue that the entire text is in a kind of code, that its gayness is never actually foregrounded and that, on the contrary, there is an elaborate strategy, throughout the novel, of sidestepping the issue and as it were displacing it in a series of evasive and subtly coded ways. What I offer below are some examples of how the text is queered so that its queerness is at once invisible and obvious.

One starting point is a simple fact of textual evolution whereby Wilde and his editors successively queered the text by making crucial material less and less explicit. The evidence from the manuscript and typescript, then the 1890 magazine publication of the first, shorter (and to my mind much superior) version, then the familiar and longer 1891 book version is clear – and is very helpfully laid out in the excellent Norton Critical Edition (edited by Michael Gillespie). Wilde himself and his editors went out of their way to cloud the issue when it came to, for instance, Basil's love for Dorian which is more strongly worded in 1890 (Carson in the trial strategically quoted from that version) than 1891 and even more strong and explicit in the manuscript and typescript. Two examples among many: the 1890 version has Basil say to Dorian 'somehow I have never loved a woman' (oddly, Carson failed to read that out) and Wilde took that out for the book version. And Wilde's editor, working on the magazine typescript, removed a sentence that Basil says about how the painting revealed his 'secret': 'there was love in every line, and in every touch there was passion' (in Gillespie: 250).

Also subject to successive editing and toning down were materials dealing with (or, rather, not really dealing with) Dorian's night-time activities in the roughest parts of London. Again, two examples: 1890 and 1891 have Dorian going at night to 'dreadful places' where he would stay 'until he was driven away'. That last phrase was the editor's: the original read 'till they almost drove him out in horror and had to be appeased with monstrous bribes' – which, by suggesting that Dorian was paying for or asking to pay for sexual practices that caused horror even in these dreadful places, is as close as any version gets to naming something truly dreadful, especially in today's culture. (What's in my mind is indeed truly dreadful but you'll have your own horrors to fill that textual gap so we'll keep our horrors to ourselves.) On the next page the magazine editor cut a sentence saying that women prostitutes used to curse Dorian 'seeing in him a corruption greater than their own and knowing but too well the horror of his real life' (Gillespie: 270–271). But in 1890 and 1891 it's exactly that knowledge of Dorian's 'real life' and of that 'greater' corruption that become unavailable to the reader.

There are more subtle ways in which the text queers itself in coded or displaced materials. Here I have three examples, one focused on a particular word, another on Lord Henry's private life, which receives little critical attention, and the third on Wilde's enormous debt to a novel that, in a sense, he openly plagiarised – which one might also say of his debt to the Conclusion in Walter Pater's 1868 book *The Renaissance* with its insistence that it's 'not the fruit of experience, but experience itself' that is crucial and its instruction 'to burn always with this hard gem-like flame, to maintain this ecstasy' for 'success in life' (in Gillespie: 334). Lord Henry clearly knows these famous pages by heart. Pater himself, incidentally, then had reservations, removing the Conclusion from the second edition as he thought it might potentially mislead young men who happened to come across the book. Young men misled, as if by Dorian.

In the novel's opening pages, where he establishes the triangular network between Henry, Basil and Dorian, Wilde is at pains to set up a kind of eroticised force-field and it's as if energised by a single word, 'fascinate'. Dorian fascinates Basil; Dorian fascinates Lord Henry; Lord Henry fascinates Dorian – and the word (repeated later in the novel in relation to Dorian's power over other young men) is clearly coded for the spell-binding power of seduction, which in the form of Lord Henry's seductive words makes Dorian feel 'awakened' and, in other barely disguised eroticised words, 'vibrating and throbbing', his features 'quiver[ing]' and 'trembling' (Chapter 2). The word 'fascinate', from the 17th century onwards, had senses that Wilde is clearly aware of – suggesting as it does the power that a serpent (Satanic or femme fatale) has to deprive a victim (typically a young man) of the power to escape or resist and to paralyse his faculties. This is the coded, queered language of an older man seducing a boy.

I'm sure we can agree that Lord Henry's wife is very cruelly treated by the novel – and the cruelty is Wilde's as well as her husband's, as Wilde clearly expects his readers to share in the contempt they both have for her, with her 'shrill voice', her efforts to 'look picturesque, but [she] only succeeded in looking untidy', her 'perfect mania for going to church' and her 'silly sudden laugh'. When his wife leaves the room Lord Henry tells Dorian that women are merely 'decorative' and 'never have anything to say' (Chapter 4); later he tells him that 'women appreciate cruelty, downright cruelty, more than anything else' (Chapter 8). The casualness of this misogyny from Lord Henry is, even by the standards of the time (and by Wilde's standards), excessive and I think the answer to its problematic status in the novel comes towards the end when Lord Henry (and again, it's suspiciously casual) refers to 'my own divorce-case and Alan Campbell's suicide' (Chapter 19), the first time we hear of both events. Campbell's suicide, you'll remember, would have been due to his secret gay life, which Dorian exploited, and so the effect of Lord Henry's news of the two events, and of his misogyny generally, is to yoke together himself and Campbell into a coded queer zone, as if it was his own secret gay life (mutedly suggested in his fascinated feelings for Dorian) that, like Campbell's, led to the stated outcome.

The source-text that takes up so much space in this novel (for me, disproportionately so, unbalancing and even bloating the narrative) is Joris-Karl Huysmans' *A rebours*, the decadent cult classic of 1884, published just a few years before Wilde wrote. This is the book that Lord Henry gives to Dorian, bewitching him as it indeed bewitched Wilde. (It was mentioned in Wilde's first trial but the judge ruled against it being cited further.) All of Dorian's collecting obsessions derive from this source. But one crucial difference between the novels is that, for Dorian, his collecting obsessions coexist with his nocturnal sexual indulgences (which we saw were successively made less and less explicit); for the hero of *A rebours* his sexual history is a series of memories of events much earlier than his current collecting mania which thereby becomes a kind of sad substitute.

Two comments: the effect of this in the Wilde is that the more obsessively Dorian collects, and at the same time, as is hinted, collects sexual exploits, the more the collecting of objects comes to seem coded for and a displaced version of his sexually obsessive seeking out of more and more outrageous sexual acts – the collecting of objects, which Wilde can write about, thereby being a queered version of what he can't write about. The other thing to say is that because the Wilde novel so openly owes such a debt to the Huysmans novel, Wilde must have expected his more alert and knowledgeable readers, particularly those with the same sexual tastes, to compare the vivid and detailed memories of the protagonist's unusual sexual history in *A rebours* (that come, as it happens, at the exact centre of that novel) with the reticencies and elisions in the Wilde. These memories in the Huysmans include entanglements with a very masculinised female acrobat who disappoints the hero for being too feminine in bed (and in mind) and a female ventriloquist with whom he can only reach orgasm when she pretends to be someone threatening to come into the room to discover them. (I'll let that little item pass without comment.) But the last relationship of this group of three is the most telling: in it the hero says he 'never ... submitted to a more seductive, more compelling servitude, never ... experienced such dangers, yet never ... felt more painfully fulfilled'.

This relationship, which 'lasted for months', is not with a lady performer; it is with a 'very young man' who 'looked as if he should be in school' (he's seen carrying 'a hard-backed school book' when they meet) and who has 'great liquid eyes', a 'nose stippled in gold' and a mouth 'like a cherry' (Huysmans, trs. Baldick: Chapter 9). A queer reading of the Wilde novel might add that this boy is partly Dorian but is, more suggestively, the boys that Dorian (by inference and in literary parallel) and Wilde want (and in Wilde's case got, at least in the later form of rent-boys who pretended to be younger than they were). And that's exactly why he or they are so absent from *The Picture of Dorian Gray*.

Oh, and those homo-erotic descriptors (the eyes and mouth) are also easy to apply to an iconic figure in a fairy-tale story many of you will know, Wilde's own 'The Happy Prince', written just four years after *A rebours*. I doubt I'm the first to connect Huysmans' 'very young man' with Wilde's playwright in the fairy-tale, a 'young man in a garret' whose 'lips are red as a pomegranate, and he has large and dreamy eyes'. The homo-erotic (peder-astic) descriptors also fatefully evoke Bosie Douglas whom Wilde met soon after publishing *Dorian Gray* – and I'll just leave you with that, an acutely ironic glimpse of the future and what many of you, I'm sure, know about the abominable Bosie, about whom I will restrain myself from saying any-thing more (in case I'm incited to acts of violence against the desk currently in front of me).

Thank you.

Further Reading

Neil Bartlett, *Who Was That Man?* (Profile: 1988).

Richard Ellman, *Oscar Wilde*, new ed. (Penguin: 1988).

Joris-Karl Huysmans trs. Robert Baldick, *Against Nature (A rebours)* (Penguin: 2003).

Peter Raby ed. *The Cambridge Companion to Oscar Wilde* (Cambridge U.P.: 1997).

Will Self, *Dorian: An Imitation* (Viking: 2002).

Alan Sinfield, *The Wilde Century: Oscar Wilde, Effeminacy and the Queer Move-ment* (Cassell: 1994).

John Sloan, *Oscar Wilde: Authors in Context* (Oxford U.P.: 2009).

Oscar Wilde, *The Picture of Dorian Gray*, ed. Michael Patrick Gillespie (Norton: 2007).

Oscar Wilde, *The Complete Short Stories* (Oxford U.P.: 2010).

9 The Fallen Woman
Emma Bovary and (Many) Others

Let me start the lecture, which is at the centre of this book and makes for what are I hope strong connections with the opening and closing lectures (as well as with a couple of other lectures in the book that deal with 'fallenness'), with Michel Foucault and his *History of Sexuality*. The first volume of this was published in 1976 and it underpins most modern thinking about sexuality in the Victorian period. Foucault was the most accessible and readable of the troika of male French intellectual heavy-weights who dominated so-called post-structuralism from the 1970s and helped form many aspects of modern theory. (The other two were the Jacques, Derrida and Lacan.) Foucault argued that power operates not to repress sex (the fallacy of the 'repressive hypothesis' in Victorian society) but the opposite – to produce, construct and regulate sex through discourse (a key word for Foucault), the discursive production of sexuality and of sexual subjects. For Foucault discourse, and discursive formations, refer to all the ways by which language in society operates to constitute knowledge and forms of subjectivity, and to exert mechanisms of power and control, both through domination and resistance.

Far from being silent about sex, the Victorian age, with its rage to classify, saw, in Foucault's words, the 'dispersion of devices invented for speaking about it, for having it be spoken about, for inducing it to speak of itself ... a whole network of varying, specific, and coercive transpositions into discourse ... a regulated and polymorphous incitement to discourse' (Foucault, trs. Hurley 1998: 34). Instead of repressing different sexualities, they were isolated and incorporated in power mechanisms through the discourses of (for instance) medicine, the law and education. An important idea that Foucault adds is that, though discourses exert power, they can also be the point of resistance to power, what he calls reverse discourse, the starting point for the formation of oppositional identity. The identification of varieties of homosexuality made possible, again in Foucault's words,

> a strong advance of social controls into this area of 'perversity'; but it also made possible the formation of a 'reverse' discourse: homosexuality began to speak in its own behalf, to demand that its legitimacy or

'naturality' be acknowledged, often in the same vocabulary, using the same categories by which it was medically disqualified.

(101)

This reverse discourse took a decisive step forward during and because of the Oscar Wilde trials which I touched on in the *Dorian Gray* lecture.

The Victorian period saw the solidifying of four strategic locations or unities centred on sex with their 'specific mechanisms of knowledge and power' (103). Foucault identified these as: the 'hysterisation of women's bodies'; the 'pedagogisation of children's sex'; the 'socialisation of procreative behaviour'; and the 'psychiatrisation of perverse pleasure' (104–105). These correspond to the emergence of four ideologically necessary bodies or figures, saturated with anxiety and subjected to the need to police and control: the hysterical/fallen woman, disqualified in both medicine and society; the self-pleasuring boy, requiring surveillance as a permanent threat; the Malthusian couple (Malthus was a late-18th-century political theorist and advocate of middle-class birth-control); and the 'perverse' adult, the 'other', pathologised against the 'normal', 'healthy' man.

**

Let me move towards a focus on the hysterical/fallen woman. There are three binary opposites I want to present, where one side of the pair is positioned to naturalise, authorise and legitimise the other. The first is the famous fallen woman/angel in the house pairing. The fallen woman is the ideologically necessary 'other' that naturalises and legitimises its opposite, the upper middle-class bourgeois chaste wife and mother, the 'angel in the house' (the term comes from an 1858 poem by Coventry Patmore), chaste in the sense of having limited or no sexual appetite and accepting sex only as the means to procreate; this idealised figure is no less ideological but her demonised 'other', the fallen 'unnatural' woman, is positioned to make the angel seem 'natural' and normal. (Behind this binary opposite, incidentally, is the Eve/Lilith othering that I talked about in the lecture on the myth of the Fall.) The most celebrated statement about the appetite-free middle-class woman was made by the mainstream Victorian doctor William Acton (unusually, he was sympathetically understanding about prostitution). In a much reprinted book he said this:

> The majority of women (happily for society) are not very much troubled with sexual feeling of any kind ... There can be no doubt that sexual feeling in the female ... requires positive and considerable excitement to be roused at all; and even if roused (which in many instances it never can be) it is very moderate compared with that of the male ... [Many women] do not feel any sexual excitement whatever. Others, again, immediately after each period, do become, to a limited degree, capable

of experiencing it; but this capacity is often temporary, and may entirely cease till the next menstrual period. Many of the best mothers, wives, and managers of households, know little of or are careless about sexual indulgences. Love of home, of children, and of domestic duties are the only passions they feel. As a general rule, a modest woman seldom desires any sexual gratification for herself. She submits to her husband's embraces, but principally to gratify him; and, were it not for the desire of maternity, would far rather be relieved from his attentions.

(Acton 1865: 112–113)

The passive, sexually quiescent wife at the domestic centre is herself ideologically necessary to naturalise and legitimise another opposite – the active, aggressive male ego in its pursuit of capitalist and colonial/imperialist acquisition, as if all that male cruelty and aggression is normalised in order to uphold the sanctity and chastity of the home. This is what historians call the 'two spheres' theory, hers in the home, his in the 'world'. Her 'chastity' and absence of sex-drive serves the additional function of legitimising its opposite, his raging sexual appetite, thereby legitimising also his recourse to prostitutes, thus rounding the circle back to the fallen woman. A point to add is that the ideological connection between the male sex drive and the world of capitalist activity sheds light on the standard Victorian slang term for the male orgasm – spending.

And behind that binary opposition of the two spheres is the last of my three, the slow shift that sexual-historian Thomas Laqueur has described (in a classic 1990 study) from the so-called one-sex model to the two-sex model of distinguishing between men and women. By the beginning of the 19th century heterosexual, penetrative intercourse became the norm of human sexuality, thereby marginalising the diversity of practices that had flourished before. Laqueur shows that around the same time two earlier models of sexual difference and sexuality became replaced. In one case, the earlier one-sex model, which posited women as biologically inferior men (their sexual organs the 'same' but smaller and inside), was replaced by a two-sex model which argued that women's and men's bodies were incommensurate. A lovely example of the one-sex model is in *Twelfth Night* (subject of a later lecture), though it's never commented on in any edition I've seen. Viola, disguised as a boy, says that 'a little thing would make me tell them how much I lack of a man' (Act 3, Sc. 4). S/he doesn't mean that, as a boy, she only has a small penis ('thing'); she means that, as a girl, she has a clitoris which is her little penis.

In the other case, a model of human generation, which believed that the woman's clitoral orgasm was necessary for conception, was replaced by an understanding of ovulation and menstruation which meant that the female orgasm could, as it were, become a functionless irrelevance and thereby edited out of common knowledge. It is widely agreed that Victorian men (including some doctors), and certainly many women, had little or no knowledge of female orgasm or of the clitoris. The case has been made that the vibrator was invented to relieve doctors of the task of manually coping with 'hysterically' frustrated women. Do look at the excellent webpages by the medical archivist Lesley Hall (www.lesleyahall.net) for a properly informed discussion of this as well as of the issue of whether or not Victorian doctors practised clitoridectomy for 'hysteria'. One of them, Isaac Baker Brown, certainly did but was not in mainstream practice. In an astonishing footnote, William Acton (quoted above) advises against excision of the clitoris in cases of 'nymphomania', but not out of humane concern but because he was fully convinced that for most women there was no particular sexual sensation in the clitoris.

The clitoris was Freud's famous blind-spot, arguing as he did that clitoral orgasm was an inferior analogue to 'real' vaginal orgasm. The notorious Victorian *My Secret Diary* by the anonymous Walter devotes thousands of pages to his enjoyment of women's genitalia but I gather (you'll be glad to hear I've only sampled this text in Steven Marcus' important 1964 book *The Other Victorians*) that there isn't a single mention there of the clitoris as the source of women's sexual pleasure.

The fallen woman, especially the prostitute, was also an ideologically necessary figure, as Lynda Nead argues in her excellent study of what she calls 'myths of sexuality' in the period (Nead 1990), and this was for pressing socio-political reasons. Prostitutes were a conveniently visible manifestation (and the fallen woman a conveniently narratable story: temptation, fall, decline, death) of what Victorians were most fearful of, the threat of imperial decline. Prostitution was argued to lead to deterioration of character for nation as well as person – in effect (as was argued), the decline and fall of empire. This, of course, evokes Gibbon's hugely popular *Decline and Fall of the Roman Empire* (Dickens makes great fun with that book in his last novel) and Victorians were very exercised by the spectre of their empire declining in the same way, from internal degeneracy as made all-too present by 'deviant' women and their power over men. Equivalently, after the wave of French and then other European revolutions from 1848, English moralisers emphasised the presumed connection between prostitution and revolution: France itself became from this time an emblem of sexual license and degeneracy. French novels of the period (as we'll see with *Madame Bovary*) are notably more explicit than English ones.

**

Of Foucault's four sites or bodies, that of the deviant, hysterical or fallen woman was, in the mid- and late 19th-century period, the site of the most discursive anxiety, replaced only at the end of the century, and made very public in the Wilde trials, by the homosexual man. The fallen woman was the site where discourses conveniently clustered together: medical/biological (the notion that women were intrinsically weaker bodies, delicate and prone to fall), legal (thereby 'justifying' women as men's property, their exclusion from public affairs, the grotesquely double standards obtaining in the divorce laws), political (as apparent in social reform movements such as the battle over the Contagious Diseases Act and in Dickens' involvement in Urania Cottage for rescued fallen-women) and of course literary, with the fallen-woman narrative becoming so pervasive in Victorian and earlier fiction (to say nothing of poems by Tennyson, Rossetti and others), from Jane Austen (four examples of fallen women) onwards, through Charlotte Bronte, Hawthorne, Flaubert, Gaskell, Dickens (at least seven), George Eliot (at least seven), Hardy, James, Tolstoy and beyond, later becoming a cliched formula, as we'll see. (The classic critical discussion is Nina Auerbach's 1980 article 'The rise of the fallen woman', later in her 1984 book.) Fallenness also becomes broader and broader in terms of definition, encompassing (as Deborah Logan shows in her 1998 book) unmarried mothers, seamstresses, alcoholics, the mentally ill, the childless and the anorexic.

The psychic roots of the literary treatment of fallenness are easily traced back to Eve or the Eve/Lilith 'othered' opposition. Eve is the exemplary fallen woman and the story of her fall (temptation, fall, punishment) is what we might call the exemplary narrative, the one that answers to the most fundamental psychic needs, including the need to blame the woman. The fallen woman, as opposed to the more generalised prostitute, is a figure necessarily embodying narrative or history: George Eliot, who wrote with varying degrees of conflicted sympathies for fallen women in her fiction, very pertinently said that 'the happiest women, like the happiest nations, have no history' (*The Mill on the Floss*, Book 6, Chapter 3).

The pervasiveness of the fallen women formula in fiction (and in painting: do take a look at the dedicated section of the 'Victorian Web', and especially seek out Augustus Egg's 'Past and Present' triptych) suggests a fascinated concentration on a usefully compacted emblem of what the Victorians took as particularly indicative about their anxieties, and in an emotional response range from what we might call the punitively prurient (or *Daily Mail* sense) to the richly sympathetic. It's almost as if there's an obsessive compulsive need for the Victorian mind to keep looking for, writing about, picturing – and, especially, finding the fallen woman, with the act of finding her being itself a narrative trope, the subject of the pictures and the stories, the woman and child finding the errant father, the father finding the fallen woman, with or without child, the woman alive or, most typically, drowned. Bizarrely but quite logically fallenness becomes not just the deviant exception to the angelic rule but the opposite – so that the angelic ideal becomes the anomaly (and, for ordinary women, an impossible role-model) and fallenness a kind of norm.

**

Let me now quickly sample some literary fallen women that interest me (and which form part of a much longer study I've been working on about fallenness and narrative) and then I'll move equally quickly to two sharply contrasting examples in a bit more detail before I end with the greatest of all fallen-women novels, *Bovary* (well, greatest before *Anna Karenina*, which couldn't have been written without *Bovary*).

Among Jane Austen's examples, I'm most struck by the weirdly duplicating narratives of the two Elizas in *Sense and Sensibility*, mother and daughter both seduced in their teens, both bearing illegitimate children, the one narrative nested within the other (of the first it is asked 'can we wonder that ... she should fall?') and both nested within Colonel Brandon's narrative (Chapter 31). The intentional awkwardness of the duplicated names and stories, as well as the awkwardness of Brandon's clumsy narrative delivery, seems designed to naturalise (or try to) what the novel positions as the opposite of the fallen woman story, Marianne's 'conversion' from potentially-falling 'sensibility' (after all, Willoughby entered her life by carrying her when she fell on the hill) into a quiet, modest and safely eligible heroine of 'sense' after her illness. But whether this conversion is successfully naturalised enough to be credible for modern readers is open to question.

Dickens' Martha Endell (in *David Copperfield*: the name puns on end-all) and Nancy (in *Oliver Twist*) are fallen-prostitutes though the texts are muted about saying so. The closest Nancy gets to uttering the taboo word is when she talks of 'riot and drunkenness, and – and – something worse than all' (Chapter 40). But Dickens does allow Martha's and Nancy's profession to emerge in coded form when they both gesture towards the Thames and say they know they will end up there, where they belong, fallen, defiled and drowned, as if that's all that fallen women are or do, fulfil a pattern, fall.

Martha's 'story' and its relations with her as-if sister and double Little Em'ly's story are subtly patterned together in a kind of elaborate game of shadows and mirrors. The lack of any narrative back-story for how Martha drifted into prostitution (in terms of 'character' she is little more than a persistently drifting shadow), at one end, and her formulaically managed emigration and marriage into respectability, at the other end, have the effect of telescoping any claim she might have to a meaningful novelistic life to two 'pictures' in the novel. One is Martha being physically rescued from (end-all) suicidal drowning in the Thames (the illustration for this in the first edition is closely related to the equivalent picture in the Augustus Egg 'Past and Present' triptych) and, in the other, pictured as 'white and hurried' and identifying herself as 'a ghost that calls her [Em'ly] from beside her open grave', she physically rescues Em'ly from the brothel in which Em'ly is 'upon the brink' of undergoing a terminal fall into a 'black pit of ruin'. Echoing Nancy again, Martha calls to Emily to 'rise up from worse than death' (Chapter 51). But Martha as fallen woman in the novel is a kind of absence.

A particularly intriguing example is the apparently random and even punitive death of the fallen Hetty Sorrel in *Adam Bede*. Her sentence for infanticide having been commuted to transportation (in line with Eliot's evident sympathy for her plight) she is nonetheless killed off coming home from her sentence in a way that can only suggest a kind of wilful exclusion from the benevolent happiness of the rest of the novel's ending. We've reached, perhaps, the limits of Eliot's sympathies. It's as if, having fallen, Hetty can't 'fit in' to the narrative in its drive towards closure. Miss Wade's narrative in *Little Dorrit* is a particularly interesting example of a narrative that also can't be seen or allowed to 'fit': as if 'fallen' into the otherwise smooth machine of the novel's master-narrative.

Her chapter is titled 'The History of a Self-Tormentor' (Book 2, Chapter 21) and this awkwardly inserted narrative (sheets of paper taken by Miss Wade 'from an inner drawer' and given, for no good reason, to Clennam who then reads them) has an uncertain textual status and identity: nested within the main narrative and baldly presented without any comment at either end from Clennam or Dickens it's like an embarrassing interloper, a bad or 'fallen' mini-novel, too deviant and illicit to be 'handled' by the mechanics of the rest of the narrative. (Of course, Dickens could very easily have made the narrative fit more plausibly and naturalistically.) In this sense Miss Wade's narrative is like pornography – the most demonised and definitively fallen of Victorian textual genres – which it also resembles in its claim to be a 'history' rather than a fiction; and, for that matter, 'self-tormentor' doesn't need much translating into 'masturbator'.

If Miss Wade's narrative is 'bad' or 'fallen' it is so in order to naturalise and legitimise the main narrative of the novel – and we saw the same, in the *Emma* lecture, of Emma's bad or fallen matchmaking or story-telling naturalising the 'good' matchmaking that is the main narrative. (And you'll recall that Emma's bad narrative of the Dixon/Jane secret affair starts from the fact that he caught her when she nearly fell out of a boat, like Willoughby with Marianne who fell running on the hill.) So bad narratives positioned to naturalise good ones, to empty the latter of ideology, duplicates what I said much earlier: fallen women are the bad 'other' to naturalise the chaste angel-wife-mother. I'd just add that another 'bad' or fallen story-teller, like Emma, is Mrs Sparsit in *Hard Times*. Her determination to invent the story of Louisa Gradgrind becoming Harthouse's fallen woman – step by step on the staircase erected in her mind, and she's a woman said to appear and disappear suddenly from storey to storey in her house (nice pun on storey/story) – is there in the novel to 'naturalise' Louisa's running away from Harthouse's seductiveness (from the chance of at least some fulfilled sex in her life), back to her father, falling at his feet, and becoming a kind of unfallen fallen-woman, pseudo-mother to other women's children (this is exactly how Little Em'ly ends up as well), for the rest of her life. That may not be a very successfully 'naturalised' narrative outcome for Louisa, for many readers. For me it's just depressing evidence of Dickens' fear of sexually satisfied women. But at least the fallen Little Em'ly had a sex-life, unlike Louisa.

Miss Wade (swayed from the path? swayed before her fall?), the only more or less fully realised lesbian in Dickens, has a beauty with a 'wasted look'. In Marseilles she is seen in company as 'solitary' and 'lonely of her own haughty choice' and, after what in retrospect seems a brilliantly ironic remark – 'I am not much used to the society of young ladies, and I am afraid I may not show my appreciation of it' – she withdraws from the company to her room. On her way she encounters Tattycoram, her alter-ego or double or her own sexualised body, seen 'passionate ... flushed and hot' as she 'pluck[s] at her lips ... heaving between whiles', with her neck 'freshly disfigured with great scarlet blots'. Tattycoram correctly identifies Miss Wade as her embodied self – 'you seem to come like ... my own – whatever it is – I don't know what it is' (she later supplies the word 'temper' – temperament/ sexuality) while Miss Wade stands looking at her 'tearing hand ... with a strange attentive smile' and 'her hand upon her own bosom'. Then Tattycoram's 'passionate exclamations trail off into broken murmurs as if she were in pain' (Book 1, Chapter 2).

The 'history' of Miss Wade, once one can look beyond its rather awkwardly sustained paranoia, is in one sense utopian, in its record of her passionate homoerotic love as a twelve- year-old for her 'chosen' schoolfriend, as pure in its intensity of longing as anything in Dickens. The erotic intensity is quite startling and carries considerable pathos, not least in this passage which ends in a moving variation on the archetypal fallen-woman's fate, death by drowning.

> I loved that stupid mite in a passionate way ... I so loved that unworthy girl that my life was made stormy by my fondness for her ... When we were left alone in our bedroom at night ... she would cry and cry and say I was cruel, and then I would hold her in my arms till morning: loving her as much as ever, and often feeling as if, rather than suffer so, I could so hold her in my arms and plunge to the bottom of a river – where I would still hold her after we were both dead.
>
> (Book 2, Chapter 21)

Hardy's Tess is, of course, imaged regularly as an Eve both fallen and unfallen and there's no doubting the intensity of the reader's sympathy for her, as the most fully human adult in the novel. But the Edenic representation is complicated by suggestions that Tess evokes not just Eve but also Milton's fallen Satan, disguised as a toad at Eve's ear, and the reason may be something to do with male fear of women's un-doing sexuality. Tess serves complex emotional purposes for Hardy as for her two lovers; but it's Hardy's perception of her rather than Angel's which is visualised when, as she is whispering her sad sexual history into Angel's ears on their wedding-night, he describes Tess bending forward, 'at which each diamond on her neck gave a sinister wink like a toad's' (Chapter 34). Faced with the terror of Angel's response to her story, Tess' mouth is pictured, again, by Hardy, not Angel, as in male-sexual nightmare: 'her mouth had almost the aspect of a round little hole', the mouth as vagina (Chapter 35). In the subsequent scene of Angel's sleepwalking Tess wishes that 'they could only fall together' but finds that 'he did not let her fall' (Chapter 37). But he has let her fall, become fallen, as he didn't trust her to catch her.

The suggestion is that part of Hardy's psychic investment in Tess is his need to suggest that she agents her own fall, that her sexuality is her own Satan, her own fault. Tennyson's Lady of Shallot conveys the same idea: to give in to her sexuality (by looking directly at a desirable man) is to bring on her curse, make her fallen, and die: sexual desire kills her. In terms of Tess, the idea of a 'fault' is made explicit, in a way that's characteristic of Hardy's voyeuristic interest in her, when he observes that the 17-year-old girl has an 'attribute' that causes Alec's eyes to 'rivet' on her: 'a fullness of growth, which made her appear more of a woman than she really was' – that is, desirable breasts (the Tess landscape is famously described as a woman's eroticised body with its 'prominences', 'undulations' and the dangers of its 'recesses ... apt to engender dissatisfaction with its narrow, tortuous, and miry ways' (Chapter 2): other novelists connect landscape and women's body, including Proust, as we'll see), breasts remarkably described as 'a fault which time would cure' (Chapter 5). This is at one with the erotic charge in the narrative when Hardy describes Tess working in the fields, his claim that 'the eye returns involuntarily' to look at her, thus her fault not the voyeur's, and that 'she seduces casual attention' because 'she never courts it', a famous come-on, or excuse, for voyeurs and worse, a charge that's close to erotic-sadistic when this voyeuristic eye – 'a bit of her naked arm is visible' – dwells on the 'feminine smoothness' that 'becomes scarified' and 'bleeds' (Chapter 14).

Let me now move to two contrasting examples, forty years apart, the first one, though earlier, brilliantly sceptical about the stereotypically demonised fallen woman (like, for instance, Bronte's Bertha or Stephen Blackpool's unnamed estranged wife in Dickens' *Hard Times*), and the other, the later one, a depressingly clear sign of how formulaic the formula had become. The earlier book is Hawthorne's wonderful *The Scarlet Letter* (1850, set in Puritan New England in 1649), a story that starts with the Puritan society forcing the adulterous Hester Prynne to stand for hours on a scaffold with a scarlet A on her dress. She refuses to disclose who is the father of her child Pearl. When the novel opens, there's a subtle association of ideas between a 'wild rose-bush' with its delicate gems and the two 'token[s] of her shame': her baby (Pearl – a gem) and the scarlet letter that she herself has designed 'with so much fertility and gorgeous luxuriance of fancy'. There's a flickering suggestiveness in the wordplay which allows us to read the 'rose-bush' with its 'gems', the 'fertility' and 'fancy' of the letter's design and, above all, the letter A itself, 'enclosing her in a sphere', as Hester's vagina (fancy), displayed and, as it were, defiantly unfallen or in refusal of fallenness (Chapter 2).

That is, the intended Puritan punishment – the fallen woman's shameful display on the scaffold of the letter signifying Adulterer – gets brilliantly re-written by Hester's otherwise signifying body as the celebration of autonomous sexuality. It's in this sense of a refusal to bow to the coercion of signification that Hester also refuses to be 'fallen' in another subtly intimated way. Early in the novel it's said to be 'marvellous' that Hester, rather than become the 'general symbol' of 'woman's frailty', 'the figure, the body, the reality of sin' (that is, Eve), 'did not flee' to England or elsewhere, 'with the world before her' – a clear echo of the end of *Paradise Lost* (as we saw in *Great Expectations*: 'the world was all before them') and, again, it's a radical revision of stereotype (Chapter 5).

'Adulterer' is never 'fixed' to the signifier A which refuses again the coercion of meaning, allowing for other readings like 'Able', for Hester's ministering to other fallen women – with their 'trials of wounded, wasted, wronged, misplaced, or erring and sinful passion' (Chapter 24): those first four adjectives carry considerable political force, though weakened by the last two; and 'Able' is brilliantly punning on 'Abel' in so far as Hester is earlier said to carry her 'mark' like that which 'branded the brow of Cain' (Chapter 5); to which we can add 'Alpha' for vagina (both 'Alpha and Omega' and 'ABC' were 19th-century slang terms for the vagina). The Indians who 'fastened' their eyes on the A see it as a badge of 'high dignity' (Chapter 22). That is, in Gabriel Josipovici's words, 'the letter forms part of a conventional, not a natural, language, and how we read it depends on … what language game we are playing' (Josipovici 1971: 169).

The connection or identification established at the outset between the child Pearl and the scarlet letter is elaborated later in a way that allows us to see Pearl as an emblem of Hester's unfallen, defiantly sexuality; like the letter, Pearl is Hester's sexuality incarnate. There's such a close bond between child and scarlet letter that she won't let her mother throw it away: she obscurely recognises the rich suggestiveness of the letter as herself. In this sense we can connect the presentation of the letter and of Pearl with the argument in *Aristotle's Masterpiece*, the most popular of Early Modern and 18th-century sex-manuals, that the fallen woman's fallen sexuality would be visible, as a narratively inevitable consequence, on her infant's body as a deformity, the mark of the mother's sin. In Pearl's beauty and bodily perfection, her pearl-ness, we can measure Hawthorne's radical rewriting of the stereotype.

Despite this revisionary representation of a fallen woman, it is the case that the novel won't let Hester ever properly shed her guilt, as 'a woman stained with sin' (Chapter 24: and we saw 'erring and sinful' used above). This takes me to my second instance, which I offer as a particularly pure and particularly coercive and depressing mini-narrative of the fallen woman, at the end of the Victorian period. It's from a rather surprising text, Jerome's *Three Men in a Boat* (1889), often cited as the funniest of all books, a fictionalised travelogue boat-trip up the Thames with many wildly comic episodes. And this 'serious' episode. One of the three young men sees something black floating on the water, near Goring.

> It was the dead body of a woman ... We found out the woman's story afterwards. Of course, it was the old, old vulgar tragedy. She had loved and been deceived – or had deceived herself. Anyhow she had sinned – some of us do now and then ... Left to fight the world alone, with the millstone of her shame around her neck, she had sunk ever lower and lower. For a while she had kept both herself and the child on the twelve shillings a week that twelve hours drudgery a day procured her ... and one day, I suppose, the pain and the dull monotony of it all had stood before her eyes plainer than usual, and the mocking spectre had frightened her ... She had made one last appeal to friends, but, against the chill wall of their respectability, the voice of the erring outcast fell unheeded; and then she had gone to see her child – had held it in her arms and kissed it, in a weary, dull sort of way, and without betraying any particular emotion of any kind, and had left it, after putting into its hand a penny box of chocolate she had bought it, and afterwards, with her last few shillings, had taken a ticket and come down to Goring. It seemed that the bitterest thoughts of her life must have centred about the wooded reaches ... around Goring; but women strangely hug the knife that stabs them ... She had wandered about the woods by the river's brink all day, and then ... she stretched her arms out to the silent river that had known her sorrow and her joy. And the old river had taken her into its gentle arms ... Thus had she sinned in all things – sinned in living and sinned in dying.
>
> (Chapter 16)

The rhetorical and narrative strategies of that are just too manipulative, the 'fine' writing too self-consciously managed, the tone or tones evasive ('some of us [sin] now and then') and the sympathy confected. The narrator doesn't bother to make the slightest effort to account for basic narrative plausibility, how exactly it was 'we' found out afterwards such pictorially exact details of the 'old vulgar' story, referred to in the chapter-summary as 'rather a hackneyed story' – but not minor issues like her name, or the gender of the child. (Kissing her child in a weary sort of way and giving 'it' a penny box of chocolate: was someone watching them? You'll see why this passage gets me angry.)

Relief is expressed that the body is taken off their hands as they had 'no desire to be kept hanging about coroners' courts', and that callow, laddish indifference, duplicated in the gratuitous way in which the man in the 'story', the father, is not even cursorily mentioned, confirms that the story as narrated is a tissue of recycled and cliché-laden bits of other stories, narrative as an empty-category, mere fictiveness. That is what the fallen woman narrative had become by 1889, just something to throw into the mix in a comic novel for a gesture towards social 'sympathy', perhaps for readers targeted as 'sentimental women', though we can ask how they would take the throw-away remark that 'women strangely hug the knife that stabs them'. The three young men are completely unaffected, the woman and her 'story' are simply dropped, and the narrative resumes with a 'joke' about how to slip away from your hotel without paying the bill.

**

It took Flaubert five years of more or less complete agony to write *Bovary* and when he and his publishers were then immediately put on trial for 'outrage to public and religious morals' he had reason to feel vindicated, as well as pleased by the surge in sales that the notoriety brought, not that he saw much of the profits himself. (The trial transcripts can be read in full in the 2005 Norton Critical edition: 313–388. I also draw gratefully in this part of the lecture on Stephen Heath's excellent study of the novel.) Vindicated because as the trial, in effect, was over how to read the novel and what it can be supposed to be saying to its implied female readership, and as defence and prosecution could plausibly argue from diametrically opposite points of view, he could feel that he had succeeded in writing a book 'about nothing' (Heath 1992: 7), that is, one in which the author achieves a kind of complete impersonality and invisibility (present but invisible, like God, was Flaubert's intention), allowing or even forcing the reader to adjudicate (as if in a trial), to weigh his or her sympathies and degrees of moral engagement.

This allowed him to absorb himself, to merge into everyone and everything in the novel – impersonally, invisibly, unjudgmentally. After writing the scene he called The Big Fuck (Emma first making love with Rodolphe, in the forest, her first orgasm – and the landscape has an orgasm as well), he wrote to his mistress that, composing the scene, he felt as if he was more or less coming too much himself and felt he actually was the horse, the leaves and the wind described in the scene, as if personally vanished. And it was this impersonality that allowed the trial to present two plausibly opposing readings. The prosecution subtitled the novel 'the story of the adulteries of a provincial woman', called Emma's adultery 'a crime against the family' and argued that the book would corrupt young women readers. The defence subtitled it 'a story of the education given only too often in the provinces' (Emma's farmer-father places her in a convent) and argued that the book was a warning against 'over-educating' young women and therefore a warning to them. Neither case could be proved (that's the point) and so, despite the prosecution's attacks on the novel for negating the 'beautiful and good', Flaubert and the publishers were acquitted – though issued with a 'severe reprimand' because literature 'should raise and refine morals'.

The early reviews noticed the political implications of Flaubertian absorption into everything. One review accused the novel of exalting 'the imagination in discontented democracy' and a vision of 'implacable equality' treating equally 'the kitchen-maid, the chemist's boy, the gravedigger, the beggar' (in Heath: 51) – again, that's the point. What the trial and reviews didn't notice or emphasise was the political force of how the novel, with what was called Flaubert's scalpel-like incisiveness (his father was a celebrated surgeon), dissects and presents, in Heath's words, 'the stifling permanence of the bourgeoisie, the eternalisation of its mediocrity' (56) and how this traps Emma (and 19th-century women generally). Emma is routinely pictured at her window, trapped, looking out, waiting for something to happen.

Emma is in revolt against this stifling permanence and all she has as weapons are her romantic fantasies from her reading – and her body. At first her bodily revolt gets displaced on to her wish for a son: the 'idea of having a male child was like an expected revenge for all her impotence in the past. A man, at least, is free; he may travel over passions and over countries ... But a woman is always hampered. At once inert and flexible, she has against her the weakness of the flesh and legal dependence' (Part 2, Chapter 3). This passage, from the Eleanor Marx Aveling translation used in this lecture (and, here as elsewhere, lightly adapted: see Further Reading for recommended translations), may serve as an example of Flaubert's supple and flexible use of free indirect style which I talked about in the Jane Austen lecture: are these Flaubert's or Emma's thoughts and expressions? The passage slips in and out of the two idioms. No lawyer, in court, would be able to prove the case definitively. Anyway, of course, the baby is a girl. And, again before the actual adultery, her bodily weapons are her unspoken rage and her hysteria (which, as it were, 'speaks' her rage), which returns us to Foucault.

Emma's rage against her situation with the loving but infuriating Charles, while she's secretly in love with Leon, is where many students whom I've worked with find their sympathies for Emma (and there can't really be a successful reading of the novel without our sympathies for Emma being at least engaged) both challenged and enlarged. It's morally complex, of course, but the sheer agonising pain of what's she's going through, its self-punishing lacerations, dissected here (scalpel-like again) is, for me, unprecedented in the 19th-century novel.

> The housewives admired her economy, the patients her politeness, the poor her charity. But she was eaten up with desires, with rage, with hate. That dress with the narrow folds hid a distracted fear, of whose torment those chaste lips said nothing ... Then the lusts of the flesh, the longing for money, and the melancholy of passion all blended themselves into one suffering, and instead of turning her thoughts

from it, she cleaved to it the more, urging herself to pain, and seeking everywhere occasion for it ... What exasperated her was that Charles did not seem to notice her anguish. His conviction that he was making her happy seemed to her an imbecile insult, and his sureness on this point ingratitude ... She would have liked Charles to beat her, that she might have a better right to hate him, to revenge herself upon him. She was surprised sometimes at the atrocious conjectures that came into her thoughts, and she had to go on smiling, to hear repeated to her at all hours that she was happy, to pretend to be happy, to let it be believed.

(Part 2, Chapter 5)

Let me just quickly move to the very next chapter to illustrate something else about Emma's situation (which reminds me very much of the Chopin and Gilman texts I'll be talking about next, in the transgressive American women lecture): the sheer lack of properly reciprocal dialogue in this novel. People speak at each other, never properly with each other. The effect is a kind of comic but deeply sad evocation of our lonelinesses from each other, and Emma is lonelier than anyone – and the scene now when she tries to confide her unhappiness to the priest is at once the most comic and the saddest few pages in the novel. The priest is too busy keeping an eye on boys misbehaving around the church to properly attend to Emma's hesitant expressions of what she needs to talk about but even when he is sort-of listening to her there is just blankness and misunderstanding, as here (and as usual I've had to abridge the passage).

'How are you?' he added.

'Not well,' replied Emma; 'I am ill.'

'Well, and so am I,' answered the priest. 'These first warm days weaken one most remarkably, don't they? But, after all, we are born to suffer, as St. Paul says' ...

She fixed her pleading eyes upon the priest. 'Yes,' she said, 'you bring solace to all sorrows.'

'Ah! don't talk to me of it, Madame Bovary. This morning I had to go to Bas-Diauville for a cow that was ill; they thought it was under a spell... The farmers are much to be pitied.'

'Others, too,' she replied.

'Assuredly. Town-labourers, for example.'

'It is not they –'

'Pardon! I've known there poor mothers of families, virtuous women, I assure you, real saints, who wanted even bread.'

'But those,' replied Emma, and the corners of her mouth twitched as she spoke, 'those, Monsieur le Cure, who have bread and have no –'

'Fire in the winter,' said the priest.

'Oh, what does it matter?'

'What! What does it matter? It seems to me that when one has firing and food – for, after all –'

'My God! my God!' she sighed.

'Is it indigestion? You must get home, Madame Bovary; drink a little tea, that will strengthen you, or else a glass of fresh water with a little moist sugar.'

'Why?' And she looked like one awaking from a dream.

'Well, you see, you were putting your hand to your forehead. I thought you felt faint ... But you were asking me something? What was it? I really don't remember.'

'Me? Nothing. Nothing,' said Emma.

And the glance she cast round her slowly fell upon the old man in the cassock. They looked at one another face to face without speaking.

(Part 2, Chapter 6)

Communicative breakdown is vividly imaged also in perhaps the most moving and artfully formed couple of pages in the novel, later, in the middle of Emma's affair with Rodolphe when he has (of course, lying) promised to elope with her. Charles comes home in Yonville after a busy day and, thinking that Emma, like the child Berthe, is asleep, he fantasises the child's future in a series of pictures.

Ah! How pretty she would be later on when she was fifteen when, resembling her mother, she would, like her, wear large straw hats in the summer-time! From a distance they would be taken for two sisters ... She would embroider him slippers ... She would fill all the home with her charm and her gaiety. At last, they would think of her marriage; they would find her some good young fellow with a steady business; he would make her happy; this would last forever.

The play of free indirect style, in its selfless projection of a family bliss that 'would last forever', is the single most sympathetic presentation of Charles that we have. It is followed by a curt 'hinge' paragraph that starts bluntly: 'Emma was not asleep; she pretended to be', and then a mirror-image paragraph of identical length to Charles' paragraph, a geographically incoherent and pictorially grotesque fantasy of Emma's day-dreaming elopement-life with Rodolphe, brilliantly not even named – for she/Flaubert has no need to name him when the reader immediately knows that 'they' in her fantasy can't possibly refer to her and Charles (let alone Berthe) – and where 'you' (French '*on*') insinuates itself into the free indirect style.

To the gallop of four horses she was carried away for a week towards a new land, from which they would return no more ... On the ground there were bouquets of flowers offered you by women dressed in red bodices ... They would row in gondolas, swing in hammocks, and their existence would be easy and large as their silk gowns ... In the immensity of this future that she conjured up ... the days, all magnificent, resembled each other like waves ...

(Part 2, Chapter 12)

The juxtaposition of fantasies is painful but most telling is the notion that Emma's fantasy has the effect of exposing Charles' as equally fictitious, which of course it is (you know what's facing Berthe at the end of the novel itself: if you don't I won't spoil it for you) – and the opposite, that Emma's are as understandable and as 'real' as his. The pathos of his faith in the family's happiness-for-ever is sadly reproduced in the pathos of her faith in Rodolphe.

Emma's hysteria is her body in revolt and Flaubert (as Heath shows in amusing detail) stuck very closely to the medical notions of the time about the woman's illness, hysteria. (He also identified his own health problems with hysteria and was delighted when a doctor called him a hysterical old woman.) Heath very pertinently quotes from the critic Michelet, earlier in the period: 'What is woman? The illness ... What is man? The doctor' (Heath: 88). Following standard pseudo-science, the contemporary dictionary of medical science that Flaubert studied closely (and that Charles doesn't bother with) locates hysteria in the womb and lists symptoms including feelings of suffocation (Emma regularly feels these), irritability, melancholia, fog in the head (the exact words used in the little story Emma's maid tells her about a young woman she knew). Causes include a nervous temperament, flabby education (as in the trial) and an excessive imagination (in Emma's case from reading romances). Young women from about 18 are particularly prone and marriage and motherhood are the best 'cure' (though another treatment – suddenly pulling out the woman's pubic hairs – is suggested). The story that Emma's maid tells her about the girl with fog in the head ends like this: 'then, after her marriage, it went off, they say'. '"But with me", replied Emma, "it was after marriage that it began"' (Book 2, Chapter 5).

Flaubert's identification with Emma as a hysteric himself makes us realise that part of her revolt, the part best calculated by Flaubert to outrage the upholders of bourgeois 'family' ideology, once the adulteries are underway, is to usurp the role of a man. (Edna, in *The Awakening*, shows the influence of this, as we'll see in the next lecture.) Emma as a man; and Flaubert, according to Sartre's monumental study, wanted, especially when young, to be a girl. With Rodolphe she goes about in public in male clothing; she smokes; and notoriously she treats Leon as her mistress. This undermining of societal conventions has its crucial counterpart in the novel's single most scandalous sentence, of course seized on by the prosecution in the trial: Emma (and we could say that this is a very 'male' discovery) 'found again in adultery all the platitudes of marriage' (Part 3, Chapter 6). Ouch.

Before that discovery, adultery is Emma's means of revenge, imaged as political-feminist rebellion – to 'be someone'. It's both absurd and very much not absurd that, after first making love with Rodolphe, she looks at herself in the mirror and 'repeated "I have a lover! A lover!", delighting at the idea as if a second puberty had come to her' (Part 2, Chapter 9). I hope you agree that this, though based on and derived from her (first-puberty) reading of bad romances, is sad and poignant rather than a matter for our contempt. It's sad also that she believes in and trusts that Rodolphe fully reciprocates her love: of course, this is naïve but it's not contemptible. I feel that Flaubert is enlisting us in this way of responding to Emma's very human need – to find what she does not have and be what she hasn't yet been, happy and fulfilled in love: to feel for her and with her as well as assessing her critically. At least, that's what I feel; perhaps I'm as usual writing about myself. Put it like this, we (I) can't want her to be permanently trapped in her unhappy lonely marriage and in permanent rage with Charles, like an angry version of Dorothea in *Middlemarch*, Gwendolen in *Daniel Deronda* or Isabel in *Portrait of a Lady*, though I'm not of course suggesting that Emma and her novel are of a comparable degree of moral and intellectual complexity as the protagonists in those later masterpieces (though all of them come out of *Bovary*).

I think Flaubert's and our engaged sympathy with Emma as fallen-woman also has to do with the idea that adultery in the novel is not just a kind of illicit or even guilty source of enjoyment for the reader but in terms of narrative it's the crucial motor (triangulation) and dynamic of plot itself, as argued in important books by Rene Girard and Tony Tanner. Viewed in this light, what impels Emma on to her two disastrous adulterous affairs is something as-if outside her, plot itself, within whose grip Flaubert is also having to operate. He operates (surgically, again) with such subtle precision that the standard is set for the adulterous fallen-woman novels to come, especially the great *Anna Karenina* – which you must all now read.

I only want to add that *Bovary* is the necessary forerunner of much later 19th-century and early 20th-century fiction. Later French novelists called Flaubert '*le maitre*' and his influence over the great modernist masters like Proust and Joyce (and, later, Nabokov) can't be overstated. The radical narrative techniques of *Bovary* anticipate the modern novel. I have no time to explore these but would just point to Flaubert's free indirect style, mentioned above; his break-through deployment of the imperfect tense to convey the achingly repeated emptinesses of Emma's life (earlier translations often just ignored this, about which Nabokov was very cross); the modernist cinematic montage and cutting; and the lack of usual novelistic dialogue and 'action' – Proust saw that action in the novel is impression not event. As the drafts show (and I'm grateful to Brighton MA student Natasha Kennedy for this), Flaubert even toyed with adding an amazingly postmodernist ending in which Homais, while enjoying his state honour, is suddenly anxious about being only a character in a novel, invented by some upstart 'to give the impression I didn't exist'. Emma also gave a word to the language. 'Bovaryism': 'the imagined or unrealistic conception of self, based on anxiety to escape from conditions judged to be unsatisfactory'. Well, it's another legacy for this extraordinary novel. Oh, and do read Flaubert's great novel *Sentimental Education* or, please, at least his miraculous late story *A Simple Heart*.

Thanks for listening.

Further Reading

William Acton, *The Function and Disorders of the Reproductive organs [...] in their Physiological, Moral and Social Relations* (John Churchill: 1865). Available through the British Library.

Nina Auerbach, *Woman and the Demon: The Life of a Victorian Myth* (Harvard U.P.: 1984).

Gustave Flaubert, *Madame Bovary*, ed. Margaret Cohen 2nd ed. (Norton: 2005).

Gustave Flaubert, *Madame Bovary*, trs. Adam Thorpe (Vintage: 2012).

Gustave Flaubert, *Madame Bovary*, trs. Margaret Mauldon (Oxford U.P.: 2008).

Michel Foucault, *The History of Sexuality: 1. The Will to Knowledge*, trs. Robert Hurley, new ed. (Penguin: 1998).

Rene Girard, *Desire, Deceit and the Novel*, trs. Yvonne Freccero (Johns Hopkins U.P.: 1966).

Stephen Heath, *Flaubert: Madame Bovary* (Cambridge U.P.: 1992).

Gabriel Josipovici, *The World and the Book* (Macmillan: 1971).

Thomas Laqueur, *Making Sex: Body and Gender from the Greeks to Freud* (Harvard U.P.: 1992).

Deborah Logan, *Fallenness in Victorian Women's Writing: Marry, Stitch, Die or Do Worse* (University of Missouri Press: 1998).

Steven Marcus, *The Other Victorians: A Study of Sexuality and Pornography in Mid-Nineteenth Century England*, new ed. (Routledge: 2017).

Vladimir Nabokov, *Lectures On Literature* (Harcourt: 1982).

Lynda Nead, *Myths of Sexuality: Representations of Women in Victorian Britain*, new ed. (Wiley-Blackwell: 1990).

Tony Tanner, *Adultery and the Novel* (Johns Hopkins U.P.: 1979)

10 Two Transgressive American Women

Kate Chopin, Charlotte Perkins Gilman

Towards the end of the lecture on the 'fallen woman' I looked at Hawthorne's *The Scarlet Letter* and discussed the radical revision of the archetype that this important novel presents in Hester Prynne and her refusal to conform to the fallenness required in her punishment. We did note some hesitation on Hawthorne's part in how far he was prepared to subscribe to her subversive and brave defiance, a few moments of narrative confliction in which words like 'erring' and 'sinful' are used about her, but there's no doubting the novel's warm support for Hester, her sexuality and her child, as well as support for her refusal to shift blame on to the man who fathered that child. There are novels in the English treatment of fallenness, especially Elizabeth Gaskell's *Ruth*, that show extensive sympathy to the 'deviant' woman, though Bertha receives no sympathy from anyone, worryingly including Jane, in *Jane Eyre*. But I don't think there's anything in the English tradition to match what Hawthorne does with and for Hester and her 'transgressiveness', affording her a quiet and dignified heroism and selflessness. What I want to do now in this lecture is explore two later instances of American transgressive women-protagonists, in these cases in texts by women, and I'll be doing so by exploring the Puritan inheritance in American culture, which I hope you'll find useful in connecting with the actual early Puritan context in and against which Hester is having to defend her self-identity. But let me start with male authority-figures, like the Puritan community leaders in Hawthorne; but in these later texts it's doctors. And there are plenty of them.

**

There is, if I can put it this way, no shortage of doctors in Charlotte Perkins Gilman's story 'The Yellow Wallpaper' (three of them in that very short text, including the one who nearly drove Gilman herself mad) and in Kate Chopin's novella *The Awakening*. There the only sympathetically portrayed doctor in either text is Doctor Mandelet whom Edna's husband consults about his wife being 'peculiar' and 'not like herself' (Chapter 22). (She has been refusing him sex.) A little earlier we heard that Mr Pontellier 'could see plainly that she was not herself' – and Chopin adds, in one of her typically deft ironic play with words: 'That is, he could not see that she was becoming herself' (Chapter 19).

Dr Mandelet, consulted on this troubling matter of a wife not 'being' herself, has two responses, one social and one medical-psychological. The social thing he wants to know is whether Edna has been 'associating of late with a circle of pseudo-intellectual women – super-spiritual superior beings'. That is, he wants to know if she's in danger of being infected with 'New-Woman' ideology. The other approach he takes is to explain to Mr Pontellier that 'woman ... is a very peculiar and delicate organism', that 'most women are moody and whimsical' and that 'it would require an in-spired psychologist to deal successfully with them' (Chapter 22) – and, in a nice matter of timing, Freud (as Pamela Knights notes in her excellent 2000 edition of Chopin's stories) was indeed just then working on cases such as these, with *Studies on Hysteria* being published in 1895. That's midway between the Chopin (1899) and 'The Yellow Wallpaper' (1892) where the narrator is diagnosed with 'nervous depression – a slight hysterical ten-dency' and told to 'use my will and self-control and not let any silly fancies run away with me'.

And behind 'The Yellow Wallpaper' (and indeed closely related to the figure the narrator sees imprisoned behind the bars of the paper itself) is the text's most directly influential ancestor, a woman secreted in what we might locate as the origin of what Gilman's narrator calls the 'ancestral hall', the 'hereditary estate' and (perhaps?) 'haunted house' where she finds herself being treated for 'nervous weakness'. This ancestor is a woman glimpsed in terror in one of those mid-Victorian novels in what Gilman's narrator calls 'English places that you read about', glimpsed in terror by the heroine but dismissed by her husband-to-be as the imaginary 'creature of an over-stimulated brain ... Nerves like yours were not made for rough handling'. I'm sure you recognised that as Rochester talking to Jane Eyre after she sees Bertha in her bedroom (Chapter 25). And another, later trans-gressive woman wrote a novel that both defiantly and delicately answers back to Rochester and his treatment of Bertha: this, of course, is Jean Rhys' *Wide Sargasso Sea*, her justly celebrated prequel to *Jane Eyre* and you'll find a lecture on Rhys later in this book.

In Gilman's words given to her doctor-husband John who infantilises and medicalises his wife: 'I am a doctor, dear, and I know.'

**

So this lecture brings together Chopin and Gilman and invites you to think about them as transgressive, breaking the rules imposed by patriarchy and internalised by most women. But let's go right back in time in terms of American history for a moment or two to identify one particular and forma-tive context for the rules that are being transgressed. Many of you will know this, especially of course American readers, but let me spell it out anyway.

The first European settlers or colonisers in the new world of America from the 16th century were Puritans ('pure' practisers of Protestantism) fleeing persecution at home. For instance, the English Puritans were escaping from the official Church that they identified as insufficiently adherent to the tenets of proper Protestantism, too complicit with practices and beliefs from the older Catholic church from which the original Protestants were protesting when, from Luther onwards, they founded an alternative to what they saw as the corrupt, self-serving and oppressive Catholic faith. One crucial difference between the older Catholic faith and the new Protestantism was the latter's insistence that individuals should be able to communicate with God directly and without the mediation of the powerful Catholic priests who, in effect, preferred to keep ordinary people in ignorance and under their power. So the Protestant movement was always about politics, people having the status and power to commune with their God on their own terms – and, importantly, to read the Bible in their own languages as opposed to having it selectively expounded to them by priests from the original ancient languages.

The Puritan founding fathers in New England in the 1630s were driven by a sense of being, not just pure practisers of the true Protestant faith, but God's own chosen people (like the ancient Hebrews who were also escaping persecution), tasked with establishing the true church in virgin territory (the native Indians were, of course, not part of the divine plan), a new church that would be, in famous words of the time, 'a city on a hill'. This notion of being divinely chosen for the task lies very deep in the American psyche – and, as a side-effect, may explain the close affinities between American Protestantism and the power in elite American circles of the so-called Jewish lobby today. I'd just add that Zionism, the Jewish belief in Israel as their divinely appointed home (a belief strongly supported by American evangelical Christians), can be seen, in the context of the first lecture in this book, as a kind of reparation for the expulsion from Eden, the return to the promised home.

The positive and indeed revolutionary beliefs of Protestantism and Puritanism were, as I've said, about ordinary people taking their religious practices and faiths into their own lives, taking responsibility for their actions and consequences as well as their beliefs. The downside of this is that people, rather than sheltering child-like under the wings of the Catholic church and its priests, had the new burden of having to be, in effect, their own policeman and that in turn put great pressure on the need for family life to be conducted according to the utmost propriety and obedience to Christian principles. The Catholic confessional in which your sins can be effaced becomes, domesticated, the permanent burden of consciousness.

This is where we re-join our late-19th-century American women writers, because what Puritanism brought in its wake, especially for the early colonising settlers in new England (as in *The Scarlet Letter*), was a hardening of early Christian orthodox ideas about marriage and the family. If the family, rather than the local priest, becomes the focus of appropriately Christian behaviour then the need to conform has more and more urgency – and the potential for oppression within the family structures, and more widely in the community (with models of surveillance and punishment: again, I'm thinking of *The Scarlet Letter*) becomes more intense, with the battleground moving to the individually burdened conscience. Emily Dickinson (whom I spoke of in an earlier lecture and who connects closely with what I say here about Chopin and Gilman), as often, nails it in a single word: in a sly dig at old-style Catholic structures of oppression she writes about the heart having or indeed being its own 'inquisitor'. (Equivalently, she pokes fun at Poe whom she clearly didn't think much of, by saying that the 'Brain has corridors' much more terrifying than haunted houses.) Anyway, what St Paul, in *Ephesians*, says about the role of women in marriage comes into sharper focus than ever:

> Wives, submit yourselves unto your own husbands, as unto the Lord. For the husband is the head of the wife, even as Christ is the head of the church: and he is the saviour of the body. Therefore as the church is subject unto Christ, so let the wives be to their own husbands in every thing.

When we ask in what sense Chopin and Gilman are transgressive we can start by thinking about this background and context. The great Edith Wharton put the issue very sharply in 1919: 'The long hypocrisy which Puritan England handed on to America concerning the danger of frank and free ... relations between men and women' means that 'American women are not really "grown up"' (in Wharton, ed. Waid, 2003: 290–292). Gilman's narrator is infantilised by her husband. Edna Pontellier is explicitly and intentionally in revolt against her Protestant background – in her case Presbyterianism, a strictly severe version practised by her father – when she deliberately chooses to antagonise her family (she was an unloved middle-child; her mother died young) by marrying an older Creole man, the Catholic and French-derived Creoles in the New Orleans of the time considering themselves more cultured and 'civilised' than old-stock Americans. This deliberate act of family-transgression is poignantly shadowed by her other motive in marrying: her youthful infatuations with unavailable men have taught her that love will always painfully let her down so she deliberately chooses to marry someone for whom she feels 'no trace of passion', just fancying that 'there was a sympathy of thought and taste between them' – and Chopin, in another sharp ironic moment, adds 'in which fancy she was mistaken' (Chapter 7). Isolating herself from her Protestant background leads to yet more isolation in Edna's married life, and her revolt against the Pauline doctrine of being subject in everything to her husband drives the inner life of the novella, as we'll see.

The narrator of 'The Yellow Wallpaper' makes a point, as we've noticed, of calling her temporary 'ancestral' residence 'English'. She also calls it 'colonial'. And we've noticed Jane Eyre and Bertha in the 'ancestry' of the story's hauntedness. (The narrator considers burning the house down to reach the troubling yellow smell and jumping out of a window – for both of which of course see Bertha.) The narrator's husband and doctor John insists on relations between them based entirely on his knowledge and power and her ignorance and weakness: her gradually managed revolt against that power, and the embodiment of his power in the rest-cure, can be read as the revolt of the 'New (American) Woman' against the oppressions of colonial-style Englishness, as she tears off the paper (as-if the texts) of 'English places that you read about', releasing the cruelly colonised Bertha behind every English Jane (and 'Jane' makes a sudden and unexplained appearance in the narrator's last words). But, as for Edna (and Bertha), it's a victory (or a defeat) at enormous personal cost.

The 1880s in America saw the rise of 'New Woman' thinking – and also its opposite in the so-called 'cult of true womanhood' with its emphasis on piety and purity in the home. The conflict is clearly, at least at first, very one-sided in 'The Yellow Wallpaper' where a passive domesticity and un-complaining obedience is expected of the narrator, in thrall to John who 'knows'. One marker of the process of her release from this orthodoxy is the way the text keeps repeating 'John says ...' in its earlier phases (marking her internalising of what she is allowed to 'know') but then gradually the phrase disappears as she gains control and power, saying even of John 'as if I couldn't see through him!'. The 'new woman' and the 'true womanhood' can actually be seen to co-exist in the presentation of Adèle Ratignolle in *The Awakening* who is simultaneously the ultimate 'mother-woman' (Chapter 4), focused on her children, and a comfortably sensuous and erotically cherishing figure for Edna, whose troubles she intuitively understands (she quietly says '*Pauvre chérie*' as she tenderly strokes Edna's hand in Chapter 7).

Adele's motherly warmth is a reminder that Edna was deprived of that warmth in her childhood (and that Dickinson said she never really had a mother). One of the subtlest indicators of the sheer loneliness facing the narrator in 'The Yellow Wallpaper', and the reason why we are her only confidantes (though a nice touch about her increased later power is that she ends up not even trusting us with her secrets: 'I have found out another funny thing, but I shan't tell it this time!'), is the sudden revelation, a few pages in, that 'we just had Mother and Nellie and the children down for a week'. John polices whom his wife can and can't see so he must have correctly assumed what we must, in shock, take on board as well. Her own mother (and, presumably, sister) have been staying for a week and this vulnerable, unhappy young woman, separated from her baby whom she's been told she 'can't' see and therefore, perhaps, has not been able or allowed (or both) to bond with (so she's separated from the baby for no good reason: and is she even ill at all before or when the text starts?), and forbidden to 'work' (which is her writing: she's a writer in effect censored and silenced in John's miniature police-state), has not been able, not felt it somehow appropriate, to confide in her mother, let alone give her any inkling of her predicament. That is such a painfully clear sign of her helplessly silent isolation, and nothing in this powerful short text makes me feel sorrier for her.

We can trace, in both texts, a process of release for the narrator and for Edna, as each of them 'awakes' into their sexualised bodies. Like Emily Dickinson who in a powerful poem, as we saw in the earlier lecture, writes about tugging at her bars and Edna (like Bertha) pacing in frustration up and down in her room (as we'll see later), the narrator is in a series of prisons: the house, the room, the bed, her body. (The house itself, as often pointed out, may even be a working or an ex-asylum.) Identifying the woman behind the wallpaper and the need to release her is not only an emblem of releasing all women from the 'bars' of patriarchy but also the need to escape from an internalised sense of her own hystericised body (internalising what is actually John's hysterical fear of the woman's body: she senses this as the paper's 'yellow smell'): she gradually achieves this release through a new sense of her sexual self-sufficiency, figured in her reading of the paper and the room. Starting 'at the bottom ... where it has not been touched' her examination of the pattern in the paper is as sexually suggestive as the later detail of the 'funny mark' by the skirting board, a 'long, straight, even *smooch*, as if it had been rubbed over and over ... Round and round and round – round and round and round – it makes me dizzy!'.

It is with her shoulder in that smooch and a rope round her body, after the seamlessly subtle way the text suggests her merging with the woman behind the paper ('I pulled and she shook. I shook and she pulled'), that John at the end sees her creeping on all fours, probably naked and with bleeding hands and mouth (from tearing at the paper and gnawing at the bed) – and this makes him faint. Doctors don't faint – unless perhaps they see their perceived child-wife sexually satisfying herself. (Or openly menstruating? There's a subtle emphasis on the moon in the text.) A victory over the fainting husband, addressed now as 'young man', but also a defeat. The transgressive woman is now a free adult – and the opposite of free. If we dare think about what will happen when John wakes up, we will remember Dickinson's cool awareness that those who disagree with the conventions of patriarchal control are dangerous and will need to be 'handled with a chain'.

**

There's something symptomatic about the early reviews of *The Awakening*. They're clearly rattled about something and feel the need to go on the attack. Here's a sample, strung together from ten reviews. 'Not a healthy book ... a morbid book ... unhealthily introspective and morbid ... unwholesome in its influence ... decidedly unpleasant ... disagreeable ... repellent ... essentially vulgar ... there was no need for a second [Creole]

Madame Bovary ... we wish that [Chopin] had not written the novel'. That last reviewer said he was 'well-satisfied' at the ending (which I won't give away here) and that really takes me aback, as I'm sure it does for you (if you know the ending). Another review casually refers to Edna's multiple affairs (in Chopin, ed. Culley, 1994: 163–173). For that matter, the cheap Dover paperback edition on its back cover speaks of the book's 'honest treatment of female marital infidelity' and Chopin's portrayal of a woman 'who seeks and finds physical love outside the straitened confines of her domestic situation' (Chopin, ed. Smith, 1993). So what's all that about and how can this most delicate of novels be so crudely man-handled (the rattled reviewers are clearly men) and indeed misread, as Dickinson was? A woman seeking and finding physical love sounds like a book with lots of sex with lots of partners. (Edna has sex once, possibly twice, with a man she doesn't even like, and of course never with Robert.) Whatever is going on in these reviews and mis-readings, the result was that the book was out of print for sixty years and only returned – perhaps appropriately – in French in 1953 (and the authoritative Harvard edition of Dickinson was published in 1955).

Actually, I think we can all see what's going on. There's a felt need to mis-represent and attack the novel because of what is actually scandalous about it, which can't be directly faced: the fact that, like 'The Yellow Wall-paper' though in a more fully as well as more subtly developed way, the book is about a 'solitary soul' (its original title), a solitary body waking up to its own autonomous sexual power and identity. And it's Hester's defiant autonomous sexuality that we explored in *The Scarlet Letter*. Edna wakes into herself, to belong to herself as opposed to being a prized commodity-possession of her husband. Edna resolves 'never again to belong to another than herself' (Chapter 26): as we saw much earlier, far from being 'not herself' (as he thinks) she is 'becoming herself' (Chapter 19). Most scandal-ously, this self is one that can (as at the end of 'The Yellow Wallpaper') do without men.

But being solitary and solitude (both words are repeated through the novel) is a poignantly ambivalent matter and the novel charts another and ironic kind of awakening. As Elaine Showalter points out, Chopin trans-lated a Maupassant story called 'Solitude', just a few years earlier, and, though the first part of the awakening in her own novel validates and cel-ebrates a (scandalous) waking into autonomous sexual self-ownership (I'll trace this process later), the final phases reveal the opposite insight, the sheer aching vacancy and loneliness that solitude means. Edna's last real-isation echoes Maupassant. His story says this: 'despite the embrace and transports of love ... we are always alone ... [in] horrible solitude which overpowers me ... each of us is alone; side by side but alone' (in Chopin, ed. Walker, 2000: 202). Edna, in her extraordinary last moments 'realised that the day would come when he [Robert], too, and the thought of him would melt out of her existence, leaving her alone' (Chapter 39).

Like Dickinson, Edna is 'different'. She is 'not a mother-woman' and I've already talked about her intentionally isolating herself from her Protestant family. But she's also a stranger among the Catholic Creoles she marries into, in effect sleep-walking out of childhood into adulthood and marriage, like, as she says herself, when she was a child 'walking through the green meadow ... idly, aimlessly, unthinking, unguided' (Chapter 7). (Here I'll add that Chopin notes that Edna is embarrassed by a book, evidently a shocking one, that her Creole friends openly discuss and that she reads in solitude: none of my four editions hazards a guess as to what this book might be so I'll guess that it's a sly glance at Paul Bonnetain's notorious 1883 novel *Charlot s'amuse*.) Anyway, this is the sleep from which Edna, aged 28, will, like a (rather mature) fairy-tale princess, awake (and I'll talk more about fairy-tale soon).

Edna's difference is also neatly figured by her being positioned, perhaps even stranded between two opposite, indeed incompatible role-models on a 'spectrum' of womanhood: the ultimate mother-woman Mme Ratignolle, radiant in her sensuousness and tender fondness for Edna, and Mlle Reisz, plain and awkward and (this is lightly suggested) lesbian – she says herself that Edna has 'captivated' her (Chapter 21). Where does the potentially New Woman position herself and how? Neither a proper mother-woman nor (according to Mlle Reisz) a properly true artist Edna is 'othered' by these two women, increasing our sense of her solitariness.

There's a sense that the direction of Edna's 'plot' – though on the surface following the usual stages of the fallen-woman story – is a series of improvisations, having to make it up as she goes along, as there are no moral, social or emotional conventions for her to follow during her particular awakening – and no language to express it, like the caged parrot of the first page speaking a 'language which nobody understood'. Thus also the novel's recourse, at crucial moments of Edna's awakening awareness, to the language of impressionistic vagueness, gesturing towards the notion, which we saw as so important in Dickinson, that the truly significant always lies beyond the expressible. After the argument between husband and wife in Chapter 3 we have this cluster of words to convey Edna's feelings: 'indescribable ... unfamiliar ... vague ... like a shadow, like a mist ... strange and unfamiliar; it was a mood'. Equivalently the language of the novel evokes impressionist painting and French symbolist poetry, the shortest chapters (like Chapter 6) being in effect poems – and the way the novel's most crucial material, especially about Edna's body and sexuality, are in coded language – figured, for instance, in notions of the sea, swimming, music, birds, clothing and (as in 'The Yellow Wallpaper') rooms and houses.

Edna's story of awakening into an attempted freedom is, in a particularly subversive formal strategy, brilliantly 'answered' by the novel's shadow narrative that as-if ironically undermines hers: the silent narrative of Mme Ratignolle's conception, pregnancy and birth – very subtly gestured towards because there are 39 chapters in the novel (mutedly evoking Mme Ratignolle's 39 week term). The moment Adele gives birth actually marks the most transgressive moment in any of these texts. Edna thinks of leaving. 'But Edna did not go. With an inward agony, with a flaming, outspoken revolt against the ways of Nature, she witnessed the scene of torture' (Chapter 37). This astonishingly evokes Edna as Milton's Satan and calls out the 'nature' of a natural childbirth as torture. Perhaps the early reviewers were too shocked by this to notice it.

Let me end by sketching the very subtly evoked stages, in coded language as suggested, by which the process of Edna's awakening is evoked. It's Edna's body that awakes. And this starts with Mme Reisz's piano playing in Chapter 9. Here a crucial distinction is made between the rather adolescent way Edna used to listen to music (including a piece she, wrongly but aptly, called 'Solitude'), using music to evoke sentimental pictures in her mind, and the effect, now at this party, of Mme Reisz's playing (the music of Chopin, of course; and she will only play at all on Edna's request).

> The first chords ... sent a keen tremor down Mrs Pontellier's spinal column ... Perhaps it was the first time she was ready, perhaps the first time her being was tempered to take an impression of the abiding truth ... She saw no pictures of solitude, of hope, of longing, or of despair. But the very passions themselves were aroused within her ... She trembled, she was choking, and the tears blinded her ... The young woman was unable to answer [Mlle Reisz]; she pressed the hand of the pianist convulsively.

This is the coded language of orgasm, by inference first orgasm (the well-tempered instrument of the body sounding properly at last, as if vibrating to Mlle Reisz's piano), and this is confirmed in the immediately following scene and chapter when Robert proposes late-night swimming and Edna, who can't swim and who has failed to respond to tuition even from Robert, suddenly can. I mentioned this scene in the Dickinson lecture in relation to her poem about going to sea.

> But that night she was like the little tottering, stumbling, clutching child, who of a sudden realises its powers, and walks for the first time alone ... A feeling of exultation overtook her, as if some power of significant import had been given her to control the working of her body and her soul ... She wanted to swim out, where no woman had swum before ... Intoxicated with her newly conquered power, she swam out alone. She turned her face seaward to gather in an impression of space and solitude, which the vast expanse of water, meeting and melting with the moonlit sky, conveyed to her excited fancy. As she swam she seemed to be reaching out for the unlimited in which to lose herself.

The eroticised language ('excited fancy') and the refrain, in both passages and later in the novel, of the phrase 'for the first time' (which I think has its origins in *Madame Bovary*), suggest an onrush of and access to new layers of sensation and pleasure available to but only by herself: not even Robert can open those doors.

Before I leave these two early passages, I want to glance briefly at a story (in Knights 2000) that Chopin wrote a few years earlier, 'The Story of an Hour' (a brilliant story and I won't give away the ending), in order to confirm the intensely eroticised nature of Chopin's language in dealing with a parallel situation (as well as confirming her pun on 'fancy' = vagina). In this story a woman hears that her husband has been killed in a train accident, goes into her room, locks it (like the narrator in 'The Yellow Wallpaper') and experiences what can only be described as an orgasmic sense of release into a sense of freedom ('Body and soul free!') in which, like Edna, she thrills with the idea that now 'she would live for herself. There would be no powerful will bending hers'.

> There was something coming to her ... she felt it, creeping out of the sky, reaching toward her... Now her bosom rose and fell tumultuously. She was beginning to recognize this thing that was approaching to possess her... When she abandoned herself ... her pulses beat fast, and the coursing blood warmed and relaxed every inch of her body. She did not stop to ask if it were or were not a monstrous joy that held her ... She was drinking in a very elixir of life... Her fancy was running riot...

Edna and Robert visit a neighbouring island in Chapter 13 of *The Awakening*. During a church service she needs to escape from 'a feeling of oppression', which evokes her childhood memory of 'running away from prayers ... read in a spirit of gloom by my father', inviting us to read the scene that follows as further throwing off the elder-male authority. Robert takes Edna to rest at Madame Antoine's cottage.

> The whole place was immaculately clean, and the big, four-posted bed, snow-white, invited one to repose ... [Edna] stretched herself in the very centre of the high, white bed. How luxurious it felt to rest thus in a strange, quaint bed, with its sweet country odour of laurel ... She looked at her round arms as she held them straight up and rubbed them one after the other, observing closely, as if it were something she saw for the first time, the fine, firm quality and texture of her flesh ... When Edna awoke ... her eyes were bright and wide awake and her face glowed ... She was very hungry ... Edna bit a piece from the brown loaf, tearing it with her strong, white teeth. She poured some of the wine into the glass and drank it down. Then she went softly out of doors, and plucking an orange from the low-hanging bough of a tree, threw it at Robert, who did not know she was awake.

When Robert then tells her 'you have slept precisely one hundred years' the fairy-tale references (including a secular Mass of bread and wine: Edna not so much becoming part of Christ's body as becoming her own body) are complete; and fairy-tales chart the rite of passage between childhood and adulthood, though not in as highly sexualised way as in this amazing passage (a writer of Chopin's subtlety would not expect readers to miss the wordplay of 'quaint' and 'country' next to each other: I spoke about 'quaint' in the opening lecture on the myth of the Fall). The bed and the room are the opposite of those in 'The Yellow Wallpaper': here they are Edna's body, liberated 'in the very centre' (of the bed, of her body) and 'immaculately clean' (a stylish pun on the Christian notion of the immaculate body).

In sharpest contrast, and now exactly parallel to the Gilman story, is her room back in their New Orleans house where Edna goes, after another row with her husband, with 'flushed' face and eyes flaming 'with some inward fire'. This is, as with Gilman's narrator and Bertha, the imprisoned animal.

> She began to walk to and fro down its whole length, without stopping, without resting. She carried in her hands a thin handkerchief which she tore into ribbons, rolled into a ball, and flung from her. Once she stopped, and taking off her wedding ring, flung it upon the carpet. When she saw it lying there, she stamped her heel upon it, striving to crush it. but her small boot heel did not make an indenture, not a mark upon the little glittering circlet.
>
> (Chapter 17)

To break that symbolic ring Edna needs to refuse to go to her sister's wedding; enjoy another fairy-tale moment in this same house (Chapter 24) but now on her own (walking 'through the house, from one room to another, as if inspecting it for the first time', trying the chairs 'as if she had never sat' on them before); then set up house by herself and earn money by painting; and then, when Robert returns, and a happy ending with him is at least possible, and after their love is mutually declared and she goes to witness the 'scene of torture' as Adele gives birth, she walks back to where she left Robert and – well, let's end before the real, and really unbearable ending itself, with one last, very moving evocation of fairy-tale. Here it is poignantly gender-inverted, Edna (like Emma Bovary) planning to act like a man, one last moment of transgression (Chapter 38).

And it will never happen. It is not a fairy-tale.

> When she thought that he was there at hand, waiting for her, she grew numb with the intoxication of expectancy. It was so late; he would be asleep perhaps. She would awaken him with a kiss. She hoped he would be asleep that she might arouse him with her caresses.

Thanks for listening.

Further Reading

Janet Beer, *Kate Chopin, Edith Wharton and Charlotte Perkins Gilman: Studies in Short Fiction* (Macmillan: 1997).

Kate Chopin, *The Awakening*, ed. Margo Culley (Norton:1994).

Kate Chopin, *The Awakening and Other Stories*, ed. Pamela Knights (Oxford U.P.: 2000).

Kate Chopin, *The Awakening*, ed. Nancy Walker (Bedford/St Martin's: 2000).

Charlotte Perkins Gilman, *The Yellow Wallpaper*, ed. Dale M. Bauer (Bedford/St Martin's: 1998).

Charlotte Perkins Gilman, *The Yellow Wallpaper and Other Stories*, ed. Robert Shulman (Oxford U.P.: 2009).

Heather Ostman and Kate O'Donoghue, edd. *Kate Chopin in Context: New Approaches* (Palgrave: 2015).

Edith Wharton, *The Age of Innocence*, ed. Candace Waid (Norton: 2003).

11 *Hamlet/Lear*
Realism/Modernism

Here's a question: 'Which is the "greatest" Shakespeare play, *Hamlet* or *King Lear*?' It's what we might call an academic question, in both senses of the word, inviting not very serious answers like 'what on earth does it matter?' or '*Anthony and Cleopatra*, actually, since you ask, thank you'. But the question does have a serious issue at its heart and it's one dealt with at length in a book by R.A. Foakes called *Hamlet versus Lear* (Foakes 1993), a book that (if I can say so) fleshes out in a great deal of detail some ideas that I'd been teaching (and I'm sure many people had been teaching) about the plays for, in my case, about fifteen years before the book came out. (The book does other things as well, of course.) One very simple starting point, as I don't want to seem to be repeating Foakes (and I want to move on to thinking about the two plays together in other ways, as my title suggests), is that another question to ask about the two plays in relation to each other might be this: 'Have these two plays always been so highly and equally highly regarded, and if not why might that be?'

The answer, unsurprisingly, is no. In Shakespeare's day the *Henry IV* plays seem to have been the most popular or at least most talked about, because of the character of Falstaff. But the simple point to make is that from the period we now call Romanticism up to about the 1950s *Hamlet* was assessed as the greatest of the plays and then from the 1960s *Lear*, as if coming from nowhere, overtook it and remains to this day as the most highly regarded.

It's not difficult to see why. *Hamlet* spoke with sudden urgency to the early Romantic writers who, like Hamlet himself (or in their reading of the play), were struggling with alienated consciousness in an uncaring and oppressive society. Hamlet can be seen as occupying a space between the two paradoxical roles of the Romantic poet: the uniquely gifted individual as the idealised embodiment of his culture and at the same time the implacable critic of that culture. This is the difference between, say, how Wordsworth and Blake saw themselves, as clear in those two poets' startlingly different evocations of London, in Wordsworth's 'On Westminster Bridge' which in effect sees the city as a disembodied, in effect unoccupied spectacle (the poet seeing from above, static as a tourist) and Blake's 'London' in which a laser-like insight (the poet having no choice but to hear the 'cries' as he paces the streets) reveals the multiple unhappinesses of the city's oppressed population.

This way of thinking about *Hamlet,* or rather Hamlet (Hamlet as romantic poet) because such readers and critics focused everything on him, starts with Coleridge (and his German contemporaries) and runs through later 19th-century and early–mid-20th-century criticism, with famous landmarks such as the chapters in A.C. Bradley's turn of the century book *Shakespearean Tragedy* (1904) and, if I can add a personal note, the intensely eloquent 1942 lecture by C.S. Lewis (he of the Narnia books), the revealingly titled *Hamlet, the Prince or the Poem* (in Alexander 1964). This had a profound effect on me when I was 17. I knew chunks of it by heart. (Today, as with Narnia, I'm afraid I can't bring myself to read its very Christianised emphases.) This tradition, Romantic-humanist-conservative (and what Foakes calls privatised), comes to a kind of sceptically humanist head with Harold Jenkins's wonderful 1982 Arden edition, now very sadly superseded. (This edition was subjected to what many of us thought at the time was a shockingly poisonous review in the *London Review of Books.* For the record, I reviewed it for an academic journal.)

The 1960s brought radical scepticism and crises of authority and faith, the threat or the actuality of global and final war and a sharpened awareness of inequalities and structural, intentional divisions. *Lear* clicked into sharper focus than ever, a process critically hastened by Jan Kott's remarkable *Shakespeare our Contemporary* (originally from 1961) which, connecting the play directly to Beckett's modernist theatre, in turn had an immediate impact on the astonishing Peter Brook/Paul Scofield RSC production and later film (1971). What Kott and Brook in effect did was to overturn Bradley's traditionalist view of the play as, first, Christian-redemptive in its consolatory ending and, second, unstageable – because Bradley was reading it applying the naturalistic/realist theatrical conventions of his period (the period of Ibsen and Shaw). More on those two points later. But I want to add before moving on that there was another essay, about thirty years before Kott's 'King Lear or Endgame', that anticipated this way of reading and understanding the truly radical nature of the play: G. Wilson Knight's 'King Lear and the Comedy of the Grotesque' (in Knight 1930), a brilliant account of the play as a grotesquely cruel comedy. In the same spirit, more modern critics like Nicholas Brooke (1963) speak of the play's relentless refusal to offer any consolation, leaving us to shuffle out of the theatre as the lights come on. That's right. Let me now move on.

** **

So far, I've been speaking in a very sketchy way of what Foakes deals with at length: the social-political history of the two plays' changing reputations. I want to turn (as often in this book of lectures) to issues of form, structure, style and genre. As I will say in the next lecture about two of Keats' odes, the differences between these two plays, written within a few years of each other, are so remarkable as to make it difficult to think they were written by the same playwright. I want to explore the antinomies the two plays offer under the headings of proto-realism (*Hamlet*) and proto-modernism (*Lear*). With realism, my emphasis is on interiorities and dimensionalities and what I'd call the novelistic; with modernism, my emphasis is on myth, ritual, meta-theatre and theatre as a cruel, ironic machine. And, again as I'll be exploring with Keats, both plays are in 'late style' compared to earlier Shakespeare but *Lear* has the effect of making *Hamlet* seem not-late-style.

So let's start a series of antinomies or oppositions and see where it takes us in terms of holding these two plays in our heads at the same time.

From the opening of *Hamlet* we're thrown into a psychological thriller (with the prospect of a 'thing' appearing), with worried and edgy characters asking each other urgent questions ('who's there?'), with demands for identities to be unfolded, and with one of the most minor characters in the play (whom we never see again after the first Act) as-if casually admitting to being 'sick at heart' (Act 1, Sc. 1). That last stroke is marvellous – we haven't the faintest idea why Marcellus feels that – and it's equivalent to the way the ground suddenly opens up under the absurd-pathetic Andrew Aguecheek in *Twelfth Night* when he says 'I was adored once too' (Act 2, Sc. 3). These are the conventions of the realist novel: they guarantee a kind of 'depth effect' (as if a third dimension has suddenly been glimpsed) and this is confirmed above all when Hamlet says in the next scene 'I have that within which passeth [= surpasses] show' (Act 1, Sc. 2). This is the burden of consciousness (shared, as we are later shocked to discover, even by Claudius), interiority as always beyond surface-show (more than 'seems'), the self we perform in and to the world as always inadequate. This is the aesthetic of Romanticism and this is what Harold Bloom meant in his memorable idea about the play marking the invention of being human.

King Lear starts as fairy-tale. (Check out the entry 'Love Like Salt' in D.L. Ashliman's terrific online encyclopaedia *Folk-Texts*.) The father and the three daughters, two 'bad', one 'good', evokes of course one of the most famous of all fairy-tales and we need to think about fairy-tales later when we consider the end of the play (if we can bear to). But this is a fairy-tale where the utterance of Cordelia's phrase 'Nothing, my lord', like a cursed-spell, unleashes chaos into and on to the play's world, 'nothing' meaning, among other things, chaos (Act 1, Sc. 1). It's not too much to say that the play moves from fairy-tale to apocalypse. The appropriate question is asked in the final moments: 'Is this the promised end?' (Act 5, Sc. 3). And, unlike in a realist text and despite her gnomic little asides – cut in the Brook/Scofield film – there's no apparently 'real' motivation behind Cordelia's utterance. In a realist text like *Hamlet* she would perhaps have been made 'sick at heart' – for instance, through not liking either of the men chosen by her father as her suitors: you get the point I'm rather labouring here. Instead, her speeches have what's been called the chaste or blank 'characterisation' of fairy-tale. And the movement towards apocalypse charts a mythic-allegorical journey into what we might call the heart of darkness, enacting on the way a process of stripping down – of everything, including clothes and language – whereas *Hamlet* keeps accumulating and enrichening its realist textures.

Hamlet's interest in realism is self-reflexive and starts with initial questions as to whether the ghost is 'real' and whether Hamlet's grief is 'real' – more than 'seems', more than a performance – and then it underpins the entire play in its brilliantly sustained inquiries into the ambivalences of seeming and acting – the entire play is a pun on the two meanings of act – and structured across a series of what we might call crises of interpretation. These crises would include the nature of what Hamlet is meaning or doing in his crucial encounters with Ophelia (more about this soon). The inquiries into acting also constitute the spine of the play through its three great public scenes/performances, all laden with overt and covert motivations, with the dumb-show (Hamlet's first encounter with Ophelia was a dumbshow) and performance of the 'Mousetrap' at the centre of the play, and the no-less performative first court scene of Act 1 (Claudius performing a very public agenda, including relations with his awkward nephew) and the fencing staged-performance at the end.

If *Hamlet* stages the realist urge to explain and interpret (Polonius' absurd 'I will find / Where truth is hid' (Act 2, Sc. 2) is the comic version), *Lear* stages trials, journeys and (if 'act' is the key pun in *Hamlet*) our human-elemental or what the play identifies as our 'animal' need for 'patience' ('I will be the pattern of all patience; / I will say nothing'; 'Thou must be patient. We came crying hither') with its pun on suffering (Act 3, Sc. 2; Act 4, Sc. 6). Self-reflexivity in *Lear* is structural and the structural principal of the play is the self-motoring, sealed-in, machine-like design that Knight called grotesque comedy, one set up to exact maximum pain on characters and, crucially, audiences. If the centre of *Hamlet* is a play, the centre of *Lear* is two trials in symbolic, appallingly ironic juxtaposition with each other (Act 3, Scs. 6 and 7): the mad trial that the mad Lear thinks he's organising for Goneril and Regan in the hut in the storm and featuring a joint-stool (that he mistakes for his daughter), followed with cruel immediacy by Cornwall and Regan's trial of Gloucester (in his own house), tied up to a chair, a chair that I've always taken as the 'same' joint-stool (from among the Globe's stage-props), a trial 'mad' in a very different sense and with its terrible blinding climax, in blatant breach of theatrical conventions, by which such brutality should only happen off-stage. And it is absolutely characteristic of this play that among its extensive repertoire of grotesquely cruel, self-generating ironies is that it 'made' this old man, at the start of the action when being fooled by Edmund's forged letter, come out with a casual joke about how he will 'not need spectacles' to read it. And the letter has just been described by Edmund as 'Nothing, my lord' (Act 1, Sc. 2), another of the play's cruel ironic strokes, making as it does Cordelia's crucial utterance of the same words in the scene immediately before now seem like an equivalent trap into which each father will have to fall.

There's a quite different degree of dimensionality in the two plays' characterisations, amounting, as suggested, to a quite different approach to the issue. *Hamlet* is like a richly textured 19th-century novel in its deployment of psychologically realised interiorities – a deployment actually made even more convincing by the way characters remain opaque and unknowable, as we are to ourselves. This is obviously the case with Hamlet himself, paradoxically the most transparently opaque character in Shakespeare (perhaps Iago is the next on that list), but it's very interestingly the case with his mother as well – it's the most interesting thing about Gertrude – and this gives yet richer plausibility to the most subtly explored Oedipal problematic in all of Shakespeare's plays.

The dimensionality of Ophelia is thrown into sharp relief when we think about Cordelia in contrast (or when we compare Claudius with Edmund): as already suggested Cordelia is always shading into mythic or allegorical counterparts, from Cinderella to Christ. And there's a meta-theatrical point to make about Cordelia: I've always wanted to emphasise the Cordelia/Fool doubling. Whether the same boy-actor did or didn't act the role on the Shakespearean stage it seems undeniable that the 'characters' are duplicated or super-imposed and indeed – at Lear's 'And my poor fool is hanged' (Act 5, Sc. 3) – as-if merge (in absence and death).

Edgar in *Lear* is the most dizzyingly allegorical or allegorised 'character', a figure of almost comically varied impersonations – at least some of which are superfluous to 'plot'. We might like to count up how many roles he plays after adopting the 'Poor Tom' mad-beggar role. So, in quick succession, there's a suddenly not-mad beggar who leads his father; a total stranger at the 'bottom' of the 'cliff' at Dover who 'happens' to see an old man fall off the 'cliff' (and then calls him 'father' meaning old-man, and in another local cruel irony twice asks his blinded father to 'look up' to see how far he's fallen); a country yokel who kills Oswald; an unknown knight in armour; the inheritor of the wounded kingdom (if that's how we respond to the ending of the play: more later). The more 'roles' he plays the less 'realistic' he becomes – which is the opposite of Hamlet. Indeed, Hamlet's 'uniqueness' is naturalised by the play's stylishly sustained habit of having him as-if bump into simulacra of himself – in for instance the shape of Fortinbras and Laertes and also in the fictionalised Pyrrhus and Lucianus. On a larger scale (as Jenkins argues especially well) Hamlet's 'realist' depth-effect is underpinned by the movement that takes him from being the subject of the first revenge plot (for his father) to being the object of the second revenge plot (for Laertes). To make a rather distant analogy, we saw in the *Emma* lecture that Emma thinks she's the subject of her sentence and learns painfully that she's the object of someone else's sentence.

Let me say a few words about how madness is treated very differently in the plays. This will give me the chance also to look at one of the scenes I've described as a typical crisis of interpretation in *Hamlet*, the so-called 'nunnery' scene. To cut through a very tangled critical thicket, let me just say simply that Hamlet's assumption of pretend-madness, his 'antic disposition', is a pretty desperate (and, in practice, pretty useless) cover for what he can't admit, his very real (and 'realist') traumatic response to the revelation of his mother's sexual appetite and his new sense of expulsion from the garden of her love. This inevitably colours his attitude towards women ('Frailty, thy name is woman!' (Act 1, Sc. 2)), Ophelia is the victim in the immediate vicinity and, of course, this comes to a head in the scene after the play with Gertrude in her closet (Act 3, Sc. 4), with the son's hysterical and self-tormenting obsessing over the mother making love with the uncle in 'the rank sweat of an enseamed bed' [= stained with semen].

Hamlet treats Ophelia in the 'nunnery' scene (Act 3, Sc. 1) with, on the face of it, bullying cruelty but the scene poses an urgent interpretive problem. Is he 'acting mad' because he knows Claudius and Polonius are hidden away watching? (Some directors hedge their bets by having Hamlet 'discover' their presence when Ophelia guiltily glances towards the hiding-place when he suddenly asks her 'Where's your father?'). My cards on the table again: Hamlet is not acting mad, he doesn't know he's being watched, his treatment is cruel, bullying and (for instance in his attack on women's make-up) off-the-wall, hysterically out of control. In a word, inexcusable. But critics and editors want to excuse and protect him (just as we'll see in the next lecture critics and biographers wanting to protect Keats from the charge of being cruel to Fanny) and the simplest way is to claim he's performing, not 'really' meaning it.

Here a prize piece of evidence (which I think has not received due attention) is the work of the enormously influential *Hamlet* critic and editor, John Dover Wilson. His New Cambridge 1934 edition of the play (with its associated textual and critical studies) was the most widely used in schools and colleges for a very long time. (I used it for A-level.) Here's what Wilson, determined to protect Hamlet, did in that edition. You'll recall that in Act 2 Scene 2 Claudius, Gertrude and Polonius are discussing how to test Polonius' theory that Hamlet has gone mad from love for Ophelia. Polonius says he'll 'loose' Ophelia to Hamlet (a word we looked at in the earlier lecture on *The Tempest*) while he and Claudius are hiding to see what happens. Wilson (I still can't quite get over my shock about this) blithely invents and inserts a stage direction having Hamlet quietly, unknown to the others, come on and off stage during this exchange just briefly enough (and for no apparent reason) so that he can hear their plans. Oh, right. Shakespeare 'improved'. (On Wilson, see Hawkes 1986.)

Before I turn to *Lear* let me make the simple point that Ophelia's real madness, consequent on Hamlet killing her father, is the play's way of as-if rebuking the idea of Hamlet's own 'antic disposition' (Act 1, Sc. 5): it has the effect of showing the latter up for what it is, desperate posturing to hide his own hysteria. Ophelia's mad speeches are psychologically very telling in their plausible and touching mix of ideas of sexual longing and loss. I put it like that as Lear's mad speeches in Act 3 and especially at Dover in Act 4, though no less acute, seem of another kind and nothing to do with personal psychology. As with madness in *Lear* generally, Lear's mad speeches are part of a larger allegorical pattern which takes in Edgar's performance of poor mad Tom, the Fool's professional 'madness', Gloucester's 'I am almost mad myself' (Act 3, Sc. 4) – a pattern that positions madness as the sole source of profound wisdom (as in Emily Dickinson's 'madness is divinest sense'): Lear 'goes mad' in order to understand just as Gloucester 'goes blind' in order to see (as he correctly says, 'I stumbled when I saw' (Act 4, Sc. 1)). Madness as divinest sense; blindness as insight.

I'd like now to turn to the differences in the two plays' treatment of dimensionality of space or geography and of time. *Hamlet* is, of all Shakespeare's plays, the most three-dimensionally realised. Elsinore and its castle, with its curtains to hide behind, its surveillance culture inside, its ramparts outside and a cliff that Horatio thinks the ghost might lure Hamlet towards and then off (the cliff 'That beetles o'er his base into the sea' (Act 1, Sc. 4): ok, time for the routine apology about Shakespeare thinking that Elsinore has cliffs) is quite the opposite of *Lear*'s symbolic or mythic landscape where Dover and its cliff are less about topography and more about symbols of liminality, edges – the edge of England, of the world, of life. The audience in *Hamlet* is meant to see the cliff that Horatio evokes; the cliff at Dover that the disguised Edgar evokes in such amazingly pictorial detail for his father – and for the audience – is a white lie, not a white cliff. The 'crows and choughs', the gatherer of samphire 'halfway down' the cliff, the fishermen, the distant boat with its buoy 'too small for sight' – this view from the top of a cliff is the most evocative scene-painting speech in Shakespeare and it's a triumph of illusionism that is anti-illusionistic (Act 4, Sc. 6). Edgar's making it up. The audience 'sees' it as the blind Gloucester undoubtedly 'sees' it and the audience has to simultaneously un-see it. I know of nothing in theatre like this (before Beckett). So the two men are standing on and have previously been walking across level ground (Gloucester asks about this and Edgar lies about it being 'horrible steep') and now a sad old man, wanting to die, is about to fall, not down a cliff, but flat on to his face, in – that phrase again – grotesque comedy and a modernist flaunting of the bare-boards of the theatrical space. This is Shakespeare's most sceptical treatment – in effect, parody – of the notion of us all being 'fallen' (which you know this book of lectures regularly invites you to think about).

Hamlet is carefully shaped and structured in the larger matters of Scandinavian history and politics as well as sharply informed by the transition between the feudal world of old Hamlet and the early-modern, early-capitalist, diplomatist world of Claudius with young Hamlet painfully stranded between the two, as he is, psychologically, between two Oedipal fathers. *Lear* charts an allegorical journey, not a political one, a journey both horizontal and vertical into the storm and darkness, to find 'unaccommodated man' (Act 3, Sc. 4), in a mythic pre-historical time, the time of fairy-tale and the end of the world. Time in *Hamlet* also has a plasticity that is novelistic – the brilliant extended centre of the play works with a kind of naturalistic flux, a seamless and linear accumulation (like the populating of the field in the 'middles' of realist novels) whereas *Lear* gives us modernist and film-like cutting between simultaneities. This is what made Bradley and others claim that *Lear* was unstageable – as it would have been given the heavy-duty naturalistic/realist staging conventions of Bradley's time.

The point can be made simply and I'm certainly not the first to make it. In Act 2, Scene 2, the disguised Kent is put in the stocks outside Glouces-ter's castle by Cornwall. He reads a letter from Cordelia and falls asleep. There follows a 20-line scene or passage in which Edgar, on the run from his father, announces how he will turn himself into poor Tom (Act 2, Sc. 3). We then return to Kent in his stocks woken by the arrival of Lear. Natu-ralistic staging would of course want to distinguish between Gloucester's castle and – presumably – some distant woods where Edgar is hiding. The last place he'll want to be is outside his father's castle. So we might have the ludicrous prospect of the curtain falling on the bits of castle-props so that they can be cleared away and a few trees wheeled on, the curtain rising for 20 lines, then falling again for the trees to be wheeled off and castle-bits heaved back into place. You get the idea. Instead the staging on the Shakespearean stage (where props were minimal and wherever possible hand-held) is modernist-symbolic. The audience sees Edgar standing in the stage-space next to the sleeping Kent. There is no 'realistic' recognition between the two but in that anti-realist, mythic space all our increasingly threatened hopes are before us – Kent, Edgar, Cordelia in the letter – but in an 'impossible' space where none of them are able to come together to help. The effect on stage of seeing Edgar stand next to Kent and their being both in and not-in the same theatrical space is very moving.

What standard editions (and this lecture) call Act 3 exploits the same issue. Film-like cutting between alternating short scenes in and outside Gloucester's castle (in the storm and on the heath), in both cases getting more 'mad' and extreme, would be ludicrously ponderous if staged with fully realist settings but work with brilliantly fluid rapidity, a modernist and jarringly ironic paralleling of simultaneities, when just performed on a bare stage – with the odd joint-stool to highlight the cruel paralleling, as discussed earlier when we looked at the climax to the Act, the two trials. The linearity and accumulation of *Hamlet* as opposed to the simul-taneities and 'cutting' of *Lear* can also be seen if we think about single and double plots. The single plot of *Hamlet* is, again, a thickly textured novelistic structure, with brilliantly integrated multiple layers, strands and modalities, radiating out from Hamlet and his psychology. *Lear*'s double plot starts with the two components in fairy-tale symbolic/ironic relations (father and three daughters; father and two sons) and both initiated, as we've seen, in the fateful words 'Nothing, my lord', but by the start of Act 3 the two plots have merged and the characters re-distributed on (as it were) moral grounds and positioned either in or outside Gloucester's castle. Then at Dover, for the great Act 4 Scene 6, madness and blindness come into ironic simultaneity in one space, releasing, as if electrically, the most dazzlingly voiced speeches – or rather speeches and tears – in Western theatre. And Lear wants his boots pulled off, which is where Beckett's *Godot* starts.

**

Let me move to the endings of these extraordinary plays. I hope it's ok if I start by going back to my schooldays again. I studied *Hamlet* some time before *Lear* (fortunately: prior exposure to *Lear* might have ruined *Hamlet* for me, as late Beethoven ruined standard-repertoire later 19th-century romantic music for me, though no loss there: the Keats lecture will say more about Beethoven) and as with many self-absorbed adolescent teenagers Hamlet spoke very personally to me. After all, C.S. Lewis wrote of not needing to cross the road to meet Hamlet as he was always wherever Lewis was. But what I found most difficult to get my head round, about the way he spoke to me, was that he spoke so very differently in Act 5, after returning to Denmark. I could hear the difference clearly as I read, but it was frustratingly difficult to account for. His language (this is what I felt as I read) seemed just to have relaxed, lost its bottled-up aggression and obsession with sex and his mother, gained a kind of rhythmic springiness and narrative lightness: 'Sir, in my heart there was a kind of fighting / That would not let me sleep ...'; 'Up from my cabin, / My sea-gown scarfed about me ...' And the jokes are just jokes (the sea-gown narrative has a witty and relaxed series of puns about as-if sexually interfering with the sleeping Rosencrantz and Guildenstern: Hamlet says he 'groped ... had my desire, / Fingered their packet ... [and] withdrew' (Act 5, Sc. 2): not that any edition I've seen, or indeed anything else I've read, mentions this), just jokes and not weapons anymore, so he can joke with the gravedigger, with the latter cast as Fool or Clown, whereas in Acts 1–4 Hamlet chooses to be his own Fool/Clown. And (apart from the explosion with Laertes over Ophelia's grave) there's a sense of opened horizons and calm philosophising. Even the speech over Yorick's skull is (though many actors clearly disagree) more wry and amused than anguished. The lesson from the skull about women's makeup ('get you to my lady's chamber ... let her paint an inch thick' (Act 5, Sc.1)) is just generic (who is this lady, all of a sudden?) and has nothing of the personal and venomous force aimed at Ophelia. And even when talking in the next scene about Claudius and Gertrude – 'He that hath killed my king and whored my mother' – he sounds, well, as if casually relating a story that's hardly bothering him or even nothing to do with him.

So what's all this about? The easy thing is to say that we're meant to think that Hamlet has 'matured' – another novelistic convention, about the protagonist growing into desired maturity in time for the ending, that we buy into without thinking (but do we buy into the idea with Jane Austen's *Emma*?) – and Shakespeare prods us in that direction when we suddenly, and if we notice it, absurdly, have to take on board from the gravedigger the 'fact' that the Wittenberg college-student Hamlet is, er, over 30. My friend and ex-student Chloe Murphy told me recently that, aged 15, she felt personally betrayed by this 'fact' sprung on her in Act 5 about her hero Hamlet being over 30. But all this doesn't explain (even if we ignore or don't pick up that very clunky piece of manipulation about his age) the development that so clearly comes out in Hamlet's language, this maturing. Where's it come from?

So here's an anecdote. The school took us to Stratford to see the Alan Howard/Trevor Nunn production, all claustrophobic white-boxes and oppressiveness in Acts 1–4. Then in Act 5, for Hamlet's return and the gravedigger scene, there was a startling and lovely change of setting and staging – outside, warm colours, soft clothing, birdsong – that matched the lovely change in Hamlet's language that I knew about. It worked. In the coach on the way back to boarding-school I filled in the story. I can even today recall the warming glow I felt when I thought I was solving the 'problem'. I told myself a story to explain what happened between Hamlet's departure towards England and his return, changed, to Denmark. In effect (of course I didn't think this at the time) I was novelistically filling in the missing bit of the novel that Shakespeare had inadvertently omitted to write.

The 'story' was this: Hamlet leaves as an adolescently bitter boy convinced that the world is against him. He rather enjoys that feeling and has no idea that Claudius has plans for him. He then discovers those plans – that he is entirely dispensable – and at the same time discovers, through a succession of mere strokes of luck (reading the death-warrant; meeting the pirates; happening to have his father's seal on him), that the world has better or at least other things to do than be centred on him. Chastened and grateful to submit to this new way of looking at the world, he returns to Denmark. And speaks a transformed language. (Years later, after school and undergraduate study, I acted Hamlet. A friend, who later became a Famous Actor, kindly passed on his assessment that I was 'quite good in Act 5'. Er, thanks.)

Of course, my teenage story was mere fiction – but that's the point. I think the novelistic nature of this play demands that we 'fill in the gaps' (I did it very crudely, probably reflecting stuff more about me than about Hamlet), in ways that modern theory talks about in 'reader-response criticism'. We are co-opted in the process of making illusionism work. (A very much more sophisticated account of the illusionary strategies of the end of *Hamlet* is in Francis Barker's compelling 1984 book *The Tremulous Private Body*.) Anyway, *Lear* could hardly be more different.

But let me say quickly, before I turn to the end of *Lear*, some more straightforward points about the end of *Hamlet*. The ending novelistically completes a process, opens out on to the restoring of a king to the kingdom, that is also a retrospective rounding off of an arc – the arc that points back to the feudal single-combat between old Fortinbras and old Hamlet and for which young Fortinbras has sought revenge in the furthest outer-frame of the play. Young Fortinbras (a military opportunist) taking over at the end of the play, and Hamlet being described as potentially 'royal' – and with instructions for his body to be carried 'like a soldier' on to a 'stage' (Act 5, Sc. 2) – have, as with the endings of so many other Shakespeare plays, local ironies that leave the audience both satisfied with closure and fretting a little with uncertainties and doubts (Hamlet ending as a sol-dier?), but this is an ending that answers to our usual and novelistic needs. Again as in a novel, the end marks the point where the narrative – Hamlet's dying need for Horatio to 'tell my story' – becomes and needs to become transmissible. The end of *Hamlet* plays by the rule-book. *Lear*, terribly, could not be more different. The death of Cordelia changes everything and breaks all the rules.

So much, quite rightly, has been said about the death of Cordelia so let me approach it as a series of issues around contexts and the audience's expectations.

At the end of the play, when Edmund reveals that he has ordered Corde-lia's death, Albany, hoping with the audience that the counter-order to save her arrives in time, says 'The gods defend her!' At exactly that moment, as if in cruel reply, we have the stage direction *Enter Lear, with Cordelia dead in his arms* – and Lear is howling in anguish (Act 5, Sc. 3). Of all the cruelly grotesque ironies in the play, this 'answer' to Albany's (and the audience's) wish is certainly the most terrible. Twice I've been in the theatre next to someone who knew nothing about the play – and on both occasions each friend audibly cried out, on Lear's entrance, 'oh, no!'

The shock of this moment depends on multiple contextual factors in play. Here, in brief, are some of these. The first context is formal-generic. The audience's expectation is that Cordelia will survive, both because Edmund has twice intimated doing 'some good' at last and because of our generic knowledge of last minute rescues that go right up to the wire before good triumphs. We are cruelly jolted against these expectations, founded as they are in sound cultural competencies on our parts. I'd add that it's especially cruel of the play to delay Edmund doing good in order to listen, as the audi-ence eagerly listens as well, to Edgar's moving account of meeting Kent over his father's dead body. The delay is terminal for Cordelia.

The next context is intertextual. All previous versions of the Lear story have the Cordelia figure surviving. Shakespeare's audience is kicked in the teeth of that knowledge. Related is the next context, which is cross-cultural as well as intertextual. The emblem of father with daughter dead in his arms is an inverted *Pieta* (just as the 'Nunnery Scene' in *Hamlet* is an inverted Annunciation). The notion of Cordelia as a Christ figure has been anticipated in Act 4, Scene 4 when she said 'O dear father, / It is thy business that I go about.' Again, Shakespeare's audience would have the expertise to hear this echo of Christ more readily than we can; but the effect of that knowledge is the opposite of that in the last context: audiences semi-consciously 'expect' Cordelia's sacrificial death.

The last context is cultural-historical: the fact that Nahum Tate's version of 1681, with Cordelia surviving in a happy ending, was the only version available to theatre-goers throughout the 18th century – and was famously endorsed by Dr Johnson. It's easy to mock Tate but not so easy to mock Johnson. And in Tate's defense we could argue that his fairy-tale ending was at least appropriate to the play's fairy-tale beginning: you'll recall that the play as fairy-tale is where we started. Johnson's evident horror at the sheer gratuitous outrage of Cordelia's death provides us all with the means with which to explore and elaborate our own emotional responses to the scene. Those responses are shaped and refined by, as well as embedded in, the contexts I've been talking about. The challenge is to respond adequately in the face of the systematic denial and reversal of our expectations and desires, the cruel manipulation wielded by the play's internal and self-sealed logic.

Final thoughts, for this has been a difficult lecture to write and I need to stop. If the end of *Hamlet* is at least partly about fulfilled and completed revenge, and then continuity and progress, and about language serving to transmit the hero's story to the long reach of history, the end of *Lear* is the 'promised end' of the world, hearts that need to break, and language reduced to Lear's howling and the five-times repeated 'never', the sheer negation of the iambic pentameter, that bedrock of Shakespearian 'style' which was used with such arrogant assurance by Lear at the start of the play, in his regal gowns and pomp. Then in the Act 3 storm he wants to strip off; then in Act 4 it's his boots. At the end: a button needs to be undone, so he can breathe, as he can't.

If the question of who becomes king at the end of *Hamlet* matters, as life goes on, it's a matter of indifference at the end of *Lear* (almost literally indifferent, as the two surviving texts give the last words to different characters – see Weis, ed. 1993), as the prevailing note is nothing to do with fulfilment and continuity but sheer exhaustion after the anguish exacted in Cordelia's death and then Lear's (Bradley's notion of a redemptive ending is really desperate stuff). The machine that is the ironically-driven, self-generating, 'late style' formal structure of the play has stopped, worn down, having worn down everything and everyone else in its grip.

There are no flights of angels, and no flights of language, to sing anyone to their rest at the end of *King Lear*.

Thank you.

Further Reading

Janet Adelman, *Suffocating Mothers: Fantasies of Maternal Origin in Shakespeare's Plays* (Routledge: 1992).

Peter Alexander ed., *Studies in Shakespeare* (Oxford U.P.: 1964).

Francis Barker, *The Tremulous Private Body: Essays on Subjection* (Methuen: 1984).

A.C. Bradley, *Shakespearean Tragedy* (Macmillan: 1904).

Nicholas Brooke, *King Lear* (Arnold: 1963).

Rosalie Colie, *Shakespeare's Living Art* (Princeton U.P.: 1974).

Rosalie L. Colie and F.T. Flahiff edd., *Some Facets of King Lear: Essays in Prismatic Criticism* (University of Toronto Press: 1974).

Jonathan Dollimore, *Radical Tragedy* (University of Chicago Press: 1984).

R.A. Foakes, *Hamlet versus Lear: Cultural Politics and Shakespeare's Art* (Cambridge U.P.: 1993).

Stephen Greenblatt, *Hamlet in Purgatory* (Princeton U.P.: 2002).

Andrew Hadfield, *Shakespeare and Renaissance Politics* (Bloomsbury: 2004).

Terence Hawkes, *That Shakespeherian Rag: Essays on a Critical Process* (Methuen: 1986).

G. Wilson Knight, *The Wheel of Fire* (Oxford U.P.: 1930).

Jan Kott, *Shakespeare Our Contemporary* (Methuen: 1967).

Sean McEvoy, *Shakespeare the Basics*, 3rd ed. (Routledge: 2012).

Kiernan Ryan, *Shakespeare* (Palgrave: 2001).

William Shakespeare, *Hamlet*, ed. Harold Jenkins (Arden 2nd series, Bloomsbury: 1982).

William Shakespeare, *King Lear: A Parallel Text Edition*, ed. René Weis (Longman: 1993).

12 John Keats

Three (or is it Two?) Poems and Thoughts on 'Late Style'

Here's quite a famous anecdote about the occasion in London at the end of 1817 when Keats, aged 22 and at the start of his meteoric poetic journey, at last met his hero Wordsworth, aged 47 and at the height of his considerable fame (and a bit grumpy as he didn't like being in London). The story has been given wider currency in Ian McEwan's novel *Enduring Love*. The painter Haydon encouraged Keats to recite his 'Ode to Pan' from the first of his long poems *Endymion*, a good choice, it might have been thought, as Keats had been influenced in some of the mythology behind the passage by Wordsworth's own poetry. Haydon takes up the story.

> I begged Keats to repeat it – which he did in his usual half-chant (most touching), walking up and down the room. When he had done I felt really as if I had heard a young Apollo. Wordsworth drily said 'A very pretty piece of Paganism' – this was unfeeling and unworthy of his high genius to a young worshipper like Keats – and Keats felt it *deeply*.
>
> (In Bate 1967: 265)

On (probably) another occasion Wordsworth was holding forth to the company on some aspect of poetry and, when Keats ventured to offer a remark in agreement, the older poet's wife touched Keats' arm with the words 'Mr Wordsworth is never interrupted' (266).

A year later, in October 1818, at the start of the single year in which all his greatest poems were written, Keats wrote one of his most revealing letters in which he contrasts what he calls the 'poetical character itself ... of which, if I am anything, I am a member', which 'is not itself – it has no self – it is everything and nothing – it has no character', with what he calls 'the Wordsworthian or egotistical sublime, which is a thing per se and stands alone'. This sense Keats had of the true 'poetical character' (which he identified pre-eminently in Shakespeare) being 'the most unpoetical of anything in existence, because he has no identity', gives to the poet the most crucial of all resources, what he called 'negative capability' – and Philip Pullman draws on and refers to this in *His Dark Materials*. It's how Lyra reads the alethiometer.

I wonder how 'deeply' Keats felt Wordsworth's barbed condescension; the letter just quoted recognises quite without ill-feeling how very different Wordsworth's poetic character was from his own. On the other hand, and I'll come back to this, Keats felt his vocation so intensely, especially when he knew he had so little time to fulfil it, that he was very conscious of his many poetic forbears whom he absorbed in his passionate reading. Wordsworth was of course among these great predecessors, as were Dante, Spenser, Shakespeare and Milton. Let me just add that in 1973 Harold Bloom took the literary world aback with a startlingly original short book called *The Anxiety of Influence* which argued that all strong poets (his word) necessarily went through a kind of Freudian Oedipal rivalry, a kind of wilful misreading (his word) of their poetic precursor-fathers (his story is, characteristically, about men) in order to find their strength and their selves – and that the true critic's task is to misread with the same intensity. (I summarise very crudely a subtle and brilliant book.) Keats' late style, however much one buys into the details of Bloom's argument, emerges from his engagement with those great poetic 'fathers', some of his odes, for instance, coming out of a 'strong' reading of Wordsworth's great 'Immortality' ode.

**

But I need now to turn to that phrase 'late style' and to do so I'm going back yet again to my teenage years at boarding school, not long after *Godot* changed my life. I was studying *Hamlet* and *King Lear* and was moved above all by how different they were. (I explored this in the previous lecture in this book.) At the same time one of my English teachers, knowing my love of classical music (especially, at one 'end', Bach and, at the other, Stravinsky), introduced me to what he coolly described as 'the best music there is: late Beethoven. And Stravinsky thought so too'. So for the ensuing months (actually, years) I soaked myself, in increasing astonishment and passionate wonder, in the last five piano sonatas and last five string quartets, borrowing and buying and analysing rival recordings. (I quietly decided to exclude the few other 'late' works that I anyway knew, like the 9th symphony which, in my schoolboy snobbery, I found a bit vulgar, apart from the first movement.)

The 'late' quartets, especially, held me in a kind of suspended awe and reverence – and I was permanently and obsessively amazed by the three greatest of them, what one book rather dramatically called the ABC of music, with their increasingly radical five, six and seven movement structures: the A minor opus 132, the B flat major opus 130, and (above all) the C sharp minor opus 131. And, as with *Hamlet* and *Lear*, what really got my schoolboy mind and heart racing was what I heard as the startling differences, formal differences, between opus 130 and opus 131. And then there was a light-bulb moment, which I bored my friends about (well, the few who still put up with me after the *Godot* business) and even wrote about in my Oxford entrance exam, when I realised I was 'mapping' the two sets of differences and reading them as equivalent – *Hamlet*/opus 130 and *Lear*/opus 131. (The 'dons' who interviewed me at Oxford did pick me up on this essay – but only to query the grammar of one of my more effusive sentences. That was a bit of a dampener.) Decades later I still think I might have been on to something, so I was delighted some years ago to be shown a learned article by the scholar-pianist Stephen Pruslin who argued that Peter Maxwell Davies' amazing 1975 masterpiece *Ave Maris Stella* combined in its form the superimposed and conceptually oppositional formal principles that structure, respectively, the opus 130 and opus 131 quartets.

What I intuitively picked up from my listening and reading about what has now come to be called 'late style' all those years ago was that, in the very few artists to whom the idea applies (because we're not just talking about final works before death but something radically different from what these few artists had achieved before), the art-works concerned were part of a dialectic or tension or dynamic, not a single and static set of defining characteristics but a process that very much depended on where the reader, viewer or listener was starting from and what he or she was looking at. And especially that it was more about form and language than 'content'. So, in the case of Beethoven, all the late quartets are 'late' in contrast to his 'middle-period' and early quartets, but it is also just as true (or rather that I felt) that opus 130 and opus 131 are 'late' in dialectical contrast to opus 127 and 132 (which precede them) *and* that opus 131 is 'late' in dialectical contrast with opus 130. And the same with Shakespeare: *Lear* makes *Hamlet* not-late. And Keats?

With Keats we're faced with what is almost a chronological absurdity. Whereas with, say, Beethoven and Shakespeare early, middle and late styles are a matter of works divided by decades, in Keats' case we're talking about a year or two or even months, such was his astonishing developmental trajectory, the speed with which he, for instance, swallowed Milton, wrote under his influence (in, for instance, his long poem *Hyperion*) and moved on. But we can agree that the great Odes, especially *Nightingale* and *To Autumn* (the latter not actually named as an ode in its title), from the amazing last great year of his creative life, 1818–1819 (a very moving account of Keats' last years is in the most sensitive and critically acute of the many biographies, by Walter Jackson Bate, which I drew on earlier), are clearly in Keats' late style and yet you won't be surprised that I want to argue here that, in relation to each other, *To Autumn* is 'late' in contrast to the *Nightingale* ode. Let me read them to you.

Ode to a Nightingale

My heart aches, and a drowsy numbness pains
 My sense, as though of hemlock I had drunk,
 Or emptied some dull opiate to the drains

One minute past, and Lethe-wards had sunk:
'Tis not through envy of thy happy lot,
  But being too happy in thine happiness,—
    That thou, light-winged Dryad of the trees,
      In some melodious plot
  Of beechen green, and shadows numberless,
    Singest of summer in full-throated ease.

O, for a draught of vintage! that hath been
  Cooled a long age in the deep-delved earth,
Tasting of Flora and the country green,
  Dance, and Provencal song, and sunburnt mirth!
O for a beaker full of the warm South,
  Full of the true, the blushful Hippocrene,
    With beaded bubbles winking at the brim,
      And purple-stained mouth;
  That I might drink, and leave the world unseen,
    And with thee fade away into the forest dim:

Fade far away, dissolve, and quite forget
  What thou among the leaves hast never known,
The weariness, the fever, and the fret
  Here, where men sit and hear each other groan;
Where palsy shakes a few, sad, last gray hairs,
  Where youth grows pale, and spectre-thin, and dies;
    Where but to think is to be full of sorrow
      And leaden-eyed despairs,
  Where Beauty cannot keep her lustrous eyes,
    Or new Love pine at them beyond to-morrow.

Away! away! for I will fly to thee,
  Not charioted by Bacchus and his pards,
But on the viewless wings of Poesy,
  Though the dull brain perplexes and retards:
Already with thee! tender is the night,
  And haply the Queen-Moon is on her throne,
    Clustered around by all her starry Fays;
      But here there is no light,
  Save what from heaven is with the breezes blown
    Through verdurous glooms and winding mossy ways.

I cannot see what flowers are at my feet,
  Nor what soft incense hangs upon the boughs,
But, in embalmed darkness, guess each sweet
  Wherewith the seasonable month endows
The grass, the thicket, and the fruit-tree wild;
  White hawthorn, and the pastoral eglantine;

Fast fading violets covered up in leaves;
　　And mid-May's eldest child,
The coming musk-rose, full of dewy wine,
　　The murmurous haunt of flies on summer eves.

Darkling I listen; and, for many a time
　I have been half in love with easeful Death,
Called him soft names in many a mused rhyme,
　To take into the air my quiet breath;
Now more than ever seems it rich to die,
　To cease upon the midnight with no pain,
　　While thou art pouring forth thy soul abroad
　　　In such an ecstasy!
Still wouldst thou sing, and I have ears in vain—
　To thy high requiem become a sod.

Thou wast not born for death, immortal Bird!
　No hungry generations tread thee down;
The voice I hear this passing night was heard
　In ancient days by emperor and clown:
Perhaps the self-same song that found a path
　Through the sad heart of Ruth, when, sick for home,
　　She stood in tears amid the alien corn;
　　　The same that oft-times hath
Charmed magic casements, opening on the foam
　Of perilous seas, in faery lands forlorn.

Forlorn! the very word is like a bell
　To toll me back from thee to my sole self!
Adieu! the fancy cannot cheat so well
　As she is fam'd to do, deceiving elf.
Adieu! adieu! thy plaintive anthem fades
　Past the near meadows, over the still stream,
　　Up the hill-side; and now 'tis buried deep
　　　In the next valley-glades:
Was it a vision, or a waking dream?
　Fled is that music:—Do I wake or sleep?

To Autumn

Season of mists and mellow fruitfulness,
　　Close bosom-friend of the maturing sun;
Conspiring with him how to load and bless
　　With fruit the vines that round the thatch-eves run;
To bend with apples the mossed cottage trees,
　　And fill all fruit with ripeness to the core;
　　　To swell the gourd, and plump the hazel shells

With a sweet kernel; to set budding more,
And still more, later flowers for the bees,
Until they think warm days will never cease,
    For Summer has o'er-brimmed their clammy cells.

Who hath not seen thee oft amid thy store?
    Sometimes whoever seeks abroad may find
Thee sitting careless on a granary floor,
    Thy hair soft-lifted by the winnowing wind;
Or on a half-reaped furrow sound asleep,
    Drowsed with the fume of poppies, while thy hook
      Spares the next swath and all its twined flowers;
And sometimes like a gleaner thou dost keep
    Steady thy laden head across a brook;
    Or, by a cider-press, with patient look,
      Thou watchest the last oozings hours by hours.

Where are the songs of Spring? Ay, where are they?
    Think not of them, thou hast thy music too, –
While barred clouds bloom the soft-dying day,
    And touch the stubble-plains with rosy hue;
Then in a wailful choir the small gnats mourn
    Among the river sallows, borne aloft
      Or sinking as the light wind lives or dies;
And full-grown lambs loud bleat from hilly bourn;
    Hedge-crickets sing; and now with treble soft
    The red-breast whistles from a garden-croft;
      And gathering swallows twitter in the skies.

**

Now that you've heard them I hope you agree that the differences in tone and voice, especially the sharp contrast between the urgent intensities and drama of the personal voice in the here-and-now *Nightingale* and the as-if voiceless and as-if motionless *Autumn*, are striking enough to make it difficult to believe that the same poet wrote both within such a short time. (I argued the same about the *Hamlet/Lear* divide.) And we'll see that where *Nightingale* is richly intertextual and allusive (the reader needs lots of footnotes), *Autumn* has a bare and cool directness of style. But before we look at the differences I know that I need to tell you what I mean by late style and how my reading of the term differs from others that are out there.

The most familiar use of the term 'late style' is that deployed by Edward Said in his book of that name, put together after his very sad early death from leukaemia. (He wrote it very conscious of his terminal illness. I was lucky enough to know him a little before he was diagnosed. He was very kind to me in both a personal and professional sense.) Said writes about the standard, earlier – and sentimental – way of thinking about late style: 'the accepted notion of age and wisdom in some last works that reflect a special maturity, a new spirit of reconciliation and serenity often expressed in terms of a miraculous transfiguration of common reality' (Said 2006: 6). Sentimental readings of Shakespeare's final 'romances' like *The Winter's Tale* and *The Tempest* would clearly fit with that way of thinking. Modern readings of *The Tempest* (including a very short and modest lecture in this book) emphasise very different aspects of the play, notably its complicity in colonialism.

Said, drawing on Theodore Adorno's remarks on late Beethoven from the 1930s, rejects that account of late style and wishes to replace it with its opposite. He asks: 'But what of artistic lateness not as harmony and resolution but as intransigence, difficulty, and unresolved contradiction?... Late style that involves a non-harmonious, non-serene tension, and above all, a sort of deliberately unproductive productiveness going *against*' (7). Summarising Adorno, Said adds that late Beethoven 'abandons communication with the established social order ... and achieves a contradictory, alienated relationship with it. His late works constitute a form of exile' (8).

Adorno was a composer himself and Said an accomplished pianist, and I am very much neither of these, so it's with considerable diffidence that I say that this is not really how late Beethoven sounds to me or has ever sounded. Nor, I suspect, despite its technical difficulties for performers and marked differences from the musical conventions of the time, including his own earlier work (though these differences are as much about returning to the musical language of vanished eras as much as anticipating the 20th-century avant-garde), did late Beethoven sound alienated and exiled to his first listeners, at least the best of them, because the most challenging contemporary music at any period needs the best listeners. But this lecture is on Keats and not Beethoven, so I'll get off this hobby-horse and say what late style means to me.

It means, as already suggested, a dialectical and dynamic process, a process of moving towards horizons of possibility for the artistic work, especially at the level of form and language, one marked above all by an ironic and self-reflecting autonomy, an aesthetic self-sufficiency that, as it were, answers only to itself – in its ironic and self-motored way. Late style positions the art-work in a kind of sealed system. It neither solicits nor is in apparent need of our attention or response. It is dialogic and dynamic in its relations between its own component parts and between itself and the impulse towards 'realist' artistic alternatives that it is always going 'beyond' and into its non-mimetic autonomies. I have come over the years to think of another mapping exercise to help clarify my thinking. For me, late style can be mapped on to the dialectic that is always in play (and not just in their respective historical periods) between what we all know as 'realism' and 'modernism'. Late style is the impulse and process of realism becoming modernism – and for me modernism is inherently ironic. In the *Hamlet/*

Lear lecture you heard that I read *Hamlet* as a proto-realist novel and *Lear* as a proto-modernist myth. I'll just add that the realist/modernist dialogue or dialectic might also be mapped on to what the critic Stanley Fish, in his readings of 17th-century texts, calls the difference between self-satisfying and self-consuming artefacts (Fish 1972).

How might we approach the two Keats odes?

The *Nightingale* ode is, unlike the other odes, a narrative but it's a narrative about wanting to be out of the narrative loop, to 'leave the world' and 'fade away', to escape at last from narratives of inevitable suffering, including that of Keats' own younger brother's death ('Where youth grows pale, and spectre-thin, and dies': Tom died of consumption, what we now call tuberculosis, and Keats, who trained in medicine, nursed him and almost certainly caught the disease then, the disease from which he died aged 25). This is a narrative about wanting narrative to stop. It's the repeated urgency of the 'I' and the 'me' wanting to be absorbed into the impersonal. For Freud this is the death-drive that is always haunting the pleasure-principle. For this lecture, I'd like to risk calling the poem a narrative of about being or becoming the Hamlet of the 'To be, or not to be' soliloquy (Act 3, Sc. 1) with his 'heartache' (Keats starts 'My heart aches'), his 'pale cast of thought' with the burden of consciousness (Keats: 'but to think is to be full of sorrow') and with Hamlet's desire for oblivion and the 'consummation' of death (in Keats' words, the 'now more than ever' realisation of it being 'rich to die'). For it's a romantic poem in the guise of (like indeed *Hamlet* itself) a proto-novel, the story of the hero's desire in the intensity of the 'now more than ever' moment (Hamlet in Act 5, Scene 2: 'If it be now, 'tis not to come ...'), a story of desire, success and (as we'll see) failure.

It is a narrative steeped not only in *Hamlet* (though the very expressive word 'darkling' is borrowed from *King Lear*) but, in its textured and intertextual web of classical, biblical and mythological referencing towards other narratives, and clear debt to Wordsworth, it makes the claim that poetic language itself ('on the viewless wings of Poesy') is the only fit means (unlike opiates and alcohol: the 'draught of vintage ... With beaded bubbles winking at the brim') to achieve the longed-for stasis and the ecstasy of oblivious union with the bird and its song. This reaches its climax at the end of the penultimate stanza when the bird-song evokes the narratives of Ruth (from the bible) and of 'magic casements' – an ironic glance at Keats' own *Eve of St Agnes*. But it's not so much a climax as a brilliantly subversive anti-climax, for at this most richly realised imaginative moment the poem collapses in the act of its own triumph, the moment where the realised vision of imagined worlds – the casements, 'opening on the foam / Of perilous seas, in faery lands forlorn' – is punctured by the very enunciation of the word 'forlorn'. At which moment the final stanza says: 'Forlorn! The very word is like a bell / To toll me back from thee to my sole self!'

The intended effect is of a 'spell' word from myth that, once uttered, achieves and destroys simultaneously. The single word 'forlorn' punctures the poem in and by its own fullness of linguistic achievement, deflating the entire process of wanting to leave narrative, returning the poet, as if 'like a bell' being tolled, to his 'sole self' (in *Hamlet* the bell is beating when the Ghost appears), and it leaves Keats now left listening no longer to the bird's rapidly disembodied and disappearing music, but just listening to himself saying to the bird 'Adieu! Adieu!' like Hamlet after encountering the Ghost who also leaves with his repeated adieus: Keats saying goodbye, waking up (but 'do I wake or sleep?'), with the return to narrative. This narrative is ironically completed in its own failure which is the success of its imagined language. The language achieves the poem and simultaneously kills it. But the language of imagination is all that the poet has. The moment at which the one word 'forlorn' completes, in triumph, stanza 7 and then immediately starts, in despair, the final stanza 8 is the poem's modernist 'turn', its expression of late style.

There's a little more I want to say about that iconic repetition of 'forlorn / Forlorn' across the two stanzas and to do so I want to turn to the stanzaic form itself. As you can see and hear, the ten-line stanza of this ode is an elegant synthesis and abridgement of the two forms of sonnet available to Keats, the Shakespearean form (the first four lines of the ode are a Shakespearian quatrain) and the (older) Italian form (the following six lines of the ode are in the form of the Italian sonnet's 'sestet'). Rather paradoxically, Keats' own sonnets use the Italian first eight lines, the 'octave', and then tend to vary in practice for the final six. By avoiding the Shakespearian final rhyming couplet Keats can move his narrative onwards through the stanzas without what would have been those 'full-stops', but there's another aspect of the debt to the Italian form that I want to suggest may have unconsciously influenced the ending of this ode.

Officially the Shakespearian sonnet form (three quatrains and a couplet) has no clear break in its structure, unlike the Italian form that breaks very firmly and visibly (sometimes with a line-space) between the octave and the sestet. But it doesn't take much close reading of Shakespeare to see that there is often a break in the sense and argument in his sonnets between lines 8 and 9 (the second and third quatrain) that betrays a rather poignant debt to the earlier model. For me, the most striking example of this break is in the most moving of all his sonnets, 104. My contention here is that Keats, who certainly read Shakespeare closely, may be unconsciously drawing on what Shakespeare does in this sonnet.

Sonnet 104 has the clearest break in the entire sequence of poems between the argument of the octave (which says to the boy that his beauty is unchanging) and the sestet (well, perhaps it is invisibly changing). The break across lines 8 and 9 is movingly underscored by the word 'yet' being deployed in both lines but in opposing senses (line 8 as 'still', line 9 as 'but'). Shakespeare says to the boy in line 8 that it's three years since he first saw him – 'Since first I saw you fresh, which yet are green' ('yet' as 'still') – and then line 9 starts: 'Ah! yet doth beauty, like a dial-hand / Steal from his figure ...' ('yet' as 'but'), the poet being forced to concede that the boy's beauty may after all be fading, stealing away but, like the hands on a sundial, so slowly as to escape notice. I want to argue that the act of enunciating the first 'yet', meaning 'still', itself forces the opposing meaning of 'but' into the poet's mind and, across the 8/9 line-break, into the poem's argument, collapsing the confidence of the first eight lines' assertion of unchanging beauty. The 'yet ... yet' repetition across the crucial line 8/9 argument-break, the first word uncomfortably forcing new recognition on to the poet, is duplicated in Keats' 'forlorn / Forlorn' repetition across the break in stanzas in his ode. I'm pretty sure I'm the first to suggest this; I expect it's a bit tenuous and far-fetched but I offer it to you here.

**

The *Nightingale* ode was written in one day, in May 1819. On another amazing day's work, September 19th, Keats wrote *To Autumn*. That, at exactly the same time, he was struggling unsuccessfully with his unfinished and intransigent *Fall of Hyperion* (where, to return to Bloom, his hyper-anxious struggle was with the uber-influential Dante and Milton, simultaneously) makes the composition of *To Autumn* even more astonishing. (A couple of days later, literally, he finally abandoned the *Fall*.)

Let's start with form. At a stroke Keats does something very remarkable with his ten-line stanza used in *Nightingale*. He adds a line. As I've already said *Autumn* has nothing of the narrative drive and energy of *Nightingale*, its need to reproduce a highly personalised and dramatically voiced longing (and of course it's also a much shorter poem), but this eleventh line, in the form of a seven-line reshaping of the six-line Italian sestet, adds further to its air of gravity and stasis, an interweaving and interlineation of sound patterns (the last seven lines, after the usual quatrain, are further and subtly differentiated between the first stanza and the other two) where rhyme is both anticipated and delayed. The rhyming couplet (the Shakespearian 'full-stop') that then yields to the actual last line which rhymes with the line a distant four lines earlier is an extraordinarily beautiful and subtle weaving of varieties of patterned sound, a counterpoint of presence and absence. This radical and yet undemonstrative and as-if indifferent reshaping, or perhaps a better word is re-tuning of the form and sound of the Keatsian stanza, is late style embodied.

I've also said that *Autumn* is, compared to *Nightingale*, as-if voiceless. Who is speaking the poem? There is an abstraction at the place where we expect a voice, or rather the voice of the poem has a kind of grave, hieratic and personality-free tonelessness, perhaps as-if evoking the 'voice' of the idea of poetry (as opposed to the rather clunky 'Poesy' named, as we saw, in *Nightingale*). And who is this as-if toneless voice addressing in its questions and its instruction ('Who hath not seen thee ...?'; 'Where are the songs of Spring?... / Think not of them...')? The notional addressee is Autumn itself, as the bird is addressed in *Nightingale* and the urn is addressed in the *Grecian Urn* ode – but the bird and the urn are, in terms of the evoked 'real' of the poems, 'there' while Autumn is, despite the allegorised pictures of the granary-worker and the gleaner (and it's symptomatically impossible to determine the figure's or figures' age or gender), a kind of ironic abstraction – ironic as there's something as-if impossible about telling Autumn not to think enviously about Spring or, for that matter, about him/her/it being a 'bosom-friend' of the sun. The more I focus on the speaker and the addressed in the poem, the more hazy they become and the more I realise that we're not dealing with the 'real' in either case.

Instead the poem gives us Autumn as process, an in-process mobility (but barely noticeable as mobile) within the intricate workings of the poem's processes (I'll be saying something similar in another lecture, on *Twelfth Night*): Autumn, in effect, not as a season but as an enactment of temporal process in and across the process of three stanzas, three being the minimum number to establish process itself. So we move from the ripeness and over-ripeness of the first stanza's late summer's 'warm days' as harvest approaches; to the harvesting, reaping and fruit-pressing of the second stanza; to the stubble-plains of post-harvest and the approach of winter in the final stanza. At the same time as the stanzas enact the seasonal processes of the stages of Autumn, they enact also the advancing and declining day, from the 'maturing' sun of the morning; to the mid-afternoon sleep of the worker; to the 'soft-dying day'. And, also simultaneously and very subtly, the different senses are evoked, from the taste and touch of the first stanza; to the sights of the second; to the increasingly vanishing sounds of the third – and that process is a gradual withdrawal and distancing between and across the senses, from the immediate touch to the distant sounds.

Day, season, year die slowly as we read, and as we move further from the scenes evoked. The process is especially subtle and moving in the wonderful final stanza where paradoxes of language exert a muted pressure to hold the process at bay – the clouds 'bloom' the 'soft-dying day'; the 'stubble-plains' have the 'rosy hue' of a youth in bloom; the gnats 'mourn' but are held in a temporal suspension, rising or sinking according to the wind as it (in a painful image) 'lives or dies'; the lambs are 'full-grown' and crying for their mothers because they are – and yet the poem won't call them – sheep (ready for slaughter); the swallows are 'gathering' for the winter-migration but have not gone, yet, because they're 'gathering'. And the process is again slowed, or slowed further, with the delicate repeating of the most modest word in the poetic lexicon: 'and'.

Who is saying and doing and writing all this art? As I've tried to suggest, the tone-free voicelessness of the poem, its enactment of process rather than the highly personalised statement of, say, desire in *Nightingale*, its as-if self-sufficiency and autonomy, its seeming obliviousness to needing to be read – all this positions the greatest (and, to return to Keats on Wordsworth, the least 'egotistical') of all short Romantic poems in the sealed space of aesthetic form-as-content, poem as mere form, the ironic place of late style.

**

There's a third poem on your sheet – but is it a poem? Well, I think so, but many don't. What I want to do now is to offer you what I hope is a reasonably original reading of a problem-text. Here's the text.

> This living hand, now warm and capable
> Of earnest grasping, would, if it were cold
> And in the icy silence of the tomb,
> So haunt thy days and chill thy dreaming nights
> That thou wouldst wish thine own heart dry of blood
> So in my veins red life might stream again,
> And thou be conscience-calmed – see here it is –
> I hold it towards you.

Of all the critical notions that swirl around the last terrible months that Keats endured, the most puzzling is about what at least some readers and critics, and I'm definitely one of them, consider his last complete poem – puzzling because an inherently implausible idea has hardened into orthodoxy and so gets repeated in each new biography or edition. This is the idea that this profoundly unsettling tiny poem, probably written a couple of months after *To Autumn* in December 1819 (on a blank page of the dreary satire 'The Cap and Bells'), is not a poem but a fragment and, while sentimental older generations (so we're told) mistook it to be connected with Fanny Brawne, it should be read instead as a fragment of a blank-verse tragedy (blank verse is unrhymed iambic pentameters, as in most of Shakespeare) that Keats may or may not have intended to write.

This orthodoxy may derive partly from the wish to protect Keats from the charge of cruelty to Fanny (like we saw those editors who wish to protect Hamlet from the charge of cruelty to Ophelia) in so far as the poem (especially if read as a completed text) has an only thinly veiled wish to make its addressee unhappy, haunted and, indeed, lifeless if that is what's required to restore life to the dead speaker. But the desire to make Fanny unhappy is exactly what Keats himself recognised and couldn't avoid persisting in throughout his letters to her. One example of many, probably from May 1820: 'Have I any right to wish you to be unhappy for me... I do not want you to be unhappy – and yet I do'.

And this is because the jealousy in Keats' love for Fanny is not just an embarrassing by-product of his love but rather what the love was constituted in and driven by. (Of all the characters in Shakespeare, Keats seems to have identified most strongly with the betrayed Troilus.) Jealousy of her possibly flirting with other men becomes inflamed to jealousy of her even having an autonomous, let alone happy, existence in the social world; and that in turn becomes inflamed, in this final poem, to jealousy of her being alive at all and the need to end that in the only way possible. Keats' letters and poems to Fanny are crucial not because they're the exception to some romantic norm but because they most purely exemplify the way love is constituted in jealousy and loss. Love thrives, and can only purely thrive, on obstacles and rivals, real or imagined, on failure and loss – and what it desires most intensely is death (the key cultural theorist here is Denis de Rougemont).

The minimum requirement suggested in any reading of 'This living hand' is that the addressee needs to be 'conscience-calmed' – or, rather, that the speaker would like to believe (perhaps against what he takes to be the evidence) that the addressee has a conscience that seeks or at least needs to be calmed, even if that might only be achievable in death. Again, probably from May 1820, and in relation to what Keats read as Fanny's 'habit of flirting with Brown': 'All this may seem savage in me. You do not feel as I do – you do not know what it is to love... Do not write unless you can do it with a crystal conscience'. But it is the final letter to Fanny that makes the case for 'This living hand' being about, and to, her in the most compelling way; and I think the importance of this letter as evidence has perhaps not hitherto been fully recognised.

> A person in health as you are can have no conception of the horrors that nerves and a temper like mine go through... If my health would bear it, I could write a poem which I have in my head, which would be a consolation for people in such a situation as mine. I would show someone in love as I am, with a person living in such liberty as you do. Shakespeare always sums up matters in the most sovereign manner. Hamlet's heart was full of such misery as mine is when he said to Ophelia 'Go to a Nunnery, go, go!' Indeed, I should like to give up the matter at once – I should like to die. I am sickened at the brute world which you are smiling with.

'I could write a poem which I have in my head...' Keats' doctors forbade him at his advanced stage of illness to read, let alone write poetry and in so far as this passage has received any attention it has been taken to refer to a poem that Keats never wrote down and so is lost to posterity. But what if it was a poem already written down some months earlier, in effect on a spare scrap of paper, as if as an *aide memoire*, but neither sent at the time nor intended for publication, and understandably now running very freshly in his head as a consoling (if cruelly consoling) picture of a man in anguished love with a woman living in liberty in what he considers the brutal world? And in the letter the thought of this unprecedented poem (which he 'could write' – that is, in my reading, write or rather copy out for her there and then) makes him turn immediately and instinctively (as so often in Keats when under this kind of intellectual challenge) to Shakespeare – and the Hamlet reference seems to me decisive.

The 'misery' Keats at this moment identifies in Hamlet emerges in the suicide considered in the 'To be, or not to be' soliloquy (a speech which I identified earlier in this lecture as richly influencing the *Nightingale* ode), immediately before the Nunnery scene, but suicide is rejected because of 'conscience' (and Keats in the letter then turns to wanting to die). Then, with Ophelia, the misery reignites in Hamlet's disgust with what he reads as her trivial social frivolities – 'You jig, you amble and you lisp… and make your wantonness your ignorance' (Act 3, Sc. 1) – and these are words that find their counterpart in (less directly brutal) letters to Fanny, as when (in two letters from May 1820) Keats expresses amazement that she 'could really what is called enjoy yourself at a party', disgust with 'fashion and foppery and tattle' and anxiety that she might 'still behave in dancing rooms and other societies as I have seen you'.

The consolation to be derived from picturing such a man wanting such a woman to pacify her conscience by restoring life to his corpse at the expense of her own life is one that the speaker knows is melodramatic. This is reflected in the very literary, lapidary movement of the syntax across the regular beat of the blank verse (aspects of the poem that might have led to the critical orthodoxy with which I began, the notion that the text is a fragment from a blank-verse tragedy) but in the astonishing last nine words syntax and punctuation collapse, the rhythm relaxes into informal speech, 'thou' becomes 'you' and the consolation sought is the warm human touch of a warm human hand. The poem in effect disappears, becomes a voice speaking, a hand offered, a moment when 'all disagreeables evaporate', not in the intensity of the act of art (as Keats suggested in a famous letter of December 1817), but after it and beyond art.

This is an intensely moving expression of a poet in effect signing off his last poem, abandoning not just blank verse but poetry itself. To read it instead in the way that current critical orthodoxy asks us to read it (as if it was a stage-prop in waiting, an embarrassing side-issue) seems a demeaning disservice to a man who lived above all for the truth of true feeling. And he knew what it was for feelings to cease – back in November 1817 a poem spoke wonderfully of 'the feel of not to feel it' (but the line was normalised by a friend of his for later publication to the far more commonplace 'to know the change and feel it'. Dickinson has 'I could not see to see'). And what touches me most about this final poem is that it gives us a poet breaking through into yet new areas of what I've called late style, the ironic self-sufficiencies of an art that answers only to itself, and in this poem beyond itself. That the poet who wrote *To Autumn* then wrote this a couple of months later, and was then (aged 25) silenced, is almost too painful to think about.

So I'll leave it there. I hope you live with Keats as intensely as he deserves. So please read (if you haven't already) the *Grecian Urn* and *Melancholy* odes, the very sexy *Eve of St Agnes*, some of the sonnets and especially the letters. If late Beethoven is the best music we have – these days, I'd add a lot of Monteverdi, a lot of Bach and most of Mahler – those from Keats are the best letters we have. Thank you.

Further Reading

Walter Jackson Bate, *John Keats* (Harvard U.P.: 1967).

Harold Bloom, *The Anxiety of Influence: A Theory of Poetry* (Oxford U.P.: 1973).

Denis de Rougemont, *Love in the Western World*, trs. Montgomery Belgion (Princeton U.P.: 1983).

Michael Ferber, *The Cambridge Introduction to British Romantic Poetry* (Cambridge U.P.: 2012).

Stanley Fish, *Self-Consuming Artifacts* (University of California Press: 1972).

John Keats, *Keats's Poetry and Prose*, ed. Jeffrey N. Cox (Norton: 2008).

Michael O'Neill ed., *John Keats in Context* (Cambridge U.P.: 2017).

Edward Said, *On Late Style: Music and Literature Against the Grain* (Bloomsbury: 2006).

Helen Vendler, *The Odes of John Keats* (Harvard U.P.: 1983).

13 Republicanism, Regicide and 'The Musgrave Ritual'

I hoped you enjoyed reading 'The Musgrave Ritual' (widely available online) and I also hope you found it very strange and in many ways unlike a typical Sherlock Holmes story. You're right and I'll say more about that soon.

But first a few words about detective stories in general. It has long been recognised that detective stories are exemplary narratives, very pure in the way they demonstrate some key aspects of narrative itself. Tzvetan Todorov in a famous essay from the 1960s (see H. Porter Abbott 2008, and Brooks 1992) showed how the classic whodunnit is two stories in one – the story of the crime and the story of the investigation or inquest. The investigation is the text we read and the crime is in a kind of unobtainable virtual space, only obtained, later, through the mediation or representation of the investigation. Narrative theorists have said the same about all narratives: each one consists of two elements, only one of which (the investigation) is available, is read as the text we have in front of us, is a mediated or represented version of the abstracted, virtual, second-by-second totalities of the 'real', unmediated events (the crime). Other pairs of words have been used to express this relationship between 'crime' and 'inquest' (the usual word): the Russian Formalists called them '*fabula*' and '*szujet*' and, not very helpfully, the Anglo-American tradition is to call them 'story' (very unhelpful word) and 'discourse'. Sorry if that takes a bit of getting used to, as an idea about narrative. It may be helpful if you think of 'crime', 'fabula' and 'story' as in square brackets – the point being they exist only as an unavailable non-text. There's a debate out there, which I won't talk go into now, about which of the two has precedence, comes first. Logic suggests crime/*fabula*/story but logic would appear to be unreliable in this instance.

The inquest/*szujet*/discourse goes over the ground, represents or recapitulates, in repetition, to establish the 'fabula', and in that respect 'The Musgrave Ritual' is a typical whodunnit as we see Holmes literally going over the ground (pace by pace) that the butler Brunton took in *his* investigation. More about this soon. But let me step back again and make a point about the first unusual feature of this story. What do we expect when we start reading a detective story?

Readerly expectations, when it comes to settling down to enjoy detective stories in general, and perhaps Sherlock Holmes stories in particular, are that such texts are unlikely to intervene, explicitly or implicitly, in history or historical debates. At the least, there is a presumed conservatism about the genre, with solutions to crimes standing in, as it were, for support for the status quo. But 'The Musgrave Ritual' is unusual as it emphatically engages with a famous slice of English history and I want to suggest some interesting aspects of this engagement. The story engages with mid-17th-century history and I think we have here a conflicted kind of engagement, coming as it does out of what appears as both royalist and republican, conservative and radical perspectives. I'm also going to argue that those perspectives are played out in terms of the connection between 17th-century history and the 1890s class-system. (And let me add that this lecture contributes to the 'conflicted text' thread in this book.)

What I have to say develops and builds on other critical readings of the tale, and my attempt to bring together the historical and the psychoanalytic in what I hope is an original reading will draw in particular on the brilliant material by Peter Brooks, in his *Reading for the Plot*, a book we used in the *Great Expectations* lecture (Brooks 1992). But let me now sketch in some 17th-century history and, again, I'm going back to my own school-days to do so.

At boarding school at the age of eight I had to learn a rhyme designed to make children memorise the names of the kings and queens of England, from William I to Victoria (when history, of course, stopped). The couplet dealing with the period between Mary and James II goes like this: 'Mary, Bessie, James the Vain, / Charlie, Charlie, James again'.

The rhyme celebrates, in the friendliest possible way ('Dick the Bad' and 'James the Vain' are the closest it gets to mild criticism), the unbroken chain of monarchy so that children can internalise it as a genealogy as 'true' as those in the Old Testament and as 'natural' as playground chant. This is a chain intended to be as inseparable from Englishness as the Constitution, the Class-System and what conservative critics of the Renaissance used to call the 'Great Chain of Being'. As 'naturalised' history (history masquerading as nature) it's a good example of what Roland Barthes called myth (Barthes 1973). That is, something historically constructed (and therefore potentially available to being or having been constructed – and lived – differently) is presented as an unchangeable fact of nature, 'the way things are', like the idea that the British royal family is a 'natural' feature of being 'British' or the notion that the UK *Daily Mail* is a newspaper. This is what Marx called ideology, mistaken or very partial 'truths' about the world that we've internalised as 'the way things are', and the later theorist Louis Althusser added that the state's ideological apparatuses (the family, the Church, the educational system, the mainstream media) are just as effective, or even more so, than the state's repressive apparatuses (like the criminal justice system) in keeping us as uncomplaining subjects and complicit in our own subjections. Many of you will know that Blake called this out, nearly a century before Marx, in his great poem 'London', as the 'mind-forged manacles' that keep us in our ideological prisons.

Anyway: from Charlie to Charlie. The Musgrave Ritual's version of that part of the unbroken chain goes like this.

'Whose was it?'
'His who is gone.'
'Who shall have it?'
'He who will come.'

Holmes translates at the close of the tale.

'Whose was it?' 'His who is gone.' That was after the execution of Charles. Then, 'Who shall have it?' 'He who will come.' That was Charles II, whose advent was already foreseen.

Charlie, Charlie. Now, isn't there something missing there? Between Charlie and Charlie? Don't be embarrassed if you don't know. The editing out from history of England's revolution and republic in this children's rhyme that I learned and of course never questioned is not altogether a surprise. Even today, university students in Britain express surprise on hearing about that history. The execution of Charles I comes as a considerable shock to them. So it is of particular interest that we can take a piece of mainstream popular fiction, a Sherlock Holmes short story, and read it as an engagement with this editing of history – both reproducing that act of forgetting and dramatising an urgent attempt to recover that history, the history of revolution and regicide. That is how I read 'The Musgrave Ritual'.

This case was Holmes' break-through to successful eminence. His crucial realisation is that the ritual, meaningless to the Musgrave family over the generations, may provide the answer to the other puzzles presented to him at the outset, may be what he calls the 'starting-point of this chain of events'. By realising what the butler Brunton has realised, namely that the ritual was designed to preserve the Stuart crown after the execution of Charles I, Holmes reads or re-reads (after Brunton) the ritual, traces Brunton, finds him, extrapolates a possible cause of his death in what the jilted Rachel Howells may (or may not) have done, and restores the crown itself.

Peter Brooks' discussion of this tale is placed within a Freudian economy of desire, whereby the protagonists' desire (Brunton's to obtain, Holmes's to explain), mapped in turn on to the reader's desire (to connect everything together, but by diversionary rather than summary means), is the figure of Eros, the pleasure principle, which is shadowed and completed by Thanatos, the Death instinct, in quiescence and closure (the totalising meaning that brings the chain of connectors to a halt). Brooks also makes the crucial point (and I've already signalled this unusual feature) that the *fabula* of the apparent crime or crimes opens out on to 'a deeper level of *fabula*' (26), history itself in the form of the Stuart crown which the ritual has accidentally preserved, its meaning to be restored as the history of the 'happy ending' restoration of the monarchy itself. To develop Brooks' point it might be added that the restoration of the monarchy is positioned as the totalising closure that is, in effect, the end of history and that the story neatly positions the complementary beginning of history in its mention of the oak-tree (central to the plot as plotted space) as having been 'there at the Norman Conquest', where history, in the children's history-book sense, begins. My schoolboy rhyme of the 'British' kings and queens starts 'Willie, Willie...': that's 1066 and William I. (Nobody told me at the time that he was a French invader and that the English lost that battle and therefore the country.)

But there are other unusual features of this tale, which have been well-noted in an analysis by Nils Clausson (2005). Two features he singles out for comment are, first, the very unusual nature of the crime or crimes (is throwing stolen property into a lake a crime?) and the fact that the crime that would have been much the more serious (murder as opposed to theft) is very possibly not a crime at all (it might have been an accident) nor is it solved (the possible murderer has vanished). Secondly, Clausson observes that in his 'solution' of the crime (which, despite noting that it might not have been a crime but an accident, Holmes insists on twice calling a crime) Holmes resorts not to clinical deduction but to melodramatic invention – the recycling of Gothic clichés in his presumed reconstruction of what Brunton's accomplice Rachel Howells did (or didn't do) when she found (or didn't find) her ex-lover in her power.

> What smouldering fire had suddenly sprung into flame in this passionate Celtic woman's soul...? I seemed to see that woman's figure ... flying wildly up the winding stair, with her ears ringing perhaps with the muffled screams from behind her and with the drumming of frenzied hands against the slab of stone which was choking her faithless lover's life out.

As Clausson points out, this is exactly what Holmes usually warns sternly against in crime-solving – using fantasy and not deductive logic. Despite the 'I seemed to see ...' and the 'perhaps', this is Holmes as bad novelist and this, as 'solution' (as Holmes himself puts it, he must 'reconstruct this ... drama'), is what we might describe as the bathetic level of *fabula* to complement what Brooks saw as the deeper *fabula*, the 'solution' that is recovered and reconstructed history. The two solutions (what it was that Holmes presumes Rachel did, as melodrama, and what the ritual means, as history) come pointedly together as the double-climax to the plot at the end (Rachel/Ritual), and one effect of this is to achieve an uneasy collusion between them. Mid-17th-century history – that unusual presence in the discourse of a Sherlock Holmes story – becomes, because of Holmes' equally strange excursion into what he normally demonises (mere fantasy), a history contaminated or melodramatised.

Is this a history discursively presented from a royalist or a republican perspective? It is both, and the effect of that is that we have what I've already called a conflicted as well as a contaminated history. And the contest between perspectives on or readings of history is complemented by contestation at the level of plot between three men. Rachel is a mere plot-device, her Welshness a thin excuse for an 'excitable ... temperament', and the relations between the three men are intricately patterned in ways that Eve Sedgwick, in her influential *Between Men* (1985), characterises as symptomatic in many narratives where male-male relations underpin and shadow the overt hetero-sexually driven plot. Sedgwick draws on Rene Girard whose thoughts about mediated and imitative desire we met in the *Emma* lecture.

The story starts with a pointedly ambivalent gesture: is it an act of republican mock-regicide or of royalist salute? This is Holmes's habit, in what Watson calls 'one of his queer humours', of indoor pistol practice, 'adorn[ing] the opposite wall with a patriotic V.R. [= Victoria Regina] done in bullet-pocks'. 'Patriotic' may be an irony lost on Watson. Regina/Regicide/Reginald (Musgrave's first name) are signifiers that slide together in this text, as do other names and words. As an ambivalent gesture, Holmes' pistol practice corresponds to the ambivalence in his relations with officialdom and authority. He represents and enacts (especially for the criminal) state-apparatus style authority (VR as patriotic salute) but he does so by working (in a way that becomes prototypical for later detective fiction) as a free agent, anti-authoritarian in temperament and personal habits and outside the official structures of authority (VR as republican insolence).

The relations between Holmes and Brunton are intricately established from the start. Watson notes that Holmes' 'criminal relics' had a way of 'wandering into unlikely positions' in their lodgings, and that Holmes was, after his 'remarkable feats', subject to 'lethargy during which he would lie about with his violin and his books'. The second word of the text (also noticed by Clausson) is 'anomaly'. Brunton was originally the schoolmaster 'out of place' and is the anomaly of a butler with the habit of 'wandering into unlikely positions' (in his case jobs, his master's easy-chairs, hidden cellars) and with 'extraordinary gifts – for he can speak several languages and play nearly every musical instrument', a man of 'great energy' who nevertheless 'lacked energy'. He is clearly positioned as someone whom Holmes, with his 'feats' and 'lethargy' contending, cannot but feel threatened by as rival (as if duplicated, as if Brunton makes Holmes feel 'out of place') and whom he must follow after 'upon his trail' by, literally, going over the same ground and wandering into unlikely positions.

Holmes is positioned at the outset as 'panting' for a chance to prove his gifts; Brunton, when we first hear of him, is 'insatiable' about things that Musgrave says shouldn't concern him. Most striking is the duplication (eventually revealed as such to the alert reader) of the highly emblematic picture at the story's climax (about which more below): this is prepared for at the outset when Holmes is seen 'squatting down' in front of a large box, throwing back its lid and removing what we then learn are the 'relics' of the case that 'are history', and that have wandered into their new position in his box.

When Holmes describes how the Musgrave case allowed him to 'trace my first stride toward the position which I now hold' he is not only establishing his current position of eminence as duplicate and rival to Musgrave's social eminence, in an assertion of middle-class brains over upper-class title, but he is also establishing the ground-work (what Brooks means by plot in the geographical sense: something to be paced) of the plot of the story – the tracing and then the duplicating pacing of Brunton's strides ('on the right road' and 'put[ting] myself in the man's place' are the words Holmes uses) towards the position/place where he can finally discover and out-rival Brunton himself, the lower-class servant who attempted what Brooks calls an 'attempted change of place' (26).

In his relations with Reginald Musgrave, Holmes is engaged, just as Brunton is, in out-doing, outsmarting the aristocrat, but the contradictory elements in Holmes' opening account of Musgrave reveal another tension between republican and royalist impulses, as well as contradictions in Holmes' middle-class professional's attitude towards this aristocratic (Oxford) college-friend. The first odd note struck is that while Oxford contemporaries disliked Musgrave for his 'pride' (Brunton calls himself 'proud'), Holmes considers it rather to be 'diffidence'. So which is it? Here Holmes aligns himself with a royalist reading, as he does in the same passage where he picks out for comment Musgrave's 'keen face' and 'keen interest' – the word, of course, we would more naturally associate with Holmes and his intelligence. It's not only that other descriptors of Musgrave in the passage strike a very different note – 'languid', 'suave', 'bit of a dandy' – but the entire plot hangs on the fact that Musgrave and at least most of his ancestors are not keen at all but stupid, specifically stupidly bad readers of the ritual, with none of the 'clearer insight' that Brunton (and Holmes) bring as readers to that text.

The bad reading is a particularly arrogant kind of obtuseness: the unreflecting assumption that a chain of signifiers can be so completely empty of meaning as to serve just to prop up the succession of a series of male aristocrats coming into their property. Holmes, sensing the opportunity for his career that Musgrave is about to offer him, says that he knew he 'could succeed where others failed': this is in effect what Brunton realises about his employer and his ancestors; as failed readers they give him, the servant, the opportunity to 'master' (Holmes' word) the formula.

Relations are also closely established between Musgrave (Reginald/Rex) and the Stuart kings. This is not only clear from the detail, revealed at the end, that the first Musgrave was 'the right-hand man of Charles II', but is more subtly suggested in Musgrave's opening remark to Holmes: 'you probably heard of my poor father's death ... He was carried off about two years ago. Since then I have, of course, had the Hurlstone estates to manage'. As in the children's rhyme, this reproduces the seamless transition from Charles I (who was carried off in a rather more brutal sense – off the scaffold) to Charles II.

The same seamless transition, the editing out of the republic, is shown again in the passage just cited from the last pages. We hear that the first Musgrave was 'the right-hand man of Charles II in his wanderings': we have seen how 'wanderings' applies both to Holmes and Brunton (and 'relics') but the immediate point is that in his wanderings Charles can't, by definition, yet be called Charles II – but he is, as if there was no intervening republic. In the same passage Holmes observes that 'the royal party made head in England even after the death of the king'. And, as in 'carried off', we can't help notice the potential for a ghoulish pun in 'made head'.

Peter Brooks' phrase for Brunton's crime is 'attempted usurpation' (26) and the word, with its revolutionary implications, is well-chosen. I'd like now to develop those implications, in the light of the patterns traced above between and among the three protagonists and the Stuart kings.

One starting-point is the word Musgrave uses when outlining to Holmes the mystery of Brunton's disappearance from the house. He says it was 'incredible ... that he could have gone away leaving all his property behind him' – and 'property', with its sense of house and land, allows one to realise that, in effect, what this servant who wants to 'master' really wants is his right to assert ownership and power itself, as conventionally represented by property in the form of house and land. And not just the house and land of Hurlstone but, on behalf of his class, the houses and lands of the country.

For the logic of the reading that I've been trying out in this lecture is that Brunton is, in the patterns that we have been exploring, Cromwell. And what happens to Brunton because of this presumption to Cromwell-like 'usurpation' is the richly emblematic figure presented to Holmes at the end of his tracing of Brunton's steps.

> It was the figure of a man, clad in a suit of black, who squatted down upon his hams with his forehead sunk upon the edge of the box and his two arms thrown out on each side of it. The attitude had drawn all the stagnant blood to the face, and no man could have recognised that distorted liver-coloured countenance ... He had been dead some days.

I said earlier that this might have been murder or an accident. Despite Holmes' coercive reading of it as Rachel's crime of murder, it doesn't really matter which it was, in so far as the emblematic suggestiveness of that picture is more telling than its immediate cause. I also hinted earlier that this emblem has been significantly prefigured in the picture at the outset of Holmes 'squatting down' in front of a large box, from which he takes out the 'relics' of the tale and proceeds to tell it.

But Brunton is dead and the details of the position of his head and his arms in relation to the box are unmistakeably those of a man about to be executed. That is, the vengeance meted out to this Cromwell is the duplication of what that Cromwell exacted on Charles I, regicide by execution. This Cromwell, in effect, wanted to usurp Musgrave and Hurlstone; he is punished with Mus/grave as His/grave – when (as if hurled down) the 'stone … shut Brunton into what had become his sepulchre'. He, and in effect republicanism, have been buried alive – in a sepulchre, the word with inescapably Christian-royalist connotations: Hamlet uses it about his idolised-deified father.

I've suggested that the tale positions Reginald Musgrave of Hurlstone as Charles II and his father as Charles I; Brunton-Cromwell's first name is Richard, the name of Cromwell's son who succeeded him as Protector and died on his estate at Hursley. These are signifiers again sliding into each other, as indeed might be the alphabetical closeness of the corresponding letters in the names Brunton and Cromwell. But I wouldn't push that on you.

The Musgrave ritual speaks darkly of an 'it'. Like me you naturally enough assumed that this 'it' will be the secret that Holmes will find at the end of his tracing of Brunton's steps. But the 'it' of the ritual (and it is not found by Holmes) is the apparent junk thrown into and then fished out of the lake. The crowning event of the story is Holmes' recognition or reading of the junk as the Stuart Crown. Instead, the 'it' that Holmes actually finds is the buried-alive Brunton. This 'it' is, in effect, the haunting dread itself of being buried alive, which was for Freud the crowning example of the uncanny. Nicholas Royle notes that the original German in Freud's essay speaks of being buried alive as 'the crown' in instances of the uncanny (Royle 2003).

This discovery by Holmes, of the man buried alive, is the uncanny as the return of the repressed, the repressed being the emblem of the king about to be executed, repressed for good reason, as I said from the outset of this lecture, as the fact of regicide which English history cannot bear to countenance and has to forget. I'd add that Marvell's 'Horatian Ode', dealing with the execution of Charles I, says that the king 'bowed his comely head / Down, as upon a bed' and that Musgrave is at pains to emphasise the 'handsome' Brunton's 'splendid forehead'. The return of the repressed, again; the executed king.

I started with the editing out from history of the revolution, regicide and republic, an act of forgetting, and I noted that the story duplicates this editing on the occasions when it cuts seamlessly (either explicitly or by analogy) between Charles I and Charles II. What I can now say about Brunton is that his act of attempted usurpation is an attempt to recover and assert that forgotten history, to insert himself between and among aristocrats or monarchs, in an act that will, in miniature, duplicate and reproduce that history, driven by the same goals as Cromwell's, republicanism as the desire for what is perceived as just property and propriety.

Holmes' last words about the ritual are that Brunton 'tore its secret out of it and lost his life in the venture'. In so far as Holmes is also in the business of tearing or at least teasing secrets out of family mysteries (and Brunton's tearing-out is nothing of the kind but only an act of good reading), it's difficult not to feel that the one ambitious secret-solver, following in closely patterned detail 'upon [the] trail' of the other, is a duplicated figure embodying the republican impulses – in Holmes' case at least partly repressed – that literature as well as history prefers to forget.

A very strange tale. Thank you.

Further Reading

H. Porter Abbott, *The Cambridge Introduction to Narrative*, 2nd ed., Cambridge U.P.: 2008).

Roland Barthes, *Mythologies* (Granada: 1973).

Peter Brooks, *Reading for the Plot: Design and Intention in Narrative* (Harvard U.P.: 1992).

Nils Clausson, 'The Case of the Anomalous Narrative' in *The Victorian Newsletter* 107: Spring 2005.

Arthur Conan Doyle, 'The Musgrave Ritual' in *The Memoirs of Sherlock Holmes* (Penguin: 1950).

Nicholas Royle, *The Uncanny* (Manchester U.P.: 2003).

Eve Kosofsky Sedgwick, *Between Men: English Literature and Male Homosocial Desire* (Columbia U.P.: 1985).

14 Jean Rhys

Her Texts from the 1930s

Most of you will know of Jean Rhys because of her celebrated *Wide Sargasso Sea* (1966), her last and most successful novel – well, in a sense her only successful one as it brought her fame and prizes (her dry response was that it had all come too late) after years of more or less complete neglect, years in which many of those who knew her earlier work thought she was dead. She was such a perfectionist over issues of style that she hung on to the novel, fearing that the odd word was wrong or out of place, and only allowed it to leave her hands when she dreamed of giving birth to a puny baby. It was her long-nurtured project, to answer back to *Jane Eyre* (an early version was written in about 1939) in the form of a prequel told in the voice of Antoinette, whom Rochester renames Bertha (the middle section of the novel is in his voice), and there's no doubt that the novel has an ambitiousness that belies its short length. You'll know it, if you do, because it quite properly plays a key role in numerous post-colonial university modules and courses, especially those (again quite properly, most of them) informed by feminist critical approaches.

Despite the importance of the novel, not least to her personally, there's a case that can be made (and I've made it myself) that her best work is her pre-war novels and stories, especially the three novels that follow her first and less assured novel *Quartet* (1928), novels that in retrospect can be seen as an unplanned trilogy, *After Leaving Mr Mackenzie* (1930), *Voyage in the Dark* (1934) and, the best of them, *Good Morning, Midnight* (1939: Rhys, very understandably, given the novel's radical treatment of women and sex, said that the outbreak of the war killed her novel). As a sort-of trilogy, with differently named protagonists who are in effect the same woman (and at different ages and from different narrative points of view), they have often made me think of connections with Beckett's great postwar trilogy of novels (also with three notionally different protagonists), though the latter are clearly more extreme and allegorical in their anti-realist form and style. I like to think of Rhys and Beckett in those novels standing for modernism's uncharacteristically clear and clearly felt affiliation to those abandoned and lost by society, and in Rhys' case especially to women. Rhys herself was exploited and forgotten; the novels unashamedly draw on raw and immediate memories. Compared to these three novels there's something just a little too willed and painstakingly well-made about *Wide Sargasso Sea. Good Morning, Midnight*, especially, is a more vulnerable text, if I can put it that way, as well as dealing with a woman more vulnerable and more vulnerably exposed than even Antoinette. But what we have with Rhys, as always, is a dynamic or tension between vulnerability and resilience.

So what I want to do in this lecture is to take a look at Jean Rhys' earlier work from the 1930s, specifically *Good Morning, Midnight* and also one tiny and miraculous (and biographically crucial) short story from the same time, as my impression is that her pre-war novels and stories are in comparative neglect. A small but I think telling point before I finish these introductory remarks. The title of *Good Morning, Midnight* is the first line of an Emily Dickinson poem (first published in 1929) and it's heartening to think that Rhys was reading Dickinson in the 1930s. I'd like to think she introduced Dickinson to her much older mentor and lover Ford Madox Ford in Paris (he was an advocate of 'literary impressionism') but expect it was the other way around: he taught her to refine and hone her style by reading and translating from French writers including Colette and Baudelaire. (I owe that detail, and some other details and facts, to the Jean Rhys estate, to which I'm very grateful.)

We can think about what these radically transgressive women writers share and one point to make is that they both have a pained but also ironic awareness of language's state of hopeless compromise, the near-impossibility of the most important, urgent things being communicated at all. I mentioned this in the Dickinson lecture and later we'll hear Rhys' Sasha questioning whether she even thought, let alone said, what we just heard her say. That notion of their shared understanding of the inexpressible is one reason I would offer the pre-war Rhys novels and Dickinson as very pure examples of what some of you will know as *écriture feminine*, the term coined by Helene Cixous and referring to writing that is usually repressed in patriarchy, writing that is anti-linear and marked by narrative disturbance, discontinuities, gaps and ellipses, processes of fragmentation, liquifying and dissolvings, silences and irresolutions (you might remember Dickinson's half-rhymes at the end of poems). All this is particularly true of *Good Morning, Midnight*. Rhys' regular use of ellipses ('...') might valuably be compared to Dickinson's dashes. (In quotations from Rhys below my editorial cuts are in square brackets, thus [...].) And as I started by talking about Rhys and *Jane Eyre*'s Bertha let me just add that further connections can be made with transgressive women writers explored in other earlier lectures, like Gilman's *The Yellow Wallpaper* which as we saw has Bertha in its ancestry, and Chopin's *The Awakening*, another text that Cixous might have pointed to (see Moi 1985).

**

The voice of the vulnerably exposed and isolated female at the centre of all Rhys' work can be heard from her first stories in the 1920s and the pre-war texts present the woman's life as a kind of exile – 'perpetually moving to another place which was perpetually the same' (*Voyage in the Dark*, Chapter 1) – and one marked by thwarted longings. The young woman, exiled indeed, as Rhys was, to London (and Paris) from her rich and complex childhood sensations in Dominica, had earlier been emotionally exiled from her mother. (I draw gratefully in this lecture on Carole Angier's biography.) Rhys' mother had lost a baby daughter to dysentery and Jean's birth was then intended to replace that loss – but the opposite seems to have happened, Jean becoming increasingly aware as a child that she was, especially after the birth of a more obviously loved younger sister, resented by the still mourning mother. For a child of Jean's hyper-sensitivity this is all too easily internalised in self-blame. (We noted Mrs Earnshaw's resentment of Heathcliff who was meant to replace the dead son. We also explored mother-less children in that *Wuthering Heights* lecture.)

She resents a cold and grim England and she drifts into and out of the lives of men who exploit and abandon her, always surviving but always raw to the vicissitudes of a life of edges and margins. It is a story – several novels and stories – that is evoked as banally routine and mutedly intense. And what is most startling of all about these early texts is the fraught, lyrical voice – often, in effect, poetry – in which the most distressing events (abortion; the death of a baby) are so movingly expressed, in a kind of perpetual and dynamic relation with the inexpressible. Silence, as in Beckett and as in Dickinson, is the default language (the ellipses, the dashes) that shadows these delicate, seemingly insubstantial texts, containing worlds of suffering, grief – and the undercutting ironies that always refuse sentiment.

**

Given that *Wide Sargasso Sea* was like a return from the dead for those readers who had come across the pre-war Rhys novels, there's a sharp irony in *Good Morning, Midnight* being about a return from the dead (and 'it hurts when you have been dead to come alive') as Sasha, following the 'bright idea' of drowning herself in drink in London, returns to Paris in her late thirties ('but I've never been young'), the city where much of her difficult earlier life has been transacted (Part 1). This return from drowning takes me straight to a Dickinson poem that I feel sure Rhys would have known (from the 1924 edition that we used in the Dickinson lecture) which wryly notes that drowning is 'not so pitiful / As the attempt to rise'. In the bars and restaurants and shops of Paris (if I can quote from material on Rhys in an earlier book I did) 'negotiating at once the city's painfully associative memories and the men whom magnetically she both attracts and resists, Sasha attempts something between a renewal of and a revenge on her life' (Jacobs 2001: 394). Sasha's journey also evokes for me another Dickinson poem in which the memory of pain can only with the most cautious and slowest of steps approach the past. Dressed in clothes that she hopes extinguish her – but in a fur coat that proves to be a final betrayal – Sasha is determined not to collapse faced with the everyday and casual cruelty of social encounters and one way to resist is to cultivate a calm indifference. But it's not easy when her life, like the street outside her hotel, is in 'what they call an impasse' (Part 1).

The novel is the most complex of Rhys' pre-war novels in almost every respect: in its richly dynamic and nuanced presentation of Sasha's paradoxical predicaments, needs and fears, as well as in its very subtly deployed patterns in form and style (the formal patterns come to a terrible climax that is also a trap for readers on the last page) and in the skilfully woven temporalities which make for a distinctly disorientating experience for the reader, equivalent to what Sasha is having to negotiate as the memories crowd in. For all its unwavering vision the novel is also Rhys' most bitter-comic, as Sasha is her most wryly self-aware and unillusioned narrator.

> Now then, you, X – you must go down and be born. Oh, not me, please, not me. Well then, you, Y, you go along and be born – somebody's got to be. Where's Y? Y is hiding. Well, come on Z, you've got to go and be born. Come on, hurry up, hurry up.
>
> (Part 1)

The novel is also Rhys' most expressionist and surrealist. People, bits of bodies, a whole menagerie of animals, mannequins and automata and puppets (Sasha compares herself to an automaton), places and rooms (and corridors and basements), objects, paintings, fragments of song and music, dreams, overheard remarks – all animate in often surreal, disembodied and distorted form the discourses of the novel. The novel's linguistic texture is thereby realised as projections or extensions of the raw subjectivity at the centre. The novel's Paris is both topographically exact in its verisimilitude (I once paced out its itinerary through the bars and streets) and also in an unsettling way empty, a Paris of strangers encountering each other in functionless chance, as if Sasha's own emotional state is distended in space as well as time. Sasha is determined not to posture or to cry in front of those who circle around her, often imaged as if in circus or pantomime, or indeed in expressionist theatre or opera. It's doubtless a coincidence from the period but the novel, particularly its end, evokes for me Alban Berg's great expressionist opera *Lulu*, premiered (in incomplete form) just two years before in 1937. (The opera starts with a circus animal-trainer welcoming the audience to his menagerie of animals.) Names are also expressionistically deployed in the novel: Enno in her past is evoked in and against René (no/nay) in the present; the most bullying of the bullying men (largely unnamed) is summed up in Mr Blank. More on him very soon.

**

I want to turn to one paragraph in the novel and then to a tiny Jean Rhys short story, before returning in more detail to the novel in the last section of this lecture. I started teaching the novel to 17–18 year olds in the mid-1980s in my first job at a school in the UK. The students loved the novel and were encouraged to love it further when Al Alvarez, the critic who had known Jean Rhys and championed her work, came to the school and talked about her. (He was more famously the champion of Sylvia Plath whom he also knew very well.)

One task we found we needed to do in class was to try to arrange the various narrative fragments and memories into a workable chronological order (it wasn't easy, as suggested earlier). But one paragraph, very late in the novel, seemed to fit nowhere. It suddenly appears when Sasha hears René whistling a tune. And then it as-if disappears.

> I am in a little whitewashed room [...]. A man is standing with his back to me [...] I am watching for the expression on the man's face when he turns round. Now he ill-treats me, now he betrays me. He often brings home other women and I have to wait on them, and I don't like that. But [...] I am not unhappy.
>
> (Part 4)

I remember one student saying that this (though, as often, charged and poem-like – 'now he ill-treats me, now he betrays me') weirdly had the effect of the ground of the novel suddenly giving way, collapsing into a quite separate space-time world. The best we managed was that it must belong to a memory of Sasha as the very young mistress of an abusive older man, perhaps in the Mediterranean south or on a Caribbean island, a memory never followed up or anchored by the rest of the novel. Anyway, the paragraph vanishes with only a passing remark from Sasha about her mind working like a film (so we thought this might mean she's drawing on some early fantasy). Then a few years later I read Carole Angier's biography which in turn made me re-read Rhys' astonishing story 'Good-bye Marcus, Good-bye Rose' which first appeared in *Sleep It Off Lady* in 1976, her final book, though probably at least started much earlier.

The 12-year-old Phoebe tells of the elderly war-hero Captain Cardew, visiting her Caribbean island with his much younger wife, taking Phoebe for walks and gaining her affection by treating her as a grown-up girl. On one of these walks, seated beside her in a garden, he suddenly declares her old enough to have a lover at which point his hand 'dived inside her blouse and clamped itself around one very small breast'. He only removes his hand when a couple stroll onto the scene. The walks continue, despite Phoebe's misgivings (she intuits that she wouldn't be believed if she told anyone, or that, if believed, she'd be blamed), he never touches her again, but the abuse takes a more insidious turn. He would talk ceaselessly about love and ways of making it, explaining that love was not the kind thing she'd imagined but violent and cruel. The Captain's wife, knowing what's going on, starts treating Phoebe aggressively and says something to Phoebe's mother who then treats Phoebe with silent suspicion – but I'll leave you to read the rest of the story which I don't want to spoil. (The beautifully mysterious title is not explained till the last moment.)

The story and its importance are illuminatingly discussed in Carole Angier's biography. Rhys kept notebooks about her life and used them extensively. In these notebooks there are more than one version of the story (in others the girl's age is 13 or 14). She calls the elderly man Mr Howard. On later walks he talks ceaselessly about her, about how, if she belonged to him, he wouldn't allow her to wear any clothes; his hypnotising stories are about him abducting her and making her wait naked on his guests.

In Angier's words about his stories, 'she would only be allowed to rebel enough to make it more fun to force her to submit. She would have to obey his will. And always in the end she would have to be punished'. The young Jean not only internalised the message (as she did about her mother resenting her) but she recognised what it said about submission and humiliation as true, especially that she'd need to be punished. Angier says that Rhys' 'adolescent dream of Mr Howard sank below the surface of her conscious mind'. It surfaces occasionally, is painfully reclaimed in the notebook versions and then, in Angier's words, 'from its twenty pages she distilled just one charged, enigmatic paragraph for *Good Morning, Midnight*' (Angier 1992: 26–29).

I am in a little whitewashed room ...

**

I talked earlier about the ways in which the novel is Rhys' most complex and patterned. One point to make is that the word 'exhibition' acts like a thread that holds the novel together, like a motif in an opera, though in a typically muted and subtle way. The novel starts with a dream in which Sasha is in a passage in the London underground surrounded by red placards.

> This Way to the Exhibition, This Way to the Exhibition. But I don't want the way to the exhibition – I want the way out. There are passages to the right and passages to the left, but no exit sign. [...] I touch the shoulder of the man walking in front of me. I say: 'I want the way out.' But he points to the placards and his hand is made of steel.
>
> (Part 1)

In Emily Dickinson power has a face of steel. The inexorably pointing steel hand suggests that Sasha's life and its anxious needs are not hers to control but in the hands of men. Wanting not to be seen and to see nothing, Sasha is also caught up in the larger political anxieties of the late 1930s, as the passages to the right and to the left suggest.

Determined not to make an exhibition of herself Sasha is inevitably reduced to an exhibit by bullying men, as in one of the most surreal and
also cruelly painful of all the scenes, an extended memory of working in
a prestigious Parisian clothes-salon. In this novel, as elsewhere, Rhys is
acutely aware of the way women and their bodies (especially as human
mannequins) are objectified and commodified for perusal and profit. Sum-
moned for no good reason by the English owner Mr Blank, Sasha is sent on
a surreal mission into the bowels of his shop – an equivalent nightmare to
the earlier dream with corridors and no way out – and this blank of a thug
then reduces her to tears, as if in a cruel circus-ritual that she has to perform, as he cracks the whip. Composing herself, Sasha makes the angriest
political critique in Rhys' novels, a bitter denunciation of male economic
power – 'that's the right you hold most dearly, isn't it? You must be able to
despise the people you exploit'. But: 'Did I say all this? Of course I didn't.
I didn't even think it' (Part 1).

At the novel's centre is a narrative, or rather a narrative within a narrative, a story told by a French painter about living in Notting Hill in London
many years earlier. He hears a noise outside his room and finds a woman
('half-negro') crying on the ground outside his door. She asks for whisky
and she starts a long story, switching between French and English (so he
only partially understands her), about how she came from Martinique via
Paris, is now kept by a man on the top floor and is hated by everyone in the
house and the streets, to the point where she hadn't left the house for two
years, apart from at night. Then, that day, she had ventured out and a little
girl had called her a dirty and bad-smelling woman who had no right even
to be in the house. So she drinks a bottle of whisky in despair and collapses
outside the painter's door. He adds, with unerring self-regard, that he knew
all along that what she really wanted was for him to make love to her. 'But
alas, I couldn't'. So he gives her whisky and sends her away.

Within the layers of the narrative, inside Sasha's and then inside the painter's, is the rawest of stories in which access to this unnamed and unloved
woman is so difficult. The layerings and framings, and the unsympathetic
narrating painter, have the effect of shutting us out, making us complicit in
a process of dehumanising this drunk and embarrassing woman, making
an exhibition of herself, despite telling herself not to go out except after
dark. This is woman as 'othered' in every sense. It's also a version of Bertha
in *Jane Eyre*, the woman as dark secret, taken from the colonies and in effect imprisoned on the top floor in the big English house in which she guiltily emerges at night. It's also, more ironically, a version of Sasha, who partly
and not very sympathetically recognises the woman in herself (she wonders
if the painter is getting at her in this story of a woman who drinks and is
embarrassing), and (in effect in mirror-image) a version of Jean Rhys who,
as a child, wanted to be black because she was cruelly taunted by the black
children in Dominica. All these appropriations and framings exert pressure
on the narrative presentation of this actual woman, whose post-colonial

story just needs to be listened to and who just needs sympathy, not sex (a haunting premonition of the end of the novel, about which I'll say no more), and this is confirmed after the painter's narrative when Sasha and a friend arrange the painter's canvases into a make-shift exhibition. But the canvases resist. 'They curl up; they don't want to go into frames' (Part 2).

Towards the end of the novel René and Sasha visit the Exhibition, the Paris International Exposition of the Arts and Technology of Modern Life, opened in mid-1937 and overshadowed by the increasingly edgy international situation. Ahead is the War (you'll recall that the novel was published in 1939) but we're also returned to the novel's opening dream with its anxious left/right choices: the Exhibition flaunts Russian and German pavilions on opposing sides of the Trocadéro. As Sasha and René enter by the Trocadéro, she is momentarily at peace, finding what she's always wanted in the 'cold, empty, beautiful' space. But in the novel's terrible last pages she has another vision, the world as a very different exhibit, one that again returns us to the opening dream, a vision of the world reduced to a huge steel machine set against a terrifying grey sky. (After thinking about this vision, you might like to look at some images of paintings from the period by Yves Tanguy, whose work seems to me very pertinent here.)

All that is left in the world is an enormous machine, made of white steel. It has innumerable flexible arms, made of steel. Long, thin arms. At the end of each arm is an eye, the eyelashes stiff with mascara [...] Only some of the arms have these eyes – others have lights.

(Part 4)

In the works of Jean Rhys, machines crush. But there's nothing in her work as terrifying as that machine, constructed out of fetishised women's eyes, stiff with the numberless gazes they've suffered, and lights of surveillance to search and pry into the lives exposed to the blankly grey skies that offer no hiding-place.

Shortly after Sasha meets René, he stops and stares at her and says how he must be hallucinating because walking with her makes him feel he's not with an adult but a child. What makes Jean Rhys' work so distinctive, and so unsettling, is that she has at once the unblinking insight and unarmed vulnerability of a child. René was right; and although his remark leads Sasha to the edge of crying she doesn't contradict him or show any surprise (remember she's in her late thirties). This may be the most mutedly telling moment of self-revelation, showing a different level of self-knowledge, in all the Rhys texts. Sasha, we heard earlier in this lecture, says she had never really been young but we can read that as an admission of always being held in as-if suspended childhood, one in which growing into youthfulness has been impossible.

At the end of her biography Carol Angier urges the determining influence, above all else, of the 'failure of relation between mother and child'

(Angier: 657) in what became of Rhys as a woman and a woman-writer. The biographical details touched on earlier in this lecture, the evidence of her notebooks and of 'Good-bye Marcus, Good-bye Rose', suggest a freighted sense of internalised guilt and self-punishing, self-fulfilling un-happiness, the child's saddest burden. I'm not at all sure that never properly becoming an adult (a Beckett character talks of never having been properly born) made Jean Rhys any more or less happy but it made her the writer she became.

Thank you.

Further Reading

Carole Angier, *Jean Rhys* (Penguin: 1992).

Helen Carr, *Jean Rhys* (Writers and Their Work series: Northcote House: 1996).

Nancy R. Harrison, *Jean Rhys and the Novel as Women's Text* (University of North Carolina Press: 1988).

Richard Jacobs, *A Beginner's Guide to Critical Reading: An Anthology of Literary Texts* (Routledge: 2001).

Erica L. Johnson and Patricia Moran edd., *Jean Rhys: 21ˢᵗ Century Approaches* (Edinburgh U.P.: 2015).

Sylvia Maurel, *Jean Rhys* (Macmillan: 1998).

Toril Moi, *Sexual/Textual Politics* (Methuen: 1985).

Jean Rhys, *After Leaving Mr Mackenzie*; *Good Morning, Midnight*; *Sleep It Off Lady* (Penguin: 1969, 1969, 1979).

15 *Twelfth Night*
Dream-Gift

'Dream-Gift' – let's call it that, the last of the Shakespeare lectures in this book, and let's listen first to Olivia in her surreptitious excitement about Cesario. 'I have sent after him: he says he'll come; / How shall I feast him? what bestow of him? / For youth is bought more oft than begged or borrowed' (Act 3, Sc. 4).

For youth is bought more oft than begged or borrowed. Youth is bought: Olivia and Orsino buy their youth, their arrested youthfulness and they pay in the delusions and illusions by which, like Antonio, they make pleasure of their pains. And, as Feste observes, 'pleasure will be paid, one time or another' (Act 2, Sc. 4). They pay in their own suffering and, more, in the suffering they exact from others, notably from Viola and Malvolio. The youthfulness bought is expensively paid for. The money and the gifts in circulation, gifts not disinterested, gifts exchanged in unequal exchanges, are visual reminders of this expenditure, to keep the play's protagonists young.

But 'youth is bought' refers also to the process (it's what Olivia assuredly 'means') whereby other people, young people, can be bought for one's pleasure, to meet, or to avoid meeting, certain needs and desires. 'How shall I feast him? What bestow of him?' Olivia will buy Cesario and his youthfulness by giving, bestowing on him – feasting him. She will provide him with feasts, sweetmeats, just as Antonio envisages Sebastian buying toys with his (Antonio's) money; she will watch him feasting on her wealth, thus allowing herself the illusion that she is giving herself, her sweetmeats, to him. 'How shall I feast him?' How shall I feed him? She will be sustaining him – feeding him to tumescence but not growing him up – and there is an additional sense in which Olivia requires to be eaten up by Cesario, feasted away, vanquished and digested. In the meantime she will be digesting nothing. She will wilt away by feasting on the idea of Cesario feasting: she will be eaten up by not eating, eating the air while he tastes her meat. This is how she will buy her youth, in a tissue of displacements of sexual need.

Youth is bought more oft than begged or borrowed. Part of our sense of Viola's imprisonment in the play's structures is the knowledge that both Olivia and Orsino want to buy her rather than know her, freely. 'I'll serve this duke' (Act 1, Sc. 2), she says; and, as Valentine rather sourly observes, her service ('already you are no stranger') is soon privileged over, more valuable than that of the other attendants (Act 1, Sc. 4). If Olivia pays her homoerotic desire in watching ('she made good view of me' (Act 2, Sc. 2)) and in the unequal giving of feasts (and of rings and jewels with pictures), Orsino pays his in talk, not of sexual desire, but of the loved object as a text, a book – the 'discourse' of his 'dear faith'. 'I have unclasped / To thee the book even of my secret soul.' In these alleged unburdenings Orsino buys his narcissistically pampering pleasure by hiring Cesario to help him stroke the unclasped book where his secret soul lies, in both senses. He pays for not having actually to stroke him (Cesario-Viola) or her (Viola-Cesario, who pays for it in secret anguish, for real). There's at least a grain of absurd truth in his claim to be 'best / When least in company'. Permanent attendants are required to read and fondle the unclasped book, but he can't handle the company who might want to handle or unclasp other parts of him or whose other parts ('thy small pipe', for instance) he might really want to fondle (Act 1, Sc. 4).

For all the exacting frenzy of her madness in love, Olivia wants Cesario – 'I would you were as I would have you be!' (Act 3, Sc. 1) – in as unequal a role, as exactingly as Orsino wants him. Giving away her virginity as a ring, her self as a picture in a jewel, she is spending love to be its victim, just as, though in her case more desperately, Orsino images himself as the victim to his own 'fell and cruel' desires. (Thus also his taste for music with a 'dying fall' (Act 1, Sc. 1).) Olivia too sees herself as prey, falling before the lion, if not the wolf: and what is especially, unbearably beautiful about Cesario is the 'contempt and anger of his lip' (Act 3, Sc. 1), the lip that Orsino, pretending to look at it, found 'smooth and rubious' (Act 1, Sc. 4). Orsino sees himself pursued and torn apart by the hounds of his desire; Olivia is torn apart by a quiveringly angry lip. Both want to be victim, to be hurt, to be ruled. Both, evidently, rule – but when Olivia says to Sebastian-Cesario 'would thou'ldst be ruled by me' it's symptomatically unclear what force the question holds: literal – will you? – or rhetorical – would you would? But in neither case is the reply, 'Madam, I will', the one that she expects (Act 4, Sc. 1). Behind the uncertainty is the unexpressed knowledge that Olivia wants and needs to be ruled – a source of her guilty feelings about Malvolio – and that she has to pretend the opposite. Orsino needs to be ruled, if only because he rules so ineptly, and nearly so tyrannically ('Why should I not... / Kill what I love?' (Act 5, Sc. 1)). Behind the pampering of his desires, more fell and cruel than he knows, is the need to kill what he loves, which in turn disguises the fear of being ruled by it. Both need to be loved and cannot admit to that need. It is the play's most characteristic strategy to displace this doubly hidden need and to locate it – 'I thank my stars, I am happy' – in Malvolio (Act 2, Sc. 5). I am happy. Nobody else in Shakespeare says those three words.

A chastening reminder of such needs, a standing rebuke to such relationships, is manifest in Antonio's love for Sebastian. The teasing line here (in apparently endorsing sexual orthodoxy) is the ending's claim that 'nature to her bias drew in that' (Act 5, Sc. 1), in drawing male (Sebastian) to female (Olivia). But the opposite inference is possible: nature's bias drawing Olivia to Viola. A bowl has lead bias to take it in a specific, predetermined direction. A bias in nature may only make paradoxical sense, may only be ambiguously appropriate to the play's dispersal of its sexual energies. Antonio, most 'naturally', that is least self-deludingly, wants to give himself, even his life away for his love. It is also characteristic of this play, where gifts are so problematic, that its least demanding and most open giver (his purse, despite Sebastian's evident uncertainty – 'why I your purse?' (Act 3, Sc. 3) – has only literal strings attached), that Antonio and he alone should be described as a thief. He stole Sebastian from a foamy grave, to give him life, service, and if possible everything else, all his without retention or restraint. This selfless giving ('If you will not murder me for my love, let me be thy servant' (Act 2, Sc. 1)) is, one might say, the only meaning he can find in the verb to 'live' where 'love' and 'give' merge anagrammatically in the higher term. (The main protagonists' names are in nicely anagrammatical collusion. And, to quote from an unpublished novel: Viola, inviolate, in flower.) His love is a rebuke to Orsino's and Olivia's – but his gift of knowing how to love can only be manifested in such forcefulness and clarity because the play declines to offer him the gift (or the chance to demonstrate or acquire it) of being loved, that more exacting gift from which Olivia and Orsino are in anxious retreat.

One of the play's more curious patterns invites us to examine Antonio in the light of the anonymous Captain. He, like Antonio, has a 'mind that suits / With this thy fair and outward character' and for cheering up Viola he's given gold and the promise ('I'll pay thee bounteously') of more (Act 1, Sc. 2). Antonio, like the Captain, brings the twin from the sea, a gift to Illyria, but Sebastian can only 'pay' with uncurrent thanks. Because of his selfless giving Antonio is arrested by Orsino's officers, locked up for bringing Sebastian to Illyria. In a bizarre parallel movement the Captain is reported at the end to be 'upon some action ... / now in durance, at Malvolio's suit' (Act 5, Sc. 1): for bringing Viola to Illyria he gets locked up by Olivia's officer. How precisely Malvolio manages to stalk the country locking up random strangers while in a dark house and bound remains unclear, but what is clear is the inference from this pattern: those who give and who are given to most openly, with no strings attached, most deservedly and freely, will have their freedom removed. The two figures who convey the new life into Illyria are arrested by the representatives of the two ruling figures, whose sexual maturation is arrested and which will only be freed from arrestedness by the newcomers, and only once their protectors are themselves freed from arrest.

Buying, begging, borrowing. Given our impression of Illyria as so irrecoverably on holiday that its currency must have been floated off the top of the gold standard, it's disconcerting how much money or the equivalent is exchanged. Feste, the claim to whose geographical loyalties appropriately wanders, is paid at large: but one character alone wants to, needs to pay him. Malvolio alone also needs to beg and borrow. Malvolio must beg to Feste from the cellerage where he has been 'propertied' – turned into a prop for younger actors to lean on, to learn the ropes from, into a bit of green-room lumber, part of the cultural furniture along with our father's ghost, into a sign for the display of ownership and prestige, commodified and frozen into the abstractions of his name (Ill Will, the Bad Lover) – beg, for 'candle, and pen, ink and paper'. In darkness he must beg for light, for means of communication. In his darkness and bound, writing is his last resort, as Maria's earlier writing of the spurious letter was his first resort, his first accession to happiness. He will pay, requite Feste for the means to get unpropertied, unleaned on, undehumanised, unpossessed. For they possess him by propertying him and displace that guilt by pretending that he is, in the other sense, possessed.

'Convey what I will set down to my lady: it shall advantage thee more than ever the bearing of letter did.' The buying is sealed at 'the highest degree' and as earnest of his seriousness, and sanity, Malvolio gives, unlike any of the play's other offerings in its literality, a disembodied bit of himself, of his body. 'By this hand' he is sane, and by that hand thus proffered to Feste (who presumably ignores it?) he will write, sanely (Act 4, Sc. 2). The writing 'savours', Orsino later remarks, as if wine-tasting it, 'not much of distraction'. But is the buying and begging and borrowing sealed by that hand? It is not. This letter skates, like Olivia's virginity-ring, across the play's surfaces. It is unsealed and read, not by Olivia but by Feste, who says he should have given it to her 'to-day morning' but didn't, read by him in a voice approximating to no body, tossed to Fabian, read out to the company. So much for begging, and for giving his hand, his handwriting, his 'character'. When Olivia at last looks at (reads?) the letter, and sees Malvolio, as if for the first time, she says 'Alas, Malvolio, this is not my writing, / Though, I confess, much like the character' (Act 5, Sc. 1). She means handwriting; the word records her uneasy consciousness that the treatment of Malvolio meant more, and was, in a sense, hers, in character.

The dark house is more than a bad dream; it is the nightmare of exile and loss. Nightmare is the obverse, the cellerage of every dream, as there is a dark house beneath every stage, however many boxtrees are on it, temporarily for *Twelfth Night* productions, however many handsome boys, immediately after Malvolio's ordeal, stand on it to announce that 'This is the air; that is the glorious sun' (Act 4, Sc. 3). It isn't, but there is a dark house under Sebastian's, all of their feet. And all dreams are nightmares in so far as we must waken from their poignancies to the attritions of everyday life.

'Poor lady, she were better love a dream' (Act 2, Sc. 2), says one twin; 'Or I am mad, or else this is a dream' (Act 4, Sc. 1), says the other. But the play's only literal dreaming, day-dreaming on stage, is (as usual) Malvolio's, his dream of sexual power, exercised 'having come from a day-bed, where I have left Olivia sleeping' (Act 2, Sc. 5). His literal daydream is the scape-goat burdened with all the other dreamings, the fantasies and delusions – not least Olivia's sleeping fears of awakened sexual power – and according to whose logic he can be locked up in a nightmare and bound. Anything to avoid anyone else admitting to fantasy.

The pervasive fantasy of the play, the dream for which Malvolio must be be-nightmared, is the paradox of youthfulness. For what is it to be full of youth? Youthfulness, like autumn (and we saw this in Keats' autumn), is process and transition, not stasis but change. To be filled with youth is to be both on vacation, and about to vacate, to empty. To know that you are full of youth is no longer to be young. Energy, spontaneity, emotional intensity can only be retrospectively attributed, recognised in loss. But *Twelfth Night* suspends the logic. It is full of youth but not in process, on vacation but not vacating, not in change but arrested in a May morning twelve days after Christmas, always already here and now. It is the dream of no-time (too late to go to bed now), no-place (let the garden door be shut), no-age (but I will never die). But it is a dream never quite able to be any of this. Time seeps in through the gaps in what isn't quite a sealed system, ruffling its still surface with unexpected reminders of stuff that will not endure – in Feste's songs; in the priest's lugubrious evidence, when the play is at its knottiest hyper-anxiety, of the two hours he has recently travelled, 'my watch hath told me, toward my grave' (Act 5, Sc. 1); in the first officer's cold interrup-tion of Antonio's account of devotion and rejection with 'What's that to us? The time goes by' (Act 3, Sc. 4); in the most expressive stage-direction in the canon, at the point when Olivia's passion and Viola's anguish are most rawly exposed, *Clock strikes* – and due west, with as much dignity on both sides as can be recovered, is the way towards age (Act 3, Sc. 1).

Such pressures towards dissolution notwithstanding, the dream of Illyria has a curious solidity and self-sufficiency. The world of ships and of ship-wrecks is effectively marginalised by the disarming tactic of evoking it only after the first scene has naturalised Orsino's fantasias. Everything outside the charmed Illyrian circle (perhaps even Titus' leg) is (as *The Tempest* has it) 'ten leagues beyond man's life' (Act 2, Sc. 1). The Illyrian dream is as our dreaming – recognisable, and odd; here, and somewhere else; full of me and you, needs and desires: very empty, very still, as we and desire tremble towards dissolution. Antonio, for whom, like Malvolio, the dream of de-votion turned into the nightmare of rejection, registers the precariousness as he tells how Sebastian 'grew a twenty years removed thing / While one would wink' (Act 5, Sc. 1). Not, assuredly, want to wink, because nobody in this play wants to wink, in fear of waking up. And nor do we.

Twelfth Night anticipates its own dissolution, its thirteenth day, its night. While it plays, it answers our need to believe that what we think we love we will have; what we don't know we desire will be nonetheless granted; that we will find identity and presence in fulfilment: but as dissolution threat-ens more insistently – and just as our grip on the closure of happy endings begins to fasten – its intimations are colder, of desire ever searching for an object ever beyond reach; of happy endings that are compromises, often at painful cost, usually not only to ourselves; of love as constituted in fictions and evasions, collusion and lack. The play knows this, knows that we know it, knows that we will for a time – the time it takes, for instance, to make ourselves believe that Orsino and Sebastian deserve Viola and Olivia – forget what we know, to let the charmed circle end in present joy, present laughter. When Sebastian strolls into the last scene, it is into a sudden plenitude of looking and recognition, a saturation of presence from which we cannot possibly make ourselves critically absent. This is the dream we all ache to have dreamed, the one where what we want, and know we can't have, will always be found.

But the play knows that we will be critical once we are made absent, once the couples have disappeared into the golden time to which we are now denied present access, that we will question the very nature of such fulfilments, and hear, more urgently than ever, the voice of Malvolio, the absented voice of loss and exclusion, of time's vengeance and the old world's changes. In the mean times of notorious abuse we may, if warily, take the gift of *Twelfth Night*: we need it because of the nature of our dreams and needs; we pay for it in our critical waking consciousness. All this *Twelfth Night* well knows, for it is the most dazzlingly-gifted play.

Thank you. This is one of the shortest lectures as, really, I just want you to love the play as much I do. For me it's always been the most complicatedly beautiful and moving of Shakespeare's plays. What it says about love is for me perhaps only matched by Geoffrey Hill's 'Songbook', the wonderful sequence of love poems from his 1968 book *King Log* so please read the 'Songbook' (in Hill 1985) – and, now I think about it, Hitchcock's *Vertigo* must be up there as well in its serial displacements and illusionary constructions in speaking of 'love' – and what these texts say about love is perhaps only otherwise equalled by Proust. And so I turn to Proust in our next (and next to last) lecture. Thanks!

Further Reading

Judith Butler, *Gender Trouble: Feminism and the Subversion of Identity* (Routledge: 1990).

Kate Chedgzoy, *Shakespeare, Feminism and Gender*, New Casebooks (Palgrave: 2000).

Juliet Dusinberre, *Shakespeare and the Nature of Women*, 2nd ed. (Macmillan: 1996).

Stephen Greenblatt, *Shakespearian Negotiations: The Circulation of Social Energy in Renaissance England* (Oxford U.P.: 1988).

Geoffrey Hill, *Collected Poems* (Penguin: 1985).

Jean Howard, *The Stage and Social Struggle in Early Modern England* (Routledge: 1993).

Lisa Jardine, *Still Harping on Daughters: Women and Drama in the Age of Shakespeare* (Prentice Hall: 1983).

Patricia Parker and Geoffrey Hartman edd., *Shakespeare and the Question of Theory* (Routledge: 1993).

Phyllis Rackin, *Shakespeare and Women* (Oxford U.P.: 2005).

William Shakespeare, *Twelfth Night* ed. Keir Elam (Arden 3rd series, Bloomsbury: 2014).

16 Please Read Proust

As the title suggests the penultimate lecture in this book (before we close the circle with Milton's *Paradise Lost*, returning us to the first lecture on the Fall) does something different. It's a plea to you, one that assumes that you're all inexperienced Proustians – that as many of you as possible, the readers that this book of lectures may be lucky enough to attract, take the life-changing and life-enhancing, but admittedly life-challenging, decision to read the greatest of all novels, Marcel Proust's *In Search of Lost Time* (to use the English title). Proust's novel (finished – as he proudly announced to his housekeeper Celeste Albaret – but not fully revised in 1921, and revisions would certainly have radically changed the last volumes) is some 3500 pages long, in seven volumes, usually packaged as six big books. So that's quite an ask that I'm asking.

Another personal note. As an Oxford student in the 1970s I was struck by how many of my gay friends were devotees of Proust and, more particularly, how their artistic tastes generally (as I now realise) were formed by and in imitation of the tastes of Proust's narrator (whom, following convention, I'll call Marcel, but there's no easy equivalence between narrator and author): in painting (early Italians like Giotto), in music (late Beethoven quartets – well, you'll know from the Keats lecture in this book that I was at least on the same page there – and, a bit more surprisingly, some lesser operas of Wagner as well as his great *Tristan*) and (Proust here as elsewhere following the art historian John Ruskin) everything to do with Venice. But, largely because I was lazy, I didn't read Proust in my six years at Oxford. The closest I got to him was a quotation I came across somewhere from Beckett's brilliant little 1931 book on Proust (I think the first) – where Beckett writes, with the characteristically acerbic *hauteur* of the 24-year-old genius, of 'that desert of loneliness and recrimination that men call love' (Beckett 1970: 38), which I carried around in my head as a talisman in my protractedly unhappy attempts at love (I suppose that's the word) in my (very protracted) adolescence.

Then, early in my teaching career, a friend gave me Scott Moncrieff's original English translation, completed in 1931, as he was upgrading to the first of two revisions of that translation, Terence Kilmartin's in 1981. It sat on my shelves for decades and then, for no reason that I can remember, I read it one summer when I was in my 50s. I loved it but found the English rather quaint and fusty. By then there was the 1992 second revision of Moncrieff (by D. J. Enright) which took on board further textual advances in the French original. This second revision of Moncrieff, now published by Vintage, became the standard, indeed the only English version until, to some surprise, Penguin announced in 2002 the first wholly new translation since Moncrieff, with different translators for each of the seven volumes. I bought the Penguin volumes some years after they came out and, just as an ex-student-friend was reading the Vintage version, read it and we compared experiences as we went along. It changed, as they say, my life. Better late than (etc.). So I've only read Proust twice which makes me a novice (though I've read many passages many times, especially the long section that I will be turning to soon for this lecture). As I write this, I'm about a third through my third complete reading.

A note before I go further. My French is more or less hopeless, so I can only help with the question as to which of the two current complete English versions to buy and read (the twice revised Moncrieff in Vintage – and another revision of Moncrieff is now underway from Yale – or the multiple-translators Penguin) by saying that Michael Wood, among the most subtle of modern critics, stated a clear preference for the Penguin version when he reviewed it. (Other readers found the sometimes clearly different approaches to the art of translation across the volumes a problem. This issue affects the first two volumes particularly. More on this below, with a recommended way of starting your Proust journey.) Both modern versions, particularly the Penguins, show how Proust's French was more racy and modern than was represented in the often creaky and over-elaborated Edwardian style of the Moncrieff version, which was also coy and evasive in sexual matters.

**

So how to get you to read Proust? There are many handbooks and guidebooks out there including Alain de Botton's *How Proust Will Change Your Life* (well, the book's title is appropriate; not sure about the rest of it, though) and Adam Watt's very helpful *Cambridge Introduction* and the more academic *Cambridge Companion*, the latter two done by proper Proustians unlike me. And, of course, there are the great critics and fellow-writers who very quickly recognised the astonishing nature of the novel, from Virginia Woolf who loved the novel from as early as 1922 (the last volumes in French, unrevised by Proust, weren't published till 1927), and who wrote to Roger Fry later about how she was amazed by how Proust had somehow 'solidified what has always escaped before' and of how she felt the 'vibration, saturation' and 'something sexual' in reading him (in Stern 1989: 120); to Eric Auerbach in 1925 who compared the sudden impact of the novel on the world as the casting of a spell, to Beckett in 1931 (mentioned above) and, most influential of these early voices, the chapter in Edmund Wilson's study (also from 1931) of symbolist literature, *Axel's Castle* (one typical insight: all the characters 'are sick with some form of the ideal' (Wilson 1931: 134)). A history of early and developing Proust criticism would be one approach.

But I decided to do something else – to try here to lure you into the novel by exploring one extended section, chosen to be (as if this might be possible) representative of the whole. But which section? I decided not to choose anything that gave too much away about the plot(s) and that meant avoiding some of the most famous and wonderful sections of the novel (including the deaths of certain key characters, one of which I refer to in the Introduction to this book). One candidate was the almost stand-alone 'Swann in Love' long section from the first volume, the source of much analysis and of a rather bad film (reviewed by a friend of mine as 'Not Swann, Not in Love'). This has recently been published in a stand-alone volume in Oxford World's Classics in a new translation by Brian Nelson. But I knew which section it was going to be before I worried about such things. It was going to be selected extracts from the 140 pages that form most of the last third of the second volume, *In the Shadow of Young Girls in Flower* (the Penguin version of the title). This volume is, in terms of narrative, rather more linear than others and the section I want to look at has a particular momentum which, despite the characteristic Proustian diversions and ruminations, makes it sufficiently self-contained for our purposes – though I hope it will also leave you with the desire to find out more. It also locks directly into the mainstream of the novel's many concerns, dealing as it does with the giddy disorientations of desire. I feel very close to this section of the novel and love it with a particular affection.

I want to add here that my quotations are from the Penguin translation by James Grieve which seems to me very expressive and graceful in English, as I hope these extracts make clear. I am extremely grateful to James Grieve for his most kind and generous permission to use these extracts and I also want to recommend warmly his no less excellent 1982 version of the first volume, *Swann's Way*, which at the time of writing is available free as a download from the Australian National University and is, for those lucky enough to have read it, a much more engaging read than Lydia Davis' very literal volume for Penguin. So my advice is to embark on your journey by reading James Grieve's versions of the first two volumes and then the rest of the Penguins. And just to add that all quotations below (which I won't reference separately) from *In the Shadow of Young Girls in Flower* are from Part Two: *Place-names, the Place*.

The sickly narrator, Marcel, who is here about 17, is staying on the Normandy coast in high-summer with his loved grandmother. He notices a 'little gang' of five or six girls (who internal evidence suggests are probably 15 – more on this below), at first undifferentiated in their charm and attractions, but in time and as he gets to know them, differentiated enough for him to focus his affections particularly on one, who we learn is an orphan called Albertine Simonet who's staying with her aunt in her villa. She becomes the focus of his love – but we'll see that focus waver and shift among the girls, especially in one wonderfully comic page, before settling again on her. This is the Albertine who, in later volumes and a little later in time, becomes the centre of Marcel's obsessive love in his home in Paris and that relationship, explored with scalpel-like precision in all its agonies, is the emotional heart of the entire great novel. (Edmund Wilson puts it very sharply: the Albertine story is 'the tragedy of the little we know and the little we are able to care about those persons we know best and for whom we care most' (Wilson 1931: 154).) These 140 pages delineate the arc of that early process with the girls generally, and with Albertine in particular, and contain highly characteristic reflections and acute observations about love, especially teenage love. As always in Proust the narrative occupies simultaneously a highly-charged moment by moment contemporaneity, as the teenage (but preternaturally acute as well as comically wrong-headed) Marcel experiences it, and the perspective of the later and mature writer whose development towards being the writer of the book in our hands is the unfolding and in effect retrospective story told by and within the novel.

But first a word about an issue that has come up or used to come up rather too regularly in Proust criticism, if I can put it like that. Many first-time readers of Proust will be, as I certainly was, amazed at the conviction and the insight with which the novel represents the thoughts, feelings and languages of its very considerable array of characters. The subtlety and precision of this representation of so many and such diverse characters, so richly and delicately nuanced, is one of the principal wonders of the novel. So it comes as a shock that some critics claim that Albertine (throughout the novel), and the girls in this early volume, are 'in fact' not 'really' girls but boys (the formula is sometimes 'boys with breasts tacked on') – and this is alleged to be the case on the grounds that Proust was gay. A version of this argument even surfaces in a very good stand-alone study of the first volume by Sheila Stern, when she says that when Proust transferred his own experience to what she calls a 'different sphere' he may fail to convince by emphasising 'an extreme of possessiveness which develops under threat, and is more rarely found in socially approved love-affairs' (Stern 1989: 16). Oh really?

The issue is admittedly complicated by the novel's fascinated interest in the range of sexual practices and tastes (including what it calls, in a volume title, perhaps not very happily, *Sodom and Gomorrah*, the former connoting male-homosexuality, the latter lesbianism) but it is the case that the Marcel-Albertine relationship is, as I've said, the quite brilliantly realised heart of the novel (I hope it won't be too obvious plot-spoilers to say that the 'Albertine' volumes are called *The Captive* and *The Fugitive*), and that

Albertine, throughout the whole novel, is vividly and bodily and psychologically dimensionalised. If she wasn't, Jacqueline Rose wouldn't have been able to write her recent novel *Albertine*, which I mention later and which tells the story from Albertine's point of view.

But it is also true, as argued in important recent work by Elisabeth Ladenson (especially in her book *Proust's Lesbianism*) in her countering of the 'actually, they're boys' argument, that lesbian love is, for the narrator, the most intensely and obsessively anxiety-laden site where love, in its most inscrutable and invisible way, flourishes but in the margins, the fantasies and wild speculations, the second- or even third-hand narrative-anecdotes of the novel, enragingly so for the narrator to the point of almost permanent paralysis and panic. It is nonetheless the site of the most properly satisfied, and simply satisfied, sexual love in the novel, the gay-male relations in contrast being marked by power-control, cruelty (though cruelty also attends a famous early lesbian scene) and unhappiness.

**

So let's start our account of Marcel at the sea-side in Balbec, on the Normandy coast, staying with his grandmother in the (very grand) Grand-Hôtel, seeing the little gang of girls on the beach for the first time. (For readers re-reading there's something very poignant about these pages: it's the initiating moment of the Albertine story.)

The girls are first perceived as 'a strange mass of moving colours' and like 'the odd gaggle of seagulls which turns up out of the blue to strut along the beach', and Marcel's 'inability to single out and recognise one or other of these girls' has the paradoxical effect of sending 'a ripple of harmonious imprecision through their group, the uninterrupted flow of a shared, unstable and elusive beauty'. That elusive instability later becomes the keynote of his relations with and perceptions of Albertine, including the minor but elusive matter of the exact location of her beauty-spot. Noticing, not without being charmed yet further, that the little gang made its way (in a very Proustian image drawn now from machines rather than birds) along the esplanade by 'forcing everyone who stood in their way to move aside, to give way as though to a locomotive bearing down upon them without the slightest likelihood that it would avoid pedestrians', as well as hearing some 'unlady-like' expressions, Marcel draws what he calls the 'plausible' hypothesis that these girls 'must be the extremely youthful girl-friends of racing cyclists' and that there's no possibility that they were 'chaste'. Plausibility, as we might expect, is later undermined in at least one of those assumptions.

Soon Marcel has individualised the girls, especially a bright-eyed cyclist (though she's not at first the girl he thinks he likes best: because, in a nice deflating observation, her hair is a different colour from that of his childhood love Gilberte) whose 'oblique, laughing glance' makes her seem 'obviously incapable of harbouring or offering a home to any notion of who or what I was', a perception that leads him to reflect on the 'black incognizable shadows of the ideas she forms' behind which she lies 'with her desires, her likes and dislikes, the power of her inscrutable and inexhaustible will'. This in turn leads to a revelation in Marcel's understanding. (Here as elsewhere I've had to abridge. Ellipses – ... – indicate my cuts.)

> I knew I could never possess the young cyclist, unless I could also possess what lay behind her eyes. My desire for her was desire for her whole life: a desire that was full of pain, because I sensed it was unobtainable, but also full of heady excitement, because what had been my life up to that moment had suddenly ceased to be all of life, had turned into a small corner of a great space opening up for me, which I longed to explore and which was composed of the lives led by these young girls, because what was laid out now before my eyes was that extension and potential multiplication of self that we know as happiness ... [And it was] my knowledge that, in the nature of the girls as in their every action, there was not one iota of an element that was known to me or that I could have access to, which had replaced my satiety of life by a thirst, akin to that of a drought-stricken land, for a life which my soul, having gone for ever without a single drop of it, would now absorb in great greedy draughts, letting it soak me to the roots.

The slippage here from desire for sexual possession, to desire for one person's 'whole life', to the 'multiplication of self' inherent in the desire to occupy the 'lives led by these young girls', despite or because of the sheer impossibility of any 'access to' anything about them, indicates the slippage, characteristic of Marcel's needs – as I'm sure we recognise in our own needs, especially the needs of our younger selves – between desire and the desire-for-desire, with its tendency to slip between love-objects that are, in a sense, random and content-free. There's a wonderful image a few pages later that sheds an oblique but very beautiful light on this matter, Marcel here thinking about the girls as flowers in bud.

> I knew perfectly well, having botanized so much among such young blossoms, that it would be impossible to come upon a bouquet of rarer varieties than these buds, which, as I looked at them now, decorated the line of the water with their gentle stems, like a garden-full of Carolina roses edging a cliff-top, where a whole stretch of ocean can fit between adjacent flowers, and a steamer is so slow to cover the flat blue line separating two stalks that an idling butterfly can loiter on a bloom which the ship's hull has long since passed, and is so sure of being first to reach the next flower that it can delay its departure until the moment when, between the vessel's bow and the nearest petal of the one towards which it is sailing, nothing remains but a tiny glowing gap of blue.

As Marcel begins to see more of the girls, he's faced with the issue of not knowing when or if he is going to see them and this worry is characteristically intensified.

> Then my initial uncertainty about whether I would see them or not on a particular day was aggravated by another, much more serious one, whether I would see them ever again – for all I knew, they might be leaving for America or returning to Paris. This was enough to make me begin to fall in love with them. Having a liking for someone is one thing; but to be afflicted with sadness, the feeling of something irreparable having happened, the anguish which all accompany the onset of love, what is necessary is the risk – which may even be the object to which passion in its fretfulness tries to cling, rather than to a person – of an impossibility.

The risk of impossibility constitutes the love (that can only be initiated when faced with its imminent loss) which, as we'll soon see with Marcel's love for Albertine, is always accompanied by a kind of wilful 'fretfulness'. Following very closely from that insight Marcel makes a crucial distinction.

> Loving them all, I was in love with none of them; and yet the possibility of meeting them was the only element of delight in my days, the only source of those hopes which make one feel capable of overcoming all obstacles, and which for me, if I did not see them, were often dashed and turned to rage ... They were what was always hovering agreeably in my thoughts, whenever I thought I was thinking of something else, or of nothing ... If I went to another town where I might meet them, it was the sea I looked forward to seeing. The most exclusive love for any person is always love for something else.

Increasingly and as the days pass Marcel's attention is focused on Albertine, but less for reasons of her attractions and more for her being the most enigmatic and, in her appearances, elusive of the group. Marcel gets to know the distinguished painter Elstir whose casual friendship with the girls, especially Albertine, is another reason for her being singled out. But a kind of nimbus of uncertainty, what Marcel notes now as the un-necessary relation between love's pain and Albertine, is an insistent pressure.

> Was it my initial hesitancy, my inability to choose among the different girls of the little gang, in each of whom was preserved something of the collective attractiveness that had first excited me, which added to the other causes ... [gave me] the freedom to not love her? Because it had wandered about among all her friends, before opting definitely for her, my love kept some 'slack' between it and the image of Albertine, enabling it, like a badly adjusted beam of light, to settle briefly on others

before returning to focus on her; the relation between the pain in my heart and the memory of Albertine did not seem a necessary one ...

And that 'un-necessary' relation attends a sharply comic scene when Elstir is chatting to the girls and expecting Marcel to join them, so he can be formally introduced at last. Instead Marcel (in a way that had me wincing in painful self-recognition and memories of my adolescence) intentionally stages what he calls a 'fiasco' of self-punishing, look-at-me pretending not to want to be looked at, as he pretends to be more interested in the window of an antique shop. He anticipates Elstir calling him over and intends to:

> put on the interrogative look which reveals not so much surprise as the desire to appear surprised ..., my expression a cold mask hiding annoyance at being dragged away from my study of old china, merely to be introduced to people whom I had no desire to know ... The certainty of being introduced to the girls had me not only feign indifference towards them, but feel it.

Elstir, understandably perplexed, doesn't call him over. 'It was a fiasco' – but, as Marcel says, the indifference to the girls was felt as well as feigned, such being the strategies of wrong-footing oneself in the un-necessary relations of love. Within a page or so Marcel is elaborating on how love and unattainability combine in powerfully generative ways.

> Love, mobile and pre-existing, focusses on the image of a certain woman simply because she will be almost certainly unobtainable. From then on, one thinks not so much about her, it being difficult to imagine her anyway, as about possible ways of getting to know her. A whole process of anxieties comes into play, which is enough to fixate our love on her, though she is the barely known object of it. Love having become immense, we never reflect on how small a part the woman herself plays in it ... [The] real Albertine was little more than an outline: everything else that had been added to her was of my own making, for our own contribution to our love – even if judged solely from the point of view of quantity – is greater than that of the person we love.

The insight that love is 'mobile and pre-existing' takes us back to the insight earlier that 'the most exclusive love for any person is always love for something else' and together these establish Proust as a Lacanian *par excellence*. Lacan said that love means giving something you haven't got to someone who doesn't want it. And he said, more elaborately, that love (desire) is what is left over after we subtract need (for example, for food or attention – or, I suppose, sex) from demand – demand always being the imperious call for unconditional love (from the mother). Love is the aching gap between need and demand and is not about finding a lover or a thing but about (can I put it like this?) enacting a process of 'love', turning a gap or wound into a narrative – whom do I love (whom shall I love today?) to assuage the need to place and home (though it has no home, despite its home in the mother) what I do not and cannot have, that not-having in all its rich illusionism. Marcel's aching demand for his mother's unconditional love, and even more aching awareness that he cannot have it, is the keynote of the novel's great opening pages where the child is racked and ravaged by the thought that she will not grant him the longed-for goodnight-kiss. This lecture will end with a very differently considered kiss.

Anyway, a dozen or so pages later Marcel at last formally meets Albertine, at a reception that he has persuaded Elstir to hold. Though not a fiasco, it is a meeting that reprises, as if in a minor key, the comedy of the earlier scene. On arriving after the other guests, Marcel at first thinks Albertine isn't there, seeing only

> a young lady, sitting down, wearing a silk dress, bare-headed, but whose magnificent hair was unknown to me, as were her nose and complexion, in none of which could I recognise the being I had constructed out of a young girl walking along the esplanade, pushing a bicycle ... Albertine it was, however. Yet, even after realizing this, I paid no attention to her.

Instead he follows a route, claiming it to be 'not of my own design', of meeting other guests, eating, listening to the music, 'giving to these episodes the same importance as to my introduction to Mlle Simonet, which was only one among their sequence, and which I had by now completely forgotten had been, a few minutes before, the sole object of my presence there'. A particularly comic detail is that when Elstir specifically suggests going up to Albertine for the long-awaited meeting, Marcel finishes an eclair – and elaborately continues a fatuous conversation with 'an old gentleman, whom I had just met and to whom I saw fit to offer the rose he had admired in my button-hole, about certain agricultural shows in Normandy'. (I'm sure I'm not the first to say that this is a sly evocation of *Madame Bovary*, the scene in which Rodolphe starts to seduce Emma at the madly comic agricultural show.)

The friendship develops fitfully and with Albertine reluctant to introduce Marcel to the rest of the little band, though he gets to meet Andrée, who later emerges as crucial in the novel. But one of the other girls now makes an appearance and it's the occasion of what I think is the funniest thing in the volume, perhaps the funniest in the entire novel, a wonderful evocation of the violent vicissitudes of young love ('mobile and pre-existing'), with the most brilliantly deflating punchline or coda (in brackets). The girl is Gisèle, Albertine doesn't like or approve of her ('I can't stand it when she shows her hair like that, it's very unladylike') and when Gisèle approaches and greets the two of them on the beach Albertine is 'icily silent' to her and Marcel has to specifically ask to be introduced. Gisèle, with a dazzling smile,

> went straight to my head: I told myself she was just a shy girl in love, that she had stayed with us, despite being snubbed by Albertine, for my sake, for the love of me ... She must have noticed me down on the beach, at a time when I had no knowledge of her and must have been thinking about me ever since.

(Behind those 'she must have ...' you might hear, as I do, Emma on Harriet – the friends that 'must be doing her harm' – that we enjoyed in the *Emma* lecture when we looked at free indirect style.)

In the same scene (after Gisèle eventually gives up in the face of Albertine's repeated snubbing and walks off) Albertine lets slip that Gisèle is going back to Paris with her English governess that afternoon. Back at the hotel Marcel impatiently waits for his grandmother.

> I begged her to let me go off on an excursion, unexpected but not to be missed, which might last for up to forty-eight hours ... [I] ordered a carriage and was driven to the railway-station. Gisèle would not be surprised to see me; and once we had changed trains at Doncières, we would have a corridor-train to Paris: while the English governess dozed, I would have Gisèle all to myself, slipping off with her to dark corners and arranging times and places so that we could meet after my own return to Paris ... But whatever would she have thought, if I had known how long I had hesitated in my choice between her and her friends ... This thought filled me with remorse, now that Gisèle and I were to be joined together in a requited love. In any case, I could have assured her with total veracity that I was no longer attracted to Albertine ... While the coachman urged on his horse, I could hear Gisèle assuring me of her gratitude and tenderness, in words that were a direct translation of her lovely smile and ready handshake ...
>
> A few days later, despite Albertine's reluctance to bring us together, I had made the acquaintance of the whole group of girls I had seen on the first day, all of them having stayed on in Balbec (with the exception of Gisèle, whom I had been prevented from meeting at the station by a long delay at the barrier, whose train in any case had left five minutes early because the timetable had been changed, and who now could not have been further from my thoughts), plus two or three of their other friends whom I had asked to be introduced to.

The focus (of course) returns to Albertine especially after she writes him a note in front of all the other girls, saying to him '"Make sure no one can read this." I unfolded it and read the words she had written: *I like you*'.

The French is '*Je vous aime bien*'. Translations and discussions of this in English are various: 'I love you'; 'I do like you'; 'I like you very much'; 'I really like you. Don't you see?' William Carter, in his ongoing new revision of Moncrieff, has Moncrieff's 'I love you' and in his note points out that the French words can also range in meaning to include 'I really do like you' and 'I am fond of you'. He also notes that 'I love you' may 'make Albertine seem too bold, although she may be only teasing' (Carter 2015: 532), which doesn't seem right to me. Immediately after her words, and characteristically: '"Look here!" she shouted to Andrée and Rosemonde, turning suddenly impetuous and serious, "instead of sitting about writing silly things, why don't I show you this letter I got from Gisèle this morning".' Albertine's over-reaction there surely suggests that her note wasn't a tease.

A point about the girls' age, though it means further holding up the narrative again for a moment. Gisèle's letter is about the composition she had written for (in the French) her *certificat d'études*. James Grieve, in the Penguin version we're following, has 'for her fourth-form examination', pointing us, I think, to what the editors of the scholarly *Pléiade* French edition say about this examination: that it refers to the 'superior primary' certificate that in Proust's day was taken after the third-form in the *collèges*, in the year preceding transition to more advanced secondary study at the *lycées* – and taken typically at the age of 15. Carter confirms that this superior primary certificate was awarded at the point corresponding now to the end of the 8th Grade (the end of middle or junior-high school) in the American system, again at about 15. (Andrée, the oldest of these girls, has done hers and is therefore perhaps 16; Albertine is about to.) This certificate was part of the Republic's efforts from the 1880s (and these scenes in the Proust must be set in the later 1890s) to make the education of middle-class girls more equivalent to that for boys.

But Rose's novel *Albertine* goes out of its way to invent a scene in which Albertine meets Andrée for the first time at the start of her *lycée* years (aged 16). In the Proust they've clearly known each other for years before the action of this part of the novel which means that, for Rose, Albertine must be at least 18. But the evidence from the *Pléiade* edition seems to point to Albertine, like Gisèle, being 15, which, for me at least, feels right. It fits both with the girliness of the group's games (one of which is detailed below), with Albertine's casual comment that she and the other girls should stick with each other and aren't meant to have 'gentleman-friends' – but also with Marcel's earlier guess, mentioned earlier, that the girls were the 'extremely youthful', lower-middle-class (he's wrong there) and unchaste (wrong? I'll leave that one there) girlfriends of racing-cyclists. That is, aged 15 these girls are in a suggestively ambiguous space between childhood and adulthood (in, Marcel says, the adolescence which he has only recently left himself) and this is important later – as well as applying to how Marcel himself is represented in these pages (joining in with the childish games;

visiting a brothel). But this issue of the girls' age (and the narrator's) is perhaps deliberately uncertain, as James Grieve put it to me (in correspondence quoted with permission): 'The gang of girls show the same designed, or possibly undesigned, indeterminacy of age. The uncertainty of their ages can be seen as part of a larger design. It's just that at times it reads as improvisation rather than as design.' A last point about this is that the French title for the volume refers to the young girls as being *en fleurs*: this was apparently taken by Moncrieff to be suggesting puberty (the ambiguous space, though earlier than 15 in Proust's day) which made him translate the volume's title very coyly and very freely as *Within a Budding Grove*, as even today for Vintage.

Anyway, now back to our narrative, which is nearing its climax. Even after receiving her note, and reflecting that she 'was the one who would be the great love of my life', Marcel is aware that the symptoms 'which we usually interpret as meaning we are in love' (including – wonderfully – 'rage on those days if I had been unable to find a barber to shave me and was obliged to appear unkempt to the eyes of Albertine, Rosemonde or Andrée') pertain not just to Albertine, and that the 'loving state' and the 'sweetest joy in life' permeated the whole group of girls, making it impossible for him to know 'which of them I most longed to love'.

> At the very beginning of love, as at its end, we are not exclusively attached to a single beloved: it is the yearning to love, of which that person will be the loved outcome, and later the echo left in the memory, which wanders voluptuously in a place full of charms – sometimes deriving only from contingencies of nature, bodily pleasures or habitation – interchangeable and inter-related enough for it to feel in harmony with any of them. Also, since my perceptions of the girls were at that time unsated by habit, whenever I was with them I was still able to see them, that is to be profoundly surprised by setting eyes on them.

But what Marcel calls the 'harmony of cohesion' merging the girls into one entity is 'disturbed in Albertine's favour one afternoon during a game of ring-on-a-string' – though it ends in sharp pain. Seeing the chance from the game of touching her hands, reflecting (though presumably in retrospect) that 'a squeeze from the hand of Albertine had a sensual softness which ... made you feel as though you were penetrating her, entering the primacy of her senses', anticipating how holding and pressing her hands would mark the 'first steps towards sensuous delight', and then, in the game as it develops, sensing at last 'a tiny squeeze of Albertine's hand on mine, a faint caress of her finger between my own', his joy is then immediately and savagely cut off by a 'furious' whisper from Albertine – '"Take the thing, would you! I've been trying to pass it to you for about half an hour"' – leaving him, after he fails to take the ring, 'desperate and despised, the butt of all the girls' scorn, trying to laugh it off when I felt like crying' and having to hear

Albertine say to Andrée, '"People that don't want to play properly or just try to spoil it for the others shouldn't play. Next time we play this, Andrée, we'll just make sure he doesn't come. Or if he does come, then I shan't"'.

For a week Marcel 'made little attempt to see Albertine. I pretended to prefer Andrée' (who had, with characteristic kindness, come to his rescue after the debacle of the game). He feels stuck in the 'infallible logic of love ... making it as impossible for us not to love as it is inevitable that we remain unloved'. But a very surprising development suddenly comes in the form of an amazing stroke of luck. Finding himself for a few moments alone with Albertine on the esplanade, she casually draws attention to her hair (while blushing: he immediately wants to taste those cheeks) – '"I'm doing my hair now the way you like it – look at this ringlet. Everyone makes fun of it and nobody knows who it is I'm doing it for"' – and she confirms that, because she has an early train to catch the next day, she will be staying alone at his hotel that night. '"So you can come up and sit by my bedside while I'm having my dinner. Then we can play at something, whatever you like ... We can have an evening together ... Come soon, so's we can have a nice long time all to ourselves", she added with a smile'.

After dinner with his grandmother Marcel approaches Albertine's hotel-room.

> In the corridor, I was only a few paces away from the bedroom inside which lay the precious substance of her pink body – ... a few steps that no one could now prevent me from taking, and which, as though I was walking in a new element, as though what moved slowly aside to let me through was happiness itself, I took in a mood of utmost bliss and attentiveness ... of at last coming to claim an inheritance which had always been meant for me ... I found Albertine in bed. Her white nightgown bared her throat ... I thought of the colours I had seen close at hand a few hours before on the esplanade, and which were now going to reveal their taste ... She smiled at me ... The sea, which through the window could be seen beside the valley, the swelling breasts of the closest of the Maineville cliffs, the sky where the moon had not yet reached the zenith, all of this seemed to lie as light as feathers between my eyelids, at rest upon eyeballs in which I felt the pupils had expanded and become strong enough, and ready, to hold much heavier burdens, all the mountains in the world, on their delicate surface ... I leaned over to kiss Albertine. Had death chosen that instant to strike me down, it would have been a matter of indifference to me, or rather it would have seemed impossible, for life did not reside somewhere outside me: all of life was contained within me. A pitying smile would have been my only response, had a philosopher put the view ... that after my own extinction there would continue to be swelling-breasted cliffs, a sea, a sky and moonlight. How could such a thing be possible?

There are no cliff-hangers in Proust, but I've just left you on one as a final, if unfair, inducement to read him. And to calm us all down after that erotically amazing moment let me end with another recommendation. Once you've read all of Proust do read the best book on the novel, the late Malcolm Bowie's quite brilliant *Proust Among the Stars*. You'll recall that very much less good critics say or used to say that Albertine and the other girls are 'really' boys (or boys with tacked-on breasts). Edmund Wilson was in no doubt that Marcel loves young women's bodies, you have just heard how Albertine's swelling breasts are evoked (twice) in the landscape, and Bowie says this:

> Albertine's breasts are nowhere named here but their shape is rediscovered in the cliffs, the moon, the wide horizon of the sea and the ball of the narrator's inquisitively distended eye ... Sexual arousal, and the imminence of a promised pleasure, combine to produce a heady sense of omnipotence: the deepest secrets of the natural world are already within the narrator's grasp; knowledge of them beats with his pulses.
>
> (Bowie 1998: 220–21)

So with Marcel's pulses beating with the imminence of that promised pleasure, as he leans over to kiss Albertine, I'll say thanks for listening and goodbye. The next lecture is the last lecture and then it really is goodbye.

Further Reading

[A note on translations. I've said above that, like many others, I recommend the 2002 Penguin edition to the other complete English version, the twice-revised Scott Moncrieff Vintage edition of 1992. But I recommend James Grieve's 1982 version of the first volume, *Swann's Way*, over Lydia Davis for Penguin. There are copyright issues in the USA which mean that only some of the Penguin volumes are freely available there at the time of writing. Also as I write, the first three volumes of a new version by William C. Carter have been published by Yale U.P. (2013, 2015, 2019). These have received mixed reviews and, though 'new', are fresh revisions of Scott Moncrieff, so not 'new' in the sense that the Penguin volumes (and James Grieve's *Swann's Way* – and Brian Nelson's *Swann in Love*, part of *Swann's Way*) are new. In this book I've regularly recommended the Norton Critical Editions: their *Swann's Way* (ed. Susanna Lee 2003) is as usual full of excellent contextual and critical materials but please note that the translation is the unrevised Scott Moncrieff so sadly can't be recommended.]

Celeste Albaret, *Monsieur Proust*, trs. Barbara Bray (William Collins: 1976).
Samuel Beckett, *Proust* (Grove Press: 1970).
Malcom Bowie, *Proust Among the Stars* (Columbia U.P.: 1998).
Elisabeth Ladenson, *Proust's Lesbianism* (Cornell U.P.: 1999).
Marcel Proust, *In Search of Lost Time*, ed. Christopher Prendergast (6 Volumes, Penguin: 2002).

Marcel Proust, *Swann's Way*, trs. James Grieve (Australian National University: 1982. Available online.)

Marcel Proust, *In the Shadow of Young Girls in Flower*, trs. James Grieve (Penguin: 2002).

Marcel Proust, *Swann in Love*, trs. Brian Nelson (Oxford U.P.: 2017).

Jacqueline Rose, *Albertine* (Chatto and Windus: 2001).

Sheila Stern, *Marcel Proust: Swann's Way* (Cambridge U.P.: 1989).

Benjamin Taylor, *Proust: The Search* (Yale U.P.: 2015).

Adam Watt, *The Cambridge Introduction to Proust* (Cambridge U.P.: 2011).

Edmund Wilson, *Axel's Castle: A Study of the Imaginative Literature of 1870–1930* (Farrar, Straus and Giroux: 2004).

17 *Paradise Lost*
Radical Politics, Gender and Education

Let me start with a very simple point which I made more elaborately in the first lecture in this series (the one on the myth of the Fall and its impact, to which this final lecture in the series returns): loss is structured deeply into our psychic lives. To be conscious is to be conscious of loss. The post-Freudian analyst Jacques Lacan built a massive apparatus of subtle argument from the foundational insight that the infant matures having to negotiate a series of wounding separations from the mother. We have all lost that Paradise. In Proust's famous formulation, the only Paradise we have is the one we have lost.

Another fundamental loss takes me back to what I spoke about in the Sherlock Holmes lecture: the fatuous rhyme I had to learn at boarding-school aged eight which left out (intentionally) the facts of the English Revolution of the 1640s, the civil war, the abolition of the monarchy, the republic and Commonwealth – facts that the collective memory of conservative England, even today, prefers to forget. We have, in effect, 'lost' the crucial republican years – and the relevant point here is that Milton was absolutely central in those tumultuous events. The English republic and Commonwealth years are rarely taught in English schools and I'll have more to say about education later. The English Revolution (150 years before the more famous French one) is like an embarrassment, something un-English, too 'European'.

I'm writing this lecture in the midst of Brexit hostilities in the UK; for right-wing newspapers in this country (that is, almost all of them) to be anti-Brexit or pro-European or even to be senior judges upholding constitutional law is to be a traitor, an enemy of the people or a saboteur needing to be crushed. (Those terms are all from front-pages of my country's newspapers, the worst in the Western world for stirring up hatred, and for which I feel a kind of numbing and powerless shame.) It's worth a mention that in 1988 there was widespread media and public commemoration of the anniversary of 1688 when the 'glorious revolution' stabilised relations between the restored monarchy and parliament. In 1999, 350 years after the Revolution and execution of Charles I in 1649, there was just predictably deafening silence. This collective forgetting is equivalent to the attempt, in some quarters and as I'll describe later, to wish *Paradise Lost* away, to edit it out of literary history, or to side-line it, as the English Revolution is edited or side-lined out of actual history.

The loss is personal: *Paradise Lost* arouses strong personal responses, especially from critics opposed to Milton. That these have included figures of such influence as T.S. Eliot, F.R. Leavis and Ezra Pound (who charmingly called Milton asinine) is a serious business and I'll return to it. Just to say now that there may well have been personal reasons for these antagonisms, particularly for T.S. Eliot who (sort of) had second thoughts.

Another point about the personal issue. When we think about the protagonists of the poem, of course we think (but in what order?) of Adam, Eve and Satan. God, the other fallen and unfallen angels, and the Son come way behind those first three. But we need to include Milton himself. Quite unlike in the impersonal neutrality of the voice in classical epic poetry Milton puts himself, vulnerably and movingly, in his blindness, into his poem. He's there as both the inspired prophet and, like his readers, fallen in loss, in his case the personalised loss of sight, and isolated in post-Restoration England. His voice and presence are everywhere felt but most obviously in passages such as this from Book 3 which I'd like to share.

> Thus with the year
> Seasons return; but not to me returns
> Day, or the sweet approach of even or morn,
> Or sight of vernal bloom, or summer's rose,
> Or flocks, or herds, or human face divine;
> But cloud instead, and ever-during dark
> Surrounds me, from the cheerful ways of men
> Cut off, and for the book of knowledge fair
> Presented with a universal blank
> Of nature's works to me expunged and razed,
> And wisdom at one entrance quite shut out.

As one of the protagonists Milton is emotionally invested with the others, especially Eve and Satan. It's no accident that he makes Eve such a gifted and artful poet (the only poet in the poem): Milton's own liberal-humanist education led him to argue (in *Of Education* 1644) for the centrality of poetry in the curriculum (we need him now), poetry being more 'simple, sensuous and passionate' than the more traditional subjects like logic or rhetoric (in Patrides ed. 1974: 191). And Milton's identification with Satan, which Blake was the first to see and to articulate, has roots in their shared ambitiousness, awareness of dangers and likely defeat, their sense of solitude and solitariness, turned in on themselves, their sharply felt responsiveness to light and darkness, and the two of them being driven by intense creativity and proud authorship.

**

Let me fill in some simple background points. (Just to say here that this lecture is indebted to many critical landmarks, especially David Loewenstein's very good modern book on the poem, as well as A. J. A. Waldock's close reading from the 1940s.) After a humanist education at St Paul's School in London and after Cambridge (which disappointed him) Milton devoted himself to voraciously ambitious reading and self-study in classical and contemporary literature, history, politics and theology in several languages, including Hebrew, Greek, Latin and Italian, and sought out meetings with prominent continental figures such as Galileo. From the 1620s he was driven by a sense of his literary vocation, as if his prophetically appointed destiny was to write an epic on a heroic, national or biblical topic, but on a new scale of ambition, what he called in Book 1 of the poem 'Things unattempted yet in prose or rhyme'. Epic was at the apex of all renaissance genres (which were hierarchically ranked), the most prestigious because most comprehensive and ambitious, though *Paradise Lost* also draws, as we'll see, on Shakespearian tragedy (early plans were for a tragedy) as well as consciously wanting to out-do his predecessor in English epic, Spenser's pastoral-nationalist *Fairy Queen*.

In the revolutionary and civil war years of the 1640s and then the Commonwealth years of the 1650s Milton was engaged in fierce pamphleteering (he published no poetry between 1645 and the first edition of *Paradise Lost* in 1667) – against the oppressive and corrupt clergy, against royalism and monarchy, against censorship, for divorce, for the execution of Charles, always in defence of the Commonwealth, above all for liberty. The vigilant defence of the cause of liberty was for Milton a vocation for which he felt divinely chosen, picked out to justify the English people's republic. In words that point directly to pre-French revolutionary thinking, Milton famously wrote, in *The Tenure of Kings and Magistrates* of 1649, that 'no man who knows aught [= anything] can be so stupid to deny that all men naturally were born free' (in Patrides: 255).

Milton was appointed Cromwell's secretary for foreign languages in the momentous year of 1649; was totally blind by 1652; went into hiding in 1660 after defiantly publishing the last of his pro-Commonwealth pamphlets just as the monarchy was restored; and later in the year was arrested, briefly imprisoned, and then released. He was lucky to escape with his life: the poet Andrew Marvell, MP for Hull, his friend, might have worked to protect him; Milton's very formidable reputation on the Continent might also have helped. He died in 1674 just before the expanded second edition of *Paradise Lost* was published.

Let me add a word on Milton's role in the ferment of the 1640s and 1650s. Milton was driven by the notion that, in Blake's words, 'without contraries is no progression', that social change is only possible through trial and confrontation. Milton said that what 'purifies us is trial and trial is by what is contrary'. As David Loewenstein puts it, progress is by 'challenging and disrupting tyrannical custom, mindless conformity and old orthodoxies'.

Milton sees truth as dynamic, flowing in what he called 'perpetual progression' (Loewenstein: 13–14) – and we might see there a connection to
Milton's perpetually progressing syntax across the landscape of his verse.

**

Milton's insistence on the dynamic of conflict against tradition is reproduced in the place of the poem in education and critical history. Milton
himself hoped that the role of education would be to 'repair the ruins of
our first parents' (Patrides: 182). (I'm not sure how many recent Conservative secretaries of state for education would nod their heads over that.)
The first battle over the poem was, bizarrely, over its style, whether it's
even in English at all. Not many minutes ago I read you a passage from the
poem in which Milton reflected on his blindness which I'm sure you found
marvellously supple, dynamic and musical in its rhythms and larger structures. You'll be surprised (I hope) to learn that the very influential 1930s
critic F.R. Leavis accused Milton of writing in a monotonous and heavily
predictable language, wilfully disregarding the true nature of English and
sacrificing any possibility of delicacy or subtlety. For Leavis, the language
of the poem is more like laying bricks than writing real poetry.

Leavis was at one with T.S. Eliot in attacking the poem and it's pretty
clear, in Eliot's case especially, that their focus on the poem's language
(Eliot's charges include Milton deteriorating the language and thereby exercising an influence on later poets that could only be for the worse) is standing in for unstated but broader antagonism towards the poem's politics
and unorthodox religion which Eliot (as an Anglo-Catholic royalist) particularly disliked. The larger purpose was also to displace or dislodge the
poem from its place on the English school curriculum and in that respect
they were successful, though Milton's perceived 'difficulty' (much more apparent than real) had its role to play in that. Only a few years before I took
the post-16 English literature exams Milton was dropped from compulsory
study at that level, leaving only Chaucer and Shakespeare (and Chaucer
didn't survive that much longer).

But even on language the attacks are far too narrow and partisan. The
claim that the language of the poem is mechanical, artificial, remote and
dead (Milton, more than any poet, was very sensitive to the dynamics
between Latinate and Anglo-Saxon diction) was effectively answered by
Christopher Ricks in his book *Milton's Grand Style* which explored the
poem's language as subtle, complex, sensuous and musical, and richly aware
of the need to try to return language to a state of (as if unfallen) rootedness.
Milton, again more than any other poet, hears and feels words back to their
roots and origins, and plays off the varying layers of each word's history.

What the poem's detractors unwittingly point to is that *Paradise Lost*,
like *Frankenstein* (its obvious progeny), is a conflicted text – and therefore
a contested text. I mean that there are contradictory energies in the poem,

a dialectic between the orthodox Christian story apparently being told (as if on the surface) and the radical and subversive elements that may be less obvious but are nonetheless working steadily away, not necessarily always conscious on Milton's part. This tension allows the poem to be read in contradictory ways and the Eliot/Leavis way is one side of the equation. Also on that side, and long assumed to be the only way of reading it in, say, British secondary education, is to see the poem as coming out of Milton's post-Restoration despair, sense of defeat and withdrawal from public controversy into resigned and orthodox Christianity, in a kind of disillusioned acceptance of monarchical authority (God's in the poem). This view was very widely propagated in a book called *A Preface to Paradise Lost* by (oh, look, here he is again) C.S. Lewis.

The counter-reading may be said to have its roots in Blake's insight that Milton was 'of the devil's party', that is, more instinctively sympathetic to Satan than to God, identifying in Satan's ambitious battle against arbitrary and oppressive authority (for Satan, God; for Milton, Charles) what he fought for himself in the revolutionary years. William Empson's splendidly angry *Milton's God* attacked the Christian readings head-on. The radical historian Christopher Hill, in his *Milton and the English Revolution*, argued strongly that the poem was deeply implicated in Milton's revolutionary instincts, Hill's influence is clear on important modern critics like David Norbrook and Annabel Patterson, and these counter-readings can be said to reach a kind of popular head in the Philip Pullman trilogy *His Dark Materials* (the title is from the poem) which, in relation to Lewis' 'Narnia' books, I spoke about in the first lecture.

This reading of the poem, responding to its radical and subversive energies, those that 'institutional Christianity represses' (Loewenstein: 126), recognises that *Paradise Lost*, at its paradoxical heart, undermines and questions the nature of the Fall itself. Let me move now to some examples of how this happens in the poem. Here are six points, the first three of which I need to pass over quickly, leaving the later three for fuller illustration.

The first is that Milton insists that Adam and Eve have a sex-life before the Fall, that their love-making in their 'bower' starts when they met. According to Adam in Book 8, when Eve was brought to him she was, though modesty itself, not 'uninformed / Of nuptial sanctity and marriage rites' which could only mean she knew how to make love. Milton explicitly contrasts their happy, trouble-free love-making ('wedded love') to the cynical and exploitative 'court amours' of post-Restoration sexual licence. Of course, the traditional reading of Genesis is that sex (shameful and dirty) came into the world at and as a consequence of the Fall. Milton's insistence is a very radical departure. (After the Fall their love-making is, as it were, fallen: guilty and leading to mutually recriminating argument – in a word, post-Restoration. And I'll just note here that it is Eve, not Adam, who initiates their reconciliation, a point made by Diane K. Mccolley in an excellent chapter on Milton and the sexes in the Milton Cambridge Companion.)

Related is my next point, though it's less momentous. When Adam, later in Book 8, is rebuked by the arch-angel Raphael for placing too much importance on Eve's beauty and sexual desirability he dares answering back by enquiring whether angels make love. Yes, but (I paraphrase) with no troubling membranes to get in the way. Philip Pullman's neat inversion of this is that his Regent-Angel Metatron admits to envying humans for their fleshly opportunities in sex.

The third point needs a full-length study to demonstrate properly. It is that the three protagonists, Satan, Adam and Eve, are patterned together in symmetrical and asymmetrical desires, vulnerabilities and fears that regularly evoke the humanist anxieties of Shakespearean tragedy. For many readers this emphasis on humanist interactions and mutual dependencies, an emphasis that places Satan at the ironic centre and as the most fully realised 'human' in the poem (most activated and motivated by complex human feelings, some contradictory), is what marks out *Paradise Lost* as a tragedy more than an epic.

Next is the poem's emphasis, not emphatically made and perhaps not very conscious on Milton's part, but still there and very radical, on Eve's autonomous powers, especially her sexuality. (This is what connects the poem to the autonomous sexualities presented by the transgressive American women I talked about in earlier lectures.) Let me say more about this – and admit now that in the limited time I have here in this lecture my focus will be more on Eve than the other two protagonists. The emphasis on Eve's autonomy, especially her autonomous sexuality, has the effect of undermining the orthodox re-telling of the Fall.

It has often been observed that the opening descriptions of Adam and Eve in Book 4 (seen through Satan's eyes) contain conflicted materials about Eve. The main emphasis, unsurprisingly, is on Eve's inferiority and her lower status, in line with the Pauline doctrine of the male being the head of the woman: 'For contemplation he and valour formed; / For softness she and sweet attractive grace; / He for God only, she for God in him'. But there's a contrary suggestion of Eve's agency and awareness of the control and power in her body, wearing her hair 'as a veil, down to the slender waist' (veils attract attention to what they are apparently hiding), hair described as 'dishevelled' and 'in wanton ringlets' (a student of mine once called this 'bedroom hair'; 'wanton' means sexually activated), and Milton adds that she yields the expected Pauline subjection to Adam but 'with coy submission, modest pride, / And sweet, reluctant, amorous delay' – and all of those words (slowed by the commas) are delicately pulling in paradoxical directions ('coy', as in Marvell's 'Coy mistress' poem, suggests at once modest, shy and teasingly and seductively modest/shy) with the last four words hinting at the sexual power in simultaneously being 'sweet' and 'reluctant' and exercising an 'amorous delay'. This is a woman in charge of her own powers.

Later in Book 4 we have the amazing passage where Eve tells Adam her memories of waking up into life. She finds herself near a lake that she 'with unexperienced thought' goes to, looks into and sees what she takes to be 'another sky' and 'a shape ... bending to look on me' with 'answering looks / Of sympathy and love'. God (as we later discover) leads her from this vision of herself (which of course male critics have been quick to link to the Narcissus story with the aggressive idea that women are 'naturally' narcissistic) to take her to Adam, with the promise of his being 'no shadow' and with whom she will bear 'Multitudes like thyself, and thence be called / Mother of human race'. That's quite a tempting promise but, remarkably, once she sees Adam, admittedly 'fair indeed and tall', she assesses him as 'less fair, / Less winning soft, less amiably mild, / Than that smooth watery image' to which she now starts to turn back. Adam then claims her as his, on the (perhaps rather blackmailing?) grounds that 'to give thee being I lent / Out of my side to thee', at which (in Eve's words again) 'thy gentle hand / Seized mine' and she 'yielded'.

Twice in this passage we can hear Eve justifying Adam and God's arguments over her own instincts, having as it were internalised what she's later been 'taught': she says that at the lake she would have 'fixed / Mine eyes till now, and pined with vain desire' which she can't possibly have known or thought when actually at the lake; and she ends her account, after saying how Adam's 'gentle hand seized' hers (and how exactly can Adam have seized her hand gently?), by adding that she 'from that time see [an odd present tense when we expect 'saw': hinting at this later internalising of the message?] / How beauty is excelled by manly grace, / And wisdom, which alone is truly fair'.

At the very least we can be suspicious of these after-the-event lessons that Adam's exercise in early patriarchy has made her 'see'. We can also note the way the idea that she would have 'pined with vain desire' at the lake rather coercively prefigures Satan's nearly identical words forty lines later, watching Adam and Eve's sexy embrace (his bitter pun in seeing them 'Imparadised in one another's arms' is marvellously acute), and tormenting himself with his sharp awareness of his own permanent 'fierce desire ... Still unfulfilled ... with pain of longing pines', though this does, as I mentioned earlier as typical of the poem, bring Eve and Satan into a kind of textually patterned intimacy, one which allows him, at the climax of the action, to play successfully on her emotions at the tree. And it's intriguing that when, four books later, we hear Adam's version of these same events, there's nothing about her wanting to return to her own image or about his seizing her. There's perhaps some self-justifying editing going on there in Adam's account. But the one thing we can say with some confidence is that this passage opens out the critical space for the idea that Eve can be seen as completely justified in preferring her own autonomously pleasuring self to the less fair, less soft, less mild Adam, even with the promise of being mother of human race. Mother of human race? No, thank you.

I said that Eve is a great poet, the poem's only poet. Her autonomous power is of course as-if borrowed from Milton (who wrote her poem) but it's still a very radical stroke to grant her such creative gifts in artfully structuring, weaving together effortlessly this, a little later in Book 4, which I offer to you as the most beautifully made, the most touchingly self-effacing early modern love-poem.

> With thee conversing I forget all time;
> All seasons, and their change, all please alike.
> Sweet is the breath of morn, her rising sweet,
> With charm of earliest birds: pleasant the sun,
> When first on this delightful land he spreads
> His orient beams, on herb, tree, fruit, and flower,
> Glistering with dew; fragrant the fertile earth
> After soft showers; and sweet the coming on
> Of grateful evening mild; then silent night
> With this her solemn bird, and this fair moon,
> And these the gems of Heaven, her starry train:
> But neither breath of morn, when she ascends
> With charm of earliest birds; nor rising sun
> On this delightful land; nor herb, fruit, flower,
> Glistering with dew; nor fragrance after showers;
> Nor grateful evening mild; nor silent night,
> With this her solemn bird, nor walk by moon,
> Or glittering star-light, without thee is sweet.

Monotonous, heavily predictable, no delicacy or subtlety? Simple, sensuous, passionate.

In Book 5 that now follows, Eve describes to Adam her troubling dream, Milton's brilliantly imagined premonitory version of the Fall itself. This dream differs from the latter in its clear, and potentially shocking, emphasis on sexuality as both oral and autonomous. In Eve's dream (fed to her through her ear by Satan disguised as a toad – Hardy picks up this detail during *Tess* which I spoke about in an earlier lecture), she sees what she takes to be a routine angel gazing on the forbidden tree and saying 'O fair plant ... with fruit surcharged, / Deigns none to ease thy load, and taste thy sweet ...?', and that, even today, might shock many of you with its evocation of fellatio. This angel (of course, Satan) then tempts Eve with the fruit which, tasted, he says will make her 'henceforth among the Gods / Thyself a Goddess'. Eve takes up the narrative.

> So saying, he drew nigh, and to me held,
> Even to my mouth of that same fruit held part
> Which he had plucked; the pleasant savoury smell
> So quickened appetite, that I, methought,

Could not but taste. Forthwith up to the clouds
With him I flew, and underneath beheld
The earth outstretched immense, a prospect wide
And various: wondering at my flight and change
To this high exaltation ...

There's no need to say much about that flying-orgasm as it's as explicit as it
could be in the mid-17th century but you'll note that Hardy borrowed again
from this, as if spelling out its oral sexuality, when Alec makes Tess take
the strawberry from his hand into her mouth. I'd just add that 'exaltation'
may be an aural pun on 'exultation' which, in equivalently sexualised contexts (imaged as swimming or going to sea), we noticed in Kate Chopin and
Emily Dickinson.

There's one more vital moment to consider about Eve's autonomous
power and that's in Book 9 when, having eaten the apple and fallen herself, she weighs up in her mind the arguments for and against sharing the
knowledge with Adam. Doubtless she gives into some very human jealousy
(it humanises her yet further) when fearing that, if she doesn't and if she's
punished with death, Adam will become 'wedded to another Eve, / Shall
live with her enjoying', but the crucial thought is her idea that she may not
tell him because that could 'add what wants [= lacks] / In female sex... /
And render me more equal, and perhaps, / A thing not undesirable, some-
time / Superior: for inferior who is free?'

I hope I've said enough above about Milton's own core beliefs about liberty, his sense of being divinely appointed to defend liberty against oppression of any kind, and his simple assertion that nobody of sense can possibly
deny that we are all born free – well, we can all see that Eve's words 'for
inferior who is free?' echo to the very heart of all that drove this great poet
in his politics. Eve here voices Milton at his most transparent presence.
Just as she is Milton's chosen great poet, Eve here is Milton's chosen political thinker, as well, of course, as 'first' feminist. That Milton had perhaps
unconscious proto-feminist sympathies is inherent in everything I've said
here about his Eve. I'm all too aware that the biographical record suggests
some more worrying things about his attitudes towards women, but I hope
I can insist that they don't at all undermine what the poem itself is saying
or suggesting. This is the place to say that Eve, in another departure from
patriarchal conventions, is given the last spoken words in the poem. There
isn't a single Shakespeare play that has a woman saying the last words.

To my last two points about the poem's sceptical undermining of the
orthodox telling of the Fall story which is the surface narrative.

The first of these two follows on from our discussion just now about
Eve's thoughts in Book 9 as to share or not her post-Fall knowledge with
Adam. Of course, she chooses to share and, at the poem's most humanist
moment, he chooses to fall with her, choosing this over obedience to God –
because of his love for her (thus poignantly 'answering' what we saw was

her jealousy about him enjoying another Eve and letting her die alone). When he hears Eve's news Adam is 'astonied'. (Milton added a very large number of words to the English language but this play on 'turned to stone' and 'astonished' sadly didn't make it into the mainstream.) Then he reflects to himself on what it means about his own 'ruin'.

> And me with thee hath ruined, for with thee
> Certain my resolution is to die;
> How can I live without thee, how forgo
> Thy sweet converse and love so dearly joined,
> To live again in these wild woods forlorn?
> Should God create another Eve, and I
> Another rib afford, yet loss of thee
> Would never from my heart; no no, I feel
> The link of nature draw me: flesh of flesh,
> Bone of my bone thou art, and from thy state
> Mine never shall be parted, bliss or woe.

This moment, Adam knowing exactly what it means, is a moment of enlarged human consciousness, among the most enrichening and humbling in our culture. And then when he speaks aloud to Eve he makes the same point: 'if death / Consort with thee, death is to me as life', because 'Our state cannot be severed, we are one, / One flesh; to lose thee were to lose my self'. But even, perhaps inevitably, at this deeply humanist moment, the poem shows its conflicted nature when, as Adam then eats, Milton rather primly (even misogynistically) comments that he ate 'Against his better knowledge, not deceived, / But fondly overcome with female charm' ('fond' puns on foolish). Well, we can still insist that to choose to fall because of love is to call into question the very notion of the Christian Fall itself.

Which is also the case, in fact even more the case, in my last and most subversive example.

At the end of the poem, in Book 12, the arch-angel Michael gives Adam an extended glimpse of future human history and the grateful Adam admits that it was his earlier 'folly to aspire' beyond appropriate knowledge. Well, here's another sign of the conflicted text, as it wasn't Adam aspiring to greater knowledge that made him fall but his love for Eve. Still, Adam makes the important political point to Michael that he now realises (as, we might say, does Milton in the 1660s) that progress comes 'by small / Accomplishing great things, by things deemed weak / Subverting worldly strong'. Progress through small, incremental change, deed by deed, reminds me of Lyra at the end of the Pullman books having to learn to read the alethiometer afresh through hard work rather than grace.

Michael agrees and it's his stress on love, above all other virtues, that leads to the most radical moment in the poem: that it's voiced by an archangel is especially remarkable.

> Only add
> Deeds to thy knowledge answerable, add faith,
> Add virtue, patience, temperance, add love,
> By name to come called charity, the soul
> Of all the rest: then wilt thou not be loath
> To leave this paradise, but shalt possess
> A paradise within thee, happier far.

This second paradise, built on all the human virtues, with love at their centre ('the soul of all the rest'), will be happier, and make all humans happier, than the first paradise of the Eden which Adam and Eve, and all of us, have lost. And this paradise 'happier far' takes us back to Satan's pun in Book 4 where he sees Adam and Eve 'imparadised in one another's arms', calling such sexualised love 'the happier Eden'. He was right. The logic of Michael's words is inescapable and profoundly moving: there has, in effect, been no Fall. The poem set out to tell the story of the Fall; the story has been told; the Fall as-if didn't happen. Adam and Eve leave the garden of Eden (solitary – from each other, from God – but hand in hand), and we close the book called *Paradise Lost*, with that awareness enrichening, ameliorating, and now always accompanying their and our lives.

> Some natural tears they dropped, but wiped them soon;
> The world was all before them, where to choose
> Their place of rest, and Providence their guide;
> They hand in hand with wandering steps and slow,
> Through Eden took their solitary way.

Further Reading

Dennis Danielson ed., *The Cambridge Companion to Milton* (Cambridge U.P.: 1999).

Mike Edwards, *John Milton: Paradise Lost* (Palgrave: 2013).

William Empson, *Milton's God* (New Directions: 1961).

Stephen M. Fallon, *Milton's Peculiar Grace: Self-representation and Authority* (Cornell U.P.: 2007).

Christopher Hill, *Milton and the English Revolution*, new ed. (Faber and Faber: 1997).

David Loewenstein, *Milton: Paradise Lost* (Cambridge U.P.: 2004).

John Milton, *Paradise Lost*, ed. Gordon Teskey (Norton: 2005).

John Milton, *Selected Prose*, ed. C.A. Patrides (Penguin: 1974).

Annabel Patterson, *Milton's Words* (Oxford U.P.: 2009).

Christopher Ricks, *Milton's Grand Style*, new ed. (Oxford U.P.: 1978).

Louis Schwartz ed., *The Cambridge Companion to Paradise Lost* (Cambridge U.P.: 2014).

Margarita Stocker, *Paradise Lost: The Critics Debate* (Macmillan: 1988).

A.J.A. Waldock, *Paradise Lost and its Critics* (Cambridge U.P.: 1961).

Index

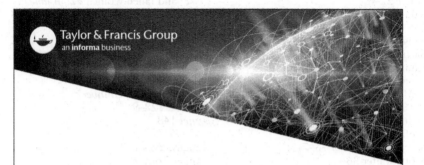